Practice-based Design Research

Practice-based Design Research

Edited by
Laurene Vaughan

BLOOMSBURY VISUAL ARTS
LONDON · NEW YORK · OXFORD · NEW DELHI · SYDNEY

BLOOMSBURY VISUAL ARTS
Bloomsbury Publishing Plc
50 Bedford Square, London, WC1B 3DP, UK
1385 Broadway, New York, NY 10018, USA
29 Earlsfort Terrace, Dublin 2, Ireland

BLOOMSBURY, BLOOMSBURY VISUAL ARTS and the Diana logo are
trademarks of Bloomsbury Publishing Plc

First published in Great Britain 2017
Paperback edition 2019
Reprinted 2019 (twice), 2020, 2021

A catalogue record for this book is available from the British Library.

A catalog record for this book is available from the Library of Congress.

ISBN: HB: 978-1-4742-6780-9
PB: 978-1-3500-8040-9
ePDF: 978-1-4742-6782-3
eBook: 978-1-4742-6781-6

Typeset by Fakenham Prepress Solutions, Fakenham, Norfolk NR21 8NN
Printed and bound in Great Britain

To find out more about our authors and books visit
www.bloomsbury.com and sign up for our newsletters.

CONTENTS

LIST OF ILLUSTRATIONS

LIST OF CONTRIBUTORS

Jonny Aspen is an Associate Professor at the Oslo Institute of Urbanism and Landscape. His research interests intersect fields such as urban theory, urban planning history and issues related to the contemporary city in terms of development and transformation and social and cultural features. More specifically, he is interested in researching: 1) inter-relations between physical surroundings and socio-cultural features; 2) issues related to 'reading the city', mapping and urban discourses; 3) issues of everyday urban living; 4) issues of social diversity and mixed cultures. He has recently become interested in new technologies, especially ICT-related technologies, and their effect on cities and urban living.

Cheryl E. Ball Dr. Cheryl E. Ball is an Associate Professor of New Media Studies in the English Department at Illinois State University. Her areas of specialization include multimodal composition and editing practices, digital media scholarship and digital publishing. She teaches writers to compose multimodal texts by analysing rhetorical options and choosing the most appropriate genres, technologies, media and modes for a particular situation. Since 2006, Ball has been editor of the online, peer reviewed, open-access journal *Kairos: Rhetoric, Technology, and Pedagogy*.

Richard Blythe is Professor in Architecture, and Dean, Architecture + Design, at RMIT University, Australia, a position he has held since June 2007. In 2010 he led the establishment of the RMIT University Creative Practice Research PhD programme in Ghent, Belgium, and was the primary author and lead researcher for the 2013 €4M EU Marie Curie ITN grant ADAPT-r. In 2013, Richard led the enlargement of this programme to RMIT's Barcelona campus. Richard was a founding director of the architecture practice, Terroir, and Company Director until 2012; he continues to contribute to the Terroir team. Richard is an Honorary Research Fellow at Queen's University, Belfast.

Eva Brandt and Thomas Binder are professors at the Royal Danish Academy of Fine Arts Schools of Architecture, Design and Conservation. With their colleagues they co-founded the CODE centre offering a master's level programme in co-design, and pursuing design research engaging open design collaborations and participatory design in the context of design anthropology, interaction design and social innovation. Their research includes contributions to methods and tools for experimental design research, and open innovation processes with a particular emphasis on participation and learning. They have been contributing to several books, such as *(Re)searching the Digital Bauhaus* (Springer 2008), *Rehearsing the Future* (Danish Design School Press, 2010), *Design Research through Practice* (Morgan Kaufman 2011) and *Design Things* (MIT Press 2011).

Ben Dalton is a Principal Lecturer in the Faculty of Arts, Environment and Technology at Leeds Beckett University, and an AHRC funded CX doctoral researcher at the Royal College of Art, London. His research is focused on the field of Identity Design, including technical, social, political and aesthetic aspects of identity in digital public space. Ben has a background in ubiquitous computing and mobile sensor networks from the MIT Media Lab, Boston, and has conducted research in the Århus University Electron-Molecular Interaction group, University of Leeds Spintronics and Magnetic Nanostructures lab, and Jim Henson's Creature Shop, London.

Pia Ednie-Brown is Associate Professor and Higher Degrees by Research Director in the School of Architecture and Design at RMIT University, Melbourne, Australia. She has a creative research practice, *onomatopoeia* (http://onomato-poeia.com.au/practice), and has edited two books, *Plastic Green: Designing for Environmental Transformation* (RMIT Press 2009) and *The Innovation Imperative: Architectures of Vitality* (Wiley 2013). Her academic writing has been published internationally.

Pelle Ehn is professor at the School of Arts and Communication at Malmö University, and one of the founders of the school and of the Interactive Institute, the associated national research institute. For the last fifteen years his research has been focused on design and digital media. His books and papers in journals and international conferences on the subject include *Computers and Democracy* (1987), *Work-Oriented Design of Computer Artifacts* (1988), Scandinavian Design – on skill and participation (1992) and Manifesto for a Digital Bauhaus (1998).

Lisa Grocott is Head of Department and Professor of Design at Monash University. She was formerly the Dean of Academic Initiatives at Parsons School of Design in New York and Director of THRVNG, a co-design research lab. Before New York, Lisa was Creative Director at Studio Anybody, an award-winning Australian design consultancy. As a practitioner/researcher her scholarship is driven by projects that enact the affordances of the speculative, solution-seeking and human-centred practice of design research. Lisa convened the international symposium Evolution: Art and Design Research and the PhD, and regularly publishes articles, chapters and conference papers on design-led research.

Neal Haslem is a communication designer, design educator and a practice-led researcher into communication design practice. His practice involves one-to-one relationships with people, enabling futures through communication design action. Neal's practice-led design research focuses on investigating the practice of communication design as an intersubjective action. Neal's practice-led research investigates the conjunction of communication design and intersubjective action through projects, writing, teaching and discourse. Ultimately, he aims, through design research, education and discourse, to initiate an 'intersubjective turn' within communication design action and research.

Henry Mainsah is a member of the Centre for Design Research at the Oslo School of Architecture and Design (AHO) in Norway. There, he takes part in several research projects connected to design, civic identity and expression. His particular specialization is building knowledge and practice about the relationship between design techniques and research methods. He is currently working on a book monograph on this topic. As a media scholar, he studies ways young people use social media in their everyday lives. Through ethnographic methods he focuses mainly on the way social network technologies are shaping society. He lectures on subjects such as qualitative research methods, youth culture, media theory and cultural identities. He received his PhD from the Department of Media and Communication, University of Oslo.

Thomas Markussen is Associate Professor of Social Design, at SDU Design, the University of Southern Denmark. In his own work and research, Markussen focuses on how design can be used as a political and critical aesthetic practice, notably in the fields of social design, design activism and design fiction. In addition, he has been involved in developing and founding a doctoral educational programme at Kolding School of Design and Aarhus School of Architecture, specifically devoted to practices and methodologies of research through design.

Katherine Moline is a Senior Lecturer in research practices, and Postgraduate Coordinator: Admissions for Masters by Research and PhDs at UNSW Art and Design. Katherine explores the cross-overs between avant-gardism in visual art and contemporary experimental design. Her particular interests are how experimental design reformulates strategies of historic artistic avant-gardes and the social impacts of design. Since co-convening the symposium *sds2k4: Experimental and Cross-Cultural Design* (2004), a collaboration between the University of New South Wales, University of Technology Sydney and the University of Western Sydney, she has curated the exhibition 'Connections: Experimental Design' (2007), and introduced international leaders in experimental and critical design to Australian audiences.

Andrew Morrison is Director of the Centre for Design Research at the Oslo School of Architecture and Design (AHO) in Norway, and Professor of Interdisciplinary Design at the Institute of Design (IDE). As coordinator of research, Andrew takes part in and leads a range of design research projects. These cover Communication Design, dynamic interfaces and social media; RFID, mediation and activity; Service Design and innovation in leadership; electronic arts installation; narrative and mobile media; practice-based research/research by design; online research mediation and design research methods.

Zoë Sadokierski is an award-winning book designer and writer. She lectures at the University of Technology Sydney School of Design, where she runs a research studio investigating the evolution of books in the digital age. She is vice president of the Australian Book Designers Association and writes a regular column on book culture and reading for *The Conversation*.

Tom Simmons is Research Leader for the School of Communication at the Royal College of Art, London, and leads on the Creative Exchange Hub based in the Royal College of Art. His creative practice and academic work is based in sound art and design, where his projects are often collaborative and interdisciplinary. He is an experienced PhD supervisor.

Marcelo Stamm is RMIT Vice-Chancellor's Senior Research Fellow, and Deputy Dean Research and Innovation, in the RMIT School of Architecture and Design; Adjunct Professor at the University of Munich LMU; Honorary Fellow of the Australian Innovation Research Centre AIRC; Honorary Research Fellow of Venice International University VIU. He is a philosopher of creativity and innovation who studied at Munich and Oxford and brings to the contemporary study of creativity and creative practice research more than two decades of work in the area of philosophical constellation research and topological research on cognitive horizons.

Cameron Tonkinwise is the Director of Design Studies at the School of Design at Carnegie Mellon University. He has a background in philosophy; his dissertation concerned the educational philosophies of Martin Heidegger. Cameron continues to research what designers can learn from philosophies of making, material culture studies and sociologies of technology. Cameron is facilitating the School of Design's creation of a new Design Studies sequence of courses that better prepare designers for a wider scope of work and the more interdisciplinary challenges of twenty-first century societies.

Teal Triggs is Professor of Graphic Design and Associate Dean, School of Communication, Royal College of Art, London. As a graphic design historian, critic and educator she has lectured and broadcast widely, and her writings have appeared in numerous edited books and design publications. She is co-editor of *The Graphic Design Reader* (Bloomsbury); her previous books include *Fanzines* and *The Typographic Experiment: Radical Innovations in Contemporary Type Design* (Thames and Hudson). Teal is Editor-in-Chief of the academic journal *Communication Design* (Routledge/ico-D), co-editor of *Visual Communication* (Sage) and Associate Editor of *Design Issues* (MIT Press). Teal is an experienced PhD supervisor in design and is co-supervising four of the CX PhD researchers.

Peter Ullmark was born in 1945 in Stockholm, became an architect in 1969 at the Royal Institute of Technology and in 1982 was awarded his PhD in building function studies at the Royal Institute of Technology, where in 1988 he became an associate professor. He was employed at the Department of Industrial Planning at the Royal Institute of Technology from 1974 to 1998, and from 1989 he was a university lecturer and research supervisor. He has run his own consultancy company in parallel, specializing in concept development for the interaction between production technology, working organization and buildings.

Laurene Vaughan is Professor of Design at RMIT University. She is Deputy Dean of Design, Games and Interaction in the School of Media and Communication (2014–16). Her recent projects include The Stony Rises Project, a curatorial exploration of vernacular practices, immigration, modes of dwelling and the crafting of landscape in the making of place. This included an associated book, *Designing Place* (Melbourne Books 2010). With Sebastien Cacquard and William Cartwright, she co-edited *Mapping Environmental Issues in the City* (Springer 2011). With Harriet Edquist she has also co-edited *Design Collectives: an approach to practice* (Cambridge Press 2012), and *Performing Digital* (Ashgate 2015) with David Carlin. Over the past twelve years, she has supervised over forty practice-based master's degree and PhD students.

Joyce Yee is a Senior Lecturer at Northumbria University, teaching interaction, service and design methodologies across undergraduate and postgraduate levels. She has recently published a book called *Design Transitions*, which looks at understanding how design practices are changing; and with Professor Paul Rodgers she co-edited *The Routledge Companion to Design Research*. Her research concerns understanding design practice in the social innovation sphere, and her next book is focused on understanding how organizations are innovating through design.

Jeremy Yuille is a designer, educator and exuberant learner. While he loves designed objects, he's more interested in framing design as a practice which creates value and connects disciplines. His work spans strategic design for civic engagement and participatory democracy, media design for immersive installations, digital platforms for archival and broadcasting, and baking creativity into education. Jeremy is a co-founder of the Design Futures Lab at RMIT, and was the inaugural manager of RMIT's innovative Master of Design Futures programme. He is also a certified scrum-master, and director emeritus of the Interaction Design Association, where he co-chaired the 2012 and 2013 IxDA Student Design Challenges and was a juror for the 2015 Interaction Awards. Jeremy is a Principal at Meld Studios Melbourne Australia.

Bonne Zabolotney is the Interim Dean of Graduate Studies at Emily Carr University. She has worked as a communication designer in Vancouver since 1993, working with a wide range of clients locally and nationally. Her most notable work can be found in the philatelic section of Canada's National Archives, which includes her 1999 stamp design recognizing the formation of the Nunavut territory. Five more of her stamp designs are also in the National Archives. She has also worked with some of the largest arts groups in Vancouver, including Vancouver Opera, Vancouver Recital Society and Vancouver International Jazz Festival.

ACKNOWLEDGEMENTS

An edited collection is always only as strong as the authors that fill the pages with their insights and ambitions. In this case I have been fortunate to work with an impressive cohort of international colleagues, all of whom have made important contributions to the evolution of practice-based design research. Contributors to this collection hail from institutions in Australia, Denmark, Europe, Norway, Sweden, the UK and the USA.

The proposal for this collection to Bloomsbury was the outcome of collaboration with Andrew Morrison and Cameron Tonkinwise and the events that were hosted in Oslo and Pittsburgh in the preceding years. In view of this, I would like also to thank the Centre for Design Research at the Oslo School of Architecture and Design, and the School of Design, Carnegie Mellon University.

I would like to express my gratitude to the School of Media and Communication at RMIT University for their ongoing support during the making of this collection. For editorial assistance, I must thank and acknowledge the very fine work of Lily Keil and Jaye Wetherburn, who have helped with the crafting of arguments and the formatting of what seemed to me endless files.

From our first email exchanges, the team at Bloomsbury have been nothing short of enthusiastic and supportive. Special acknowledgement to Rebecca Barden for seeing the vision for what this book could be, and to Abbie Sharman and Claire Constable for easing and guiding me through the process.

Finally, this edited collection would never have come to be if it wasn't for all the hard work, innovative projects and commitment to discovery that all the design students engaged in practice-based design research have done and continue to do. To my own students, to those that I have reviewed and examined, I say thank you. It isn't only students that learn through their acts of enquiry, it is the greater academic and practice community as well. I salute you and look forward to meeting those that have yet to commence their own journey.

Chapter 1

INTRODUCING PRACTICE-BASED DESIGN RESEARCH

Laurene Vaughan

The concurrent developments in design research and doctoral studies in design are interlinked phenomena. On this basis, design research may be realized as specific professional consultancy services; manifest as design roles within other allied professional organizations; or formalized within the academy as a specific programme or unit of study. The value to research of design and design-specific methods and epistemologies is becoming recognized across the material, social, economic and technology domains. Design is forming and framing policy and social change agendas, while continuing to challenge and evolve traditional design practice fields. It might even be argued that the emergent design practice fields such as interaction design, service design, user experience design and design for social innovation are playing a pivotal role in this phenomenon. Equally, the increasing pervasiveness of digital technologies from ideation phases through to manufacture or distribution methods is creating new opportunities and paradigm shifts that design specific research approaches are contributing to. All these innovations in contexts, methods and applications of design are calling for a new kind of designer, or at least an expanded capacity to undertake research with increasing sophistication. And, with this, there is the need for design educators to transform their own design practices and pedagogic capacities in order to contribute to the leadership of these exciting new domains. This leadership is being realized in the fields of practice, and in the academy.

What is the outcome of all this change you may ask? My answer would be: a profound transformation in how we understand, perform, critique and position design, as individuals and as an interdisciplinary community of practice. The world has great and increasing expectations of design and its capacity to mould how we live, work, play and survive into the future. Of course design continues to be an aesthetic and material domain of concerns, but it is also more. We have seen the rise of design thinking, design strategy, systems and playful articulations of design. So great is the expectation of what design can contribute that other professional and disciplinary domains are adopting or appropriating the language, look and feel of design, particularly when design is framed as problem-solving. But, as those of us who come from design know, design can be a practice of problem solving, but, equally, one of problem making. Design can open our known parameters, expose the intricacies of relationships, ask questions, posit answers and then explode them open again. Design is political, even when it isn't engaged in formalized politics.

The rise in practice-based design research and associated research degrees at both master's and doctoral level can be seen to be both an opportunity and a necessity for design practitioners in the future. Although graduate studies at master's level (either as an MFA or MDes) have a substantial academic heritage globally, this is changing, and we are seeing an increase in the number of people building on their graduate studies and undertaking PhDs. Typically, master's level research has focused on self-initiated creative explorations, but the new domains of design practice and the increasing realization that design research can make a vital contribution to applied projects are manifesting as an exciting era of opportunity for design and designers. The development of PhD programmes that recognize the significance of design literacies, and their capacity to contribute to the critical discourses of the academy, has been the other dimension to this pedagogic, practice and professional transformation.

Over the past five years there has been an increasing number of national funding schemes in the UK, Scandinavia, Europe and Australia supporting multi-institutional initiatives to both fund doctoral programmes and explore new intersections between industry, the academy and broader initiatives towards innovation through the support of communities of practice and student fellowships. The development of shared resources for both students and academic supervisors has been another outcome of such programmes. Examples would be the UK Creative Knowledge Exchange programme, with its various hubs of interdisciplinary and inter-institutional activity across the United Kingdom, and the European Union Marie Curie ITN funding schemes to support doctoral studies. In addition, the Australian Office of Learning and Teaching has funded both individual and large-scale multi-institutional research projects to identify best-practice models for doctoral education, while also recognizing excellence within its education community. The *Design Advanced Research Training* website (DART), an initiative of Coventry University funded through the AHRC (UK), is a model of the development of a ground-up shared resource for both PhD and other research students, as well as design researchers more broadly. The Nordic regions NORDES is a community-led initiative where academic colleagues have identified the necessity of building communities round innovation if this is to be sustainable. Its aim is to create rich learning experiences and shared resources, and to develop research capacity through summer school intensives and an international design conference. The *PhD by Design* is a UK based student led forum for discussing and critiquing the socio-cultural and institutional dimensions of doctoral degrees through practice in design.

These local, national, regional and international initiatives prompt questions regarding the integrity and intention of their origins. Do such funding schemes or regional or national developments skew or inhibit critique of practices or initiatives because of shared financial dependency and commitment to making an idea work? Or do they provide the infrastructure that allows for peer learning and peer review in a manner that institutes would find challenging in isolation? Perhaps they have the capacity to use power structures to manipulate cash-strapped institutions into aligning with government agendas through the supply of substantial financial support for institutions and students? Are they merely a means for formalizing the informal or ad-hoc initiatives that happen across the education sector at local or international level?

Academic integrity, discipline or professional relevance, new knowledge, peer review or peer assessment: there are many ways to challenge new developments, and these are necessary. As design researchers, we must challenge ourselves to look at the integrity of our ground-up initiatives and our responses to policy and funding programmes; we cannot blindly silence critique, just as we must not blindly assume that past practices or conventions are truths that we cannot transform. Not all institutional or regional initiatives are recipients of external funding. Some have come about through academic generosity and a desire for a greater community of practice or sharing of expertise. The provision of government or philanthropic funding or scholarships to support the undertaking of doctoral studies is not a new phenomenon; what is new are the large-scale initiatives, which bring together multiple institutions, academics and students, to undertake what is often industry-aligned research through design, and which evidence a growing trend across the tertiary education sector for shared resources, the expectation of doctoral education and the benefits of collaboration. A number of the chapters in this book provide case-study insights of the experience of these in practice.

With chapters by the leading proponents of practice-based design research from a range of design backgrounds and from across the world, *Practice-based Design Research* establishes grounds for the validity and importance of practice-based design research. This collection has emerged from a series of events taking place in 2013 and 2014. These include a roundtable discussion with Scandinavian colleagues at the Design Research Society, Cumulus conference in Oslo, 14–17 May 2013. The theme of the conference was 'Design Learning for Tomorrow. Design Education from Kindergarten to PhD'. Situated within this broader discussion of design education, the workshop attendees discussed the various approaches to design doctorates within their institutions, and the curriculum that had been developed to support student learning.

From 2012–13 I was the Nierenberg Chair, Distinguished Professor of Design, in the School of Design, Carnegie Mellon University, Pittsburgh PA. One of the drivers for my invitation to this role was the School's desire to re-imagine and re-boot their PhD programme. The School had an ambition to revitalize their doctoral programme by introducing a practice focus to the degree. In collaboration with Cameron Tonkinwise, and building on the conversations from the Oslo Round Table, we convened an international symposium on doctoral education in design and the role of practice. To facilitate the conversation we framed the event as *Critiquing the North American Design PhD* (Tonkinwise and Vaughan 2015). We invited participants to submit positioning statements about issues of design research, design PhD programmes, the role of practice and modes of supervision and examination. In a *designerly* manner (Cross 2007) we used the North American model as the trigger for the conversation. The North American PhD is a particular model of doctoral study, with extensive coursework and a backbone of university teacher training within its structure. This structure is unique: in Europe, the UK, Scandinavia and Australasia the focus is predominantly on extended research projects that may take between three to eight years to complete depending on full-time or part-time enrolment. This difference made it a useful device to facilitate the conversation.

In 2008, Meredith Davies (Davies 2008) noted that the development of a culture of design research has been particularly slow to develop in the USA. This could be said still to be the case, with the number of design research degrees, not only in the USA but globally, remaining fewer than in allied humanities, creative arts and technology disciplines; but this is changing. In North America, underlying this slowness is the ongoing debate as to whether the MFA should continue to be the 'terminal degree', a classification that is peculiar to North America and refers to which qualification is the one deemed to be the highest requirement for a discipline. Globally, a master's qualification has until recent times been deemed to be the required qualification for academic posts and senior positions in industry, especially when coupled with a significant body of practice experience. As the fields of design have evolved, higher qualifications in the form of PhDs or professional doctorates have largely been drawn from other disciplines or professional domains – design history, education, business or management, or social science. However, over the past ten years this has changed. Throughout Asia, Europe, Scandinavia and Australasia, the PhD is now the required qualification for ongoing academic appointments – often by government decree. Just as the professional opportunities for design research have evolved, so too has the expectation that academics across the disciplines of design would participate in, and contribute to, university research activities; and hence be required to have the base research qualification as realized across all disciplines – the PhD. The development of the design PhD has been in part a response to this. It has functioned as a means to ensure that there can be a qualification that prepares designers to be researchers, but achieves this through the literacies and practices of design.

This edited collection on practice-based design research is the outcome of the Oslo and Pittsburgh events, which themselves built on the broader body of scholarship and discourse on doctoral education which has been occurring since the late 1990s. For example, the *Re-envisioning the PhD Conference* (Washington 2000), the broad range of conferences and discussion boards established by the Design Research Society, the *Working Papers in Art and Design Research* (University of Hertfordshire 2000–8), *The Unthinkable Doctorate* (Sint-Lucas Brussels 2005), and the numerous publications in leading journals such as *Design Issues, Design Studies, International Journal of Design*. These are just some of the initiatives colleagues internationally have led and participated in, as we have worked to make sense of, and position, design research in the university and the professions, initiatives which have contributed to our greater understanding of what a design PhD is, and should be.

The majority of the authors in this edited collection have participated in both the Oslo and Pittsburgh events, as well as many others. It should be noted that, although much of the discussion in this collection is on the practice-based design PhD, the issues around the connections between design, practice and research are as relevant to master's degrees as they are to doctoral research. In this regard, I invite readers at all levels of education to translate the chapter content to their individual circumstances. Case studies and reflections on actual design research projects form a significant component of the text, providing useful and tangible insights for the reader.

PhD programmes in nonarchitectural domains of design have been available globally only within the last decade or two. Nevertheless, design PhDs, especially in the UK and Australia, New Zealand and Scandinavia, have asserted their own approaches to PhD research. It is now well established that designers can conduct design projects as part of their research processes, and submit project documentation and artefacts as evidence of research findings. Despite this having been accomplished, the knowledge base for the nature of practice-based design research remains dispersed. There is a substantial literature in the domain of practice-based art research, from the Fine Arts through the Performing Arts to Creative Writing. There are significant, although much smaller, literatures concerning practice-based architectural research and human–computer interaction research, and, as referenced above, a growing body on design research, much of which has been referenced in the chapters in this book. This particular collection on practice-based design research aims to expand the discourse by focusing on the particularities of design research *for* design across the various areas of practice and scholarship *through* design. Design here includes domains such as Products, Interactions, Services and Systems. An edited collection, this book highlights the pedagogical and the pragmatic aspects of doctoral degrees, while also presenting cases of the transdisciplinary contexts of design practice that have not yet been widely and collectively addressed in doctoral education and related research.

The book is made up of four parts, the chapters of each section presenting a different area of concern. In Part 1, 'Socio-cultural impacts of the design PhD in practice', authors present arguments for the broader social, cultural and practice implications of design PhDs and their potential to inform future directions of the academy and industry. Part 2, 'Exploring different models and approaches to design disciplines: challenges and innovations', presents five different models and approaches to doctoral education in design developed in the UK, Europe and Scandinavia. The authors present a range of approaches and curriculum initiatives that aim to honour the qualities and nuances of design knowledge and practice with the expectations of different educational systems. These research initiatives have been funded through the EU Marie Curie Framework, the UK Arts and Humanities Research Council and the Swedish government. In Part 3, 'Structures for supporting design PhD programmes', the authors reflect on a range of initiatives that they have introduced to support students and faculties in under-taking doctorates through practice in design. These range from the challenges of methodology design and alignment to the often-vexed relationship between practice and writing. Through reflections on their own research, or that of their students, the authors provide insights into, and viewpoints for, the undertaking and articulation of practice-based design research. Finally, Part 4, 'Graduate reflections on the design PhD in practice', provides a rare insight into the realities of undertaking an advanced design research degree. These seven final chapters provide insights into the joy, the pain and the discovery of having undertaken a design PhD, and the ongoing implications for the author's current design practice and research.

No text such as this can ever be regarded as complete, and this time of rapid publication and the subsequent growing body of discourse in design research makes this even more the case. Unfortunately not everyone invited to contribute to the collection was able to do so. Additionally, I have no doubt that other authors could have made a vibrant contribution to this collection. On this basis this collection represents just one more contribution to the dynamic and expanding discourse associated with design research and doctoral education through design. There will be opportunities elsewhere to expand on this.

Throughout the editorial process, I have sought to work with peers to compile an international collection of viewpoints and insights from those who have been actively seeking to establish a body of practice and literature that acknowledges and celebrates the value of design literacies. The core ambition of this process has not been confined to establishing a body of theory, or accounts 'about' practice-based design research and different doctoral programmes. I have been equally committed to providing the reader, 'through' personal accounts and insights by graduates and their supervisors, with access to what it is like to undertake such a research programme. With this in mind, I hope that this collection will provide the reader with access to the broader practice-based design research community globally: the students, alumni, academic advisors or supervisors, and the institu-tions that are leading the establishment of this exciting new domain of design practice and pedagogy.

References

Cross, N. (2007), *Designerly Ways of Knowing*. Netherlands: Birkhauser.

Davies, M. (2008), 'Why Do We Need Doctoral Study in Design?' *International Journal of Design*, vol 2. no. 3. 27 January 2016, Retrieved from http://www.ijdesign.org/ojs/index.php/IJDesign/article/view/481/223 (accessed 1 August 2016).

Tonkinwise, C., and Vaughan, L. (2013), *Critiquing the North American Design PhD*. An International Symposium at Carnegie Mellon University, School of Design. 27 January 2016, Retrieved from http://phddesigncrit.info/ (accessed 1 August 2016).

Part 1

EXPLORING DIFFERENT MODELS AND APPROACHES TO
DOCTORAL EDUCATION IN DESIGN

Chapter 2

DESIGNER/PRACTITIONER/RESEARCHER

Laurene Vaughan

A new phenomenon has emerged in recent years: practitioners in many occupations are undertaking a great deal of their own research. Traditionally, research has been the preserve of academics and scientists who have had the necessary knowledge and skills to conduct research; they have pronounced the results of their undertakings, and practitioners have been expected to abide by and implement their findings. These pronouncements have been incorporated into the profession's body of knowledge, which has been applied to practice. But things are changing. The idea that theory should be applied to practice is increasingly being recognized as an oversimplification, at the least, and at the most, as false. Many practitioners are now conducting their own research, even though it is not always referred to as such, and much of it does not get incorporated into their profession's body of knowledge.
Peter Jarvis – *The Practitioner-Researcher: developing theory from practice*

This opening text by Peter Jarvis in his 1999 publication refers to the then-emerging field of research through practice that was occurring in education, nursing and other associated fields. His rationale for its emergence was that the nature and context of work for these professionals was changing at such a pace that it was essential for practitioners to advance their education and knowledge of their fields in a manner that was not confined to traditional approaches to academic research. He notes that '(m)any practitioner-researchers are expert practitioners working toward graduate degrees as part-time students' (Jarvis 1999). These practitioners use the structures of the university as a means to formalize their professional informed expertise while working towards the award of a master's or doctoral degree.

Throughout the text, Jarvis argues that both industry and the academy need to rethink notions of expertise – particularly its ownership and application. He emphasizes that expertise acquired outside a field is not necessarily superior to, or even relevant to, the expertise of the practitioner inside the field. The 'field', in this sense, is the situation or place of everyday practice, which can include the actual physical location where action happens; or it may be the systems, materials or people that practitioners work with. As Jarvis states, 'practicing is situated and is itself a unique and ever-changing performance' (1999). This uniqueness is true for all professional or work domains, including those of design.

'Designer-practitioner-researcher' can be the title or description of an individual, their work role, or their understanding of the integration of these various aspects of their professional work. Like a molecule chain, this title can be read left-to-right or right-to-left, but at the centre of 'designer' and 'researcher' is, in effect, practice. It is now more than fifteen years since Jarvis published his text, and yet the conversation about the value of practice to research continues, not least in the area of design. It is the *value* of practitioner research for the individual, the profession and the academy which is core to Jarvis's thesis – value seen through the lenses of speed, access, deep knowledge and potential application in practice. Jarvis doesn't negate the value of traditional modes of academic and scientific research; he merely calls for the inclusion of practitioner-research to be a recognized method of achieving authoritative research outcomes. For him, this is not just a fanciful proposition – it is essential. Practitioner-researchers need the outcomes of this research from the field; it aids them in performing their profes-sional actions in more informed and effective ways, in real time, and within their spheres of influence. Practitioner-research is deeply situated, and it accepts that although there are norms of practice there are also infinite variations. The capacity to work within these variations, learn from them and subsequently transform them, should be at the heart of the research intent for future practice.

In 1993, Christopher Frayling proposed three ways of undertaking research in creative practice: research *into* the practice; research *for* the practice; research *through* the practice (Frayling 1993). This construct was not intended to be a framework for articulating practitioner-research, but the proposition that research can be undertaken: For – to use in application; Into – to understand what has been done (historically and/or theoretically); Through – to use the actions and sites of practice as a means of discovering something to be useful in articulating the intentions and outcomes of a practitioner-researcher's inquiry. Typically, these three classifications are seen separately rather than as phases, or aspects, of a practitioner-researcher's enquiry. The situated nature of practice-based enquiry ensures that research undertaken will produce knowledge that both deepens understanding and provides tangible applications for practice.

As Peter Downton states in his application of Frayling's framework to design research in particular, it is the shift from doing research *for* (actions undertaken that enable a practice to be) to applying this knowledge *through* a practice that enables new design knowledge to be seen and to exist in the world. 'Research through designing uses the knowing of doing to achieve productive outcomes which in turn indicate the knowing and the knowledge used in their production' (Downton 2003). Underpinning practitioner-research is the understanding that the practitioner-researcher has the skills and expertise in the actions of the field to be able to undertake situated research within it. Someone without this capacity will be limited to undertaking research *about* (into or for a field), which does not necessitate a level of expertise in the field of design practice. The capacity to perform (make, write, teach etc.) in a professional field of practice is essential to under-taking practitioner-research; more specifically, being a designer and possessing design expertise is the foundation to becoming a practitioner-researcher.

Doctorates and the evolution of the designer-practitioner-researcher

Despite the fact that some design PhD programmes have been running for more than twenty years, in academic terms the design PhD remains, relatively, a nascent qualification. This is not surprising, since design as an area of professional practice is also relatively nascent, as is the awarding of degrees. During this phase of becoming established, design has been under the aegis of other more established academic and scholarly domains such as architecture, art, the humanities and engineering. This has resulted in the appropriation and application of other disci-plinary structures and methodologies to design research, and this, in turn, has resulted in the production of a body of scholarship about design historically or in application. But this is changing. The time has come for design to value, embrace and articulate its own disciplinary and professionally relevant methods and modes of undertaking, disseminating and applying design research in practice.

Conventionally, within the academy the PhD is conceived of as the base quali-fication for a research career: in many disciplines this is aligned to becoming an academic. The research aim of the degree is to produce an original contribution to knowledge in the form of a thesis. Within the thesis, the student is required to provide evidence that they have read the 'literature' of their field and have positioned their research in relation to this. The outcome is a PhD graduate with a deep knowledge of a bounded topic, ready to enter the knowledge workforce as a nascent researcher and possible future professor. In this way, the graduate is both an expert and a novice, and destined for the academy where teaching would be one of a graduate's future duties. In North America it is not uncommon for doctoral programmes to include teacher training as part of the coursework of the doctoral programme, and many students also work as teaching assistants as part of this preparation for a professional life in the academy.

In the creative fields, entry to the academy was until relatively recently founded on the ingenuity and contribution of the creative practice of the future professor. This would be coupled with an appropriate academic qualification, often a master's degree. In North America, the Master of Fine Art (MFA) or Master of Design are still deemed to be the terminal degrees for the creative fields, but this is changing. In Europe, Scandinavia, Asia and Australasia, there is an expectation that the PhD will be the entry-level qualification for an academic position irrespective of the discipline of the appointment. This has created additional expectations for practitioners who may aspire to a future academic position in a creative domain such as design. Now, they must be both an expert practitioner and a credentialed researcher by virtue of the completion of a doctoral degree.

Conceiving of a doctoral programme as being a qualification for only one employment outcome has implications for what is taught, what is examined and the culture of a programme. It can create a very limited perspective on what will be researched and how the research will relate to practice outside the academy; and it is also short-sighted in that not all PhD graduates are destined for employment in universities. In 2004, less than fifty per cent of all doctoral graduates went on to pursue academic careers (Lee and Boud 2009), a trend supported by Evenson and Dubberly (2011), who note that there is an increasing demand for design researchers in commercial and private practice. This demand is based on the drive for innovation in industry and the understanding that there is a link between research, design and innovation. And just as there are changes in the destinations of PhD graduates, with many opting to work in practice, for those that go on to pursue academic careers, their employment contexts and roles are changing correspondingly, with greater expectations of innovation in research and external engagement. Whether in the academy or in industry, doctoral graduates are being perceived as being, and assuming the role of, advanced knowledge workers (Lee and Boud 2009), who are able to do more than espouse a particular topic in depth; they are able to perform as knowing subjects, able to address and engage in complex and diverse problems. This is a response to how knowledge production has shifted from being framed as a closed system to being an open system, one that is networked, responsive and expanding.

Situating design-practitioner-research as learning

When research is undertaken through practice, the site of the research is the site of the practice: this is the location where the action takes place. These everyday sites of practice are integral to research enquiry; they provide the context, means and parameters of the study. Enrolling into a doctoral programme, the designer-practitioner enters into the world of the academy and joins a community of fellow researchers. This academic site brings with it its own structures and expectations, which may align (but typically differ) to the everyday sites of practice. A challenge for doctoral programmes, PhD supervisors and examiners, is to embrace the diversity of these two sites of research for the student as they negotiate a new terrain of practice (the university) while continuing to engage with their everyday place of practice as the site of their doctoral enquiry. Maintaining the integrity of each of these situations and negotiating these transitions is essential, and quite often challenging for the practitioner-researcher.

In 1991, Jean Lave and Etienne Wenger argued for a model of situated learning that they named 'legitimate peripheral participation'. This was their attempt to articulate what they saw as the necessary integration of theory and practice within the framework of the social world, which includes the world of learning. Lave and Wenger state that 'the concept of legitimate peripheral partici-pation obtains its meaning, not in a concise definition of its boundaries, but in its multiple, theoretically generative interconnections with persons, activities, knowing, and the world'. Their definition of situated learning as a multi-sensory, socio-technical embodied phenomenon is consistent with Theodore R. Schatzki's

2001 claim that practice theorists 'conceive of practice as embodied, materially mediated arrays of human activity centrally organized around shared practical understanding'. In his definition, Schatzki is referring not only to what we may call professional practice but also to the embodied social (informal and formal) practices that exist in everyday life. This bleed crossover between the practices of the professional and non-professional situations of everyday-life and the embodied whole-person nature of being in all these situations is again articulated in Argyris's and Schön's *Theory in Practice*, where they claim that 'new knowledge/theory emerges by making explicit the informal knowledge of everyday life' (1974).

Throughout my career I have supervised a number of practitioners through their doctoral studies, and have observed them making the transition from being designers to being practitioners and researchers, and finally to becoming graduates from their degrees as designer-practitioner-researchers.

Not all professional designers conceive of themselves as having a practice. They call themselves practitioners and professional designers, but being able to name what they do as a practice rather than a job or a skill set is the first step towards undertaking a PhD. Developing this understanding is vital if they are to be able to undertake their research through practice but also emerge from their degree as the integrated future knowledge worker that Lee and Boud call for, also identified by Donald Schön and Bryan Lawson.

> Many practitioners, locked into a view of themselves as technical experts, find nothing in the world of practice to occasion reflection. They have become too skilful at techniques of selective inattention, junk categories, and situational control, techniques, which they use to preserve the constancy of their knowledge-in-practice. For them, uncertainty is a threat; its admission a sign of weakness. Others, more inclined toward and adept at reflection-in-action, nevertheless feel profoundly uneasy because they cannot say what they know how to do, cannot justify its quality or rigor. (Schön 1983)

Donald Schön's observation above is consistent with the challenge of the transition that people experience when undertaking a PhD in design. In the course of their study they transform from being designer-practitioners to becoming designer-practitioner-researchers. As Schön so succinctly comments, this is a shift for a designer from being a proficient technician, able to address the dimensions of projects in their profession, to being a professional able to understand and articulate the value or challenges of technical acts, and to place these in broader socio-cultural, technical and economic contexts. This transition is one of the profoundly significant outcomes of undertaking a research degree. The development of a framework and capacity to participate in critical reflection about practice while being engaged in the practice is one of the transferable capacities of a graduate that bridges the expectations of the university with the professional world.

On completion of their formal training in an undergraduate qualification, a novice designer, or recent graduate, enters the world of industry and adopts the title and identity of a designer. They enter the world of work armed with the knowledge and experience that has been gained through their training. This preparatory work and the accounts that they have had from their teachers and other professionals form the basis of their initial theory of what practice is, and what it will be. But this is a theory of practice that has had little opportunity to perform within the parameters of professional work. Jarvis notes that, on entering a practice, graduates 'have to make that theory their own, to legitimate it by their own pragmatic practice' (1999). This is not something that happens purely at the point of entry to the practice, this is an ongoing life work. Practices are situation specific, and this being so they must evolve in line with the changes of the world of work.

Within the domains of social theory, there has been substantial exploration of what has been named the 'practice turn' (Shatzki 2001). This turn has been established by increased recognition of the value of the social-world as the site where action happens. The social-world includes the world of work. The term 'practice' in this sense refers to the habitual actions or action patterns that can be identified within particular social groups, and the aim is to be able to classify social norms in order for normative theories of action to be established. On entering a profession, a novice designer must identify normative practices, and then decide whether to assimilate them in order to be accepted into the culture of the profession; and they must also adopt, adapt or reject them in order to establish their design contribution. This might be achieved through style, focus, method, or client preference. These may be conscious acts but often are not. Thus, the language of practice is often foreign to the world of professional design, with the designer identifying himself or herself as a designer, rather than as a practitioner-designer. Self-identification as a practitioner would be to attribute to oneself professional design skills within an organization or community while differentiating oneself from theorists, managers, or other business people.

Making the shift from designer to designer-practitioner is a significant first step for students embarking on design PhDs undertaken through practice. Students must be able to articulate what their practice is, and what their point of differentiation is, as this is the foundation for their transformation to the final stage – designer-practitioner-researcher.

It is through undertaking a research degree that students develop both the language and the rigorous framework for articulating what it is that they do in practice in their field. The structures of doctoral degrees, including modes of review and ultimately examination, demand that students should understand what they do, why this matters and what contribution it is making to their field, their clients and the academy.

Three examples of the designer-practitioner-researcher evolution

Over the past fifteen years, I have supervised a range of practitioner-researchers, who have come from a diverse range of disciplines and practice specializations. Some have been in the early years of practice, others internationally recognized for their work and their contributions – and consistent for all of them has been their capacity to transform their practice through their doctoral studies. The following are just three examples.

Student A, let us call her Amelia, came to her research degree with approximately ten years of design practice in the UK, Asia and Australia. Her passion had always been to practise within not-for-profit organizations. Working as an in-house designer in such companies was her way of being able to participate in social change while being a designer.

Amelia used her skills and expertise as a means to contribute to bigger issues. At the time that she started her research journey she had also begun to teach in a university setting. On commencing her degree, she identified herself as a graphic designer and was interested in how reflective practice might inform the development of her practice and also contribute to her new academic career.

The focus of Amelia's research was a series of design projects in which she was a participant. These projects included a political campaign and a consultative identity development project for a business collective. As she reflected on the outcomes of the projects, two important things happened. One was that she was deeply challenged by the politics of the consultative identity project, which were far less apparent in the political campaign. The second was that, through one of her supervisors, she became aware of the evolving field of participatory design in Scandinavia: as much a design movement as it was an approach and suite of methods, and a movement that strongly aligned with her interest in practising design through a values-based agenda in consultation with people. This was a transformational realization for her PhD research, a realization that focused her ongoing design-research-practice. Through this PhD research, Amelia was able to discover a bigger community of practice to connect with, and a framework that helped to position and legitimate her design approach and her contributions to the field, to the projects, and to broader design-research discourses.

By contrast, student B, we shall call her Balia, came to her doctoral project with over twenty years of professional experience in her design domain. She was nationally and internationally recognized as a leader in her field and for the integrity of her practice in the public arena. Balia wanted to undertake a PhD to upgrade her qualifications and extend her practice in new ways, particularly to practise beyond her previous scope as a leader in a large public organization. The PhD structure, as a formal time of study, provided her with the intellectual and creative space to experiment in her practice in areas impossible within the framework of her work. Despite her expertise within her domain, and her capacity to write and communicate ideas in professional contexts, the expectations and structures of the PhD programme challenged her in ways that she was unused to. This is what we might call the luxurious space of study. For an advanced practitioner, the luxury is the freedom and approval to be a student, a questioning novice, for this is rarely allowed within the formal activities of practice. During her study, Balia transformed from being a designer (someone who knew her field) to a designer-practitioner (someone able to understand the trajectory of her work and its role within the field) to a designer-practitioner-researcher, and she is now able to integrate within her field her discoveries about her own practice, with its broader connections to innovations and new projects. Her context for the practice and communication of her ideas has expanded to include engaging with the formal academic community as well as the commercial community of practice that she had known prior to her study.

Finally, student C, we can call him Carlos. Carlos came to his PhD with approximately five years of professional practice experience. He had his own studio, and worked as a contract research assistant providing technical and design expertise to formal research projects. When he entered his PhD, he had an understanding of large-scale research projects but had very little idea about doctoral studies. He enjoyed the experimentation and space of discovery of the research work compared to his outcome-driven doctoral programmes. Unlike Amelia and Balia, he undertook his design PhD on a scholarship within a funded research project. The project was a large-scale design and development project, and he was to be both a PhD student on the project and an active design-researcher in the project, working alongside the project team. During the course of his study he was to contribute to all project outcomes, including publications, and be a part of the project as a design researcher, while also fulfilling the milestones required of a PhD student.

In entering his PhD, Carlos understood his role as a designer and as a researcher in a project. He articulated what he did, not as a practice, but as skills or the expertise he contributed to projects. Throughout the course of his PhD, the three components integrated, and he emerged as a designer-practitioner-researcher. Following the completion of his PhD, Carlos continues to be engaged as a contract researcher on projects, but has also expanded his studio's business offerings to include design research. He actively translates to his world of professional design practice the research practices developed in his PhD.

Conclusion

Too often, discussions about doctoral programmes focus on programme structures or research outcomes. Not enough consideration is given to the transformation that this long and focused body of research manifests – the PhD graduate. Across the literature on the future of doctorates there is a growing awareness that the destination of doctoral graduates is changing, as are the industry and disciplinary sectors that are employing or applying doctoral expertise in their organizations. In 2009, David Boud and Alison Lee referred to this transformation as an increasing demand for *advanced knowledge workers* and we must ask ourselves: what does this mean for design? Who is an advanced knowledge worker in design? Are designers knowledge workers at all?

Skilled professional designers contribute to both our material and intellectual world – the world of commerce, culture and wellbeing. As the world of knowledge work transforms at an ever-increasing pace, fed by the affordances of digital technologies and an increasingly globalized, mobile world, designers must adapt to change and lead it, responsibly and creatively. That is the role of design – to manifest the world that we are becoming. This is the challenge for the contemporary designer.

The rise of practitioner-research in the fields of design is one means that designers can use to prepare themselves for becoming advanced in their domains; for developing the critical dexterity and rigorous processes that will enable them to practise in informed ways. Practitioner-research is deeply situated in the nuances of the practice of the researcher, and the most consistent enquiry is into the daily patterns of practice of the researcher. For design, these are the everyday acts of design practice that the designer takes from project to project, accumulating a body of expertise throughout the duration of their practice. A Design PhD undertaken through practice provides the designer with a structure that supports and enables him or her to practise as an advanced design knowledge worker – what in this chapter I have termed the designer-practitioner-researcher.

References

Argyris, C. and Schön, D. A. (1974), *Theory in Practice*. San Francisco, CA: Jossey-Bass, A Wiley Company.

Boud, D. and Lee, A. (2009), 'Framing Doctoral Education as Practice'. In D. Boud and A. Lee (eds), *Changing Practices of Doctoral Education* (pp. 10–25). New York: Routledge.

Downton, P. (2003), *Design Research*. Melbourne, Australia: RMIT University Press.

Evensen, S. and Dubberly, D. (2011), 'Design as Learning – or "Knowledge Creation" – the SECI Model'. *Interactions* 18 (1): 75–9.

Frayling, C. (1993), *Research in Art and Design*. Royal College of Art Research Papers, vol. 1, London.

Jarvis, P. (1999), *The Practitioner-researcher*. San Francisco, CA: Jossey-Bass, A Wiley Company.

Lave, J. and Wenger, E. (1991), *Situated Learning: Legitimate Peripheral Practice*. New York: Cambridge University Press.

Lawson, B. (2004), *What Designers Know*. New York: Architectural Press.

Schatzki, T. C. (2001), 'Introduction: Practice Theory'. In T. R. Schatzki, K. Knorr Cetina and E. Von Savigny (eds), *The Practice Turn in Contemporary Theory*, 1–14. New York: Routledge.

Schön, D. A. (1983), *The Reflective Practitioner*. New York: Basic Books.

Chapter 3

LOCATING NEW KNOWLEDGE IN AN UNACKNOWLEDGED DISCOURSE

Bonne Zabolotney

The political economy of design is not a typical area of academic or practical interest for designers. While not entirely *invisible* to scholars and practitioners, it is not fully defined and it is generally not discursively identified and situated within the broader discipline of design. For designers with bachelor's and master's degrees, most design practices operate within well-established relationships between design and business, engineering, manufacturing, and so on. PhD students, in contrast, are well positioned to research, study, and develop a political economy of design in order to articulate design's own knowledge of how it contributes to the world, and how designers can effect change at a meta-level. An investigation at this meta-level provides designers with areas of new knowledge to access, in order to critique or challenge existing economic, cultural or political structures. Using Communication Studies as a working model for design, we can see the possibilities of identifying and forming a framework to develop a practice around a political economy of design.

Vincent Mosco looks at two possible definitions of political economy. The first is that 'political economy is the study of the social relations, particularly the power relations, that mutually constitute the production, distribution and consumption of resources, including communication resources' (Mosco 2009). What are the existing power relations that mutually constitute the production, distribution, and consumption of resources of design? The obvious answers – clients and so-called audiences (or users) – quickly identify who hires designers and who ultimately purchases or interacts with the design, but this response doesn't acknowledge regulatory bodies (policy makers, manufacturing groups, or labour unions), technical infrastructure, and knowledge creators (universities, colleges and other groups administering information accredited by varying regulatory bodies). Understanding how power is produced, distributed, exchanged and used within the field of design becomes further complicated as it begins to implicate every person who comes into contact with design.

An example of misunderstanding or misidentifying power structures in design can be found in Charles Eames' diagram, developed to explain his collaborative and social approach to design practice (Eames [1969] 2015). This diagram displayed an overlap of three amoeba-like shapes that represented three main constituents: the 'genuine interest of the client', the 'interest and concern of the design office', and 'the concerns of society as a whole' (ibid.). These entities intersect to create a small area of shared concern, identified by Eames as a place of creative opportunity where the designer can work with 'conviction and enthusiasm', and to emphasize the designer's keen ability to pinpoint and direct their attention to a detailed issue. This diagram assists us in the initial identification of hegemonic concepts and practices within design, and verifies that, when working within the confines of this model, there is little recourse, or opportunity, for designers when the best interests of society and the interests of business no longer correspond. The first constituent – the client – is guided by market and capitalist needs and values, and may be working to their intellectual and aesthetic limits of knowledge of design. The second constituent – the designer, as a business owner and aspiring icon – is also guided by market forces and must defer to clients' 'needs'. The third constituent – society – is an ever-fluctuating heterogeneous mix of interests and social power dynamics. With this in mind, Eames inadvertently illustrates that designers and their clients probably do not address a majority of society's needs, or possibly that client's needs and society's interests may not ever intersect or overlap. For designers who are interested in locating the political, economical and social spaces in which they must work, this diagram does not account for power structures found within each of its three entities, and it falsely assumes that each of the three entities' contribution to the design project have equal power.

Mosco's second definition of political economy is 'the study of control and survival in social life' (Mosco 2009), where 'control refers specifically to the internal organization of individual and group members' while survival 'takes up the means by which [the individual and group members] produce what is needed to reproduce themselves' (ibid.). How designers organize within various professional associations based on specific design disciplines becomes political as each group competes for membership, funding through membership fees, and the ability to develop knowledge territories where each organization claims to dominate ideas about innovation, communication and technological advancement. In this sense, survival depends on reproducing the status quo: design associations regularly revive the dialogue around professional accreditation or certification – creating gateways or impediments for design professionals[1] and generating pressure for educators to teach to current practices of the professions. Many professional practitioners of design place education as subservient to design practice, demanding that educators address the demands of the professions, typically skill-based in concern, while design educators struggle to future-proof their curriculum, often choosing to teach students to demonstrate the *possibilities* of design.[2] In 'State of Design: How Design Education Must Change' (Norman and Klemmer 2014), Don Norman's call for 'educational reform' can be distilled to one concept: learn more by adapting knowledge from other fields. He does not suggest, however, where we might draw the line between design education with 'substantive knowledge' in engineering and an actual engineering education. He also does not state where new techniques of research and collaboration fit into existing forms of knowledge from disciplines related to design, nor does he explain the role of leaders in design in helping to mentor and develop emerging design practitioners.

To survive, designers must take up the work of collaborating with educators: to develop new models of curriculum, to create new insight and knowledge in the fields of design, and to remodel design practices to accept new and emerging designers who do not fit within existing and current roles of design production. Within a political economy framework, the various fields of design would be able to competently address these issues of control and survival, and the conflict between educators and professionals could be adequately examined.

Mosco also asserts that 'reality is established or constituted by many sources and cannot be reduced to the essentialism of either economics [driven by money] [...] or culture [driven by people's values]' (Mosco 2009). This positions political economy of design as susceptible to 'concepts that guide our thinking' and 'observations, or what we perceive with our senses' (ibid.). This means understanding the concepts and ideas that guide our thinking, as well as our aesthetic sense of the world. Aesthetics in design is often relegated to a superficial experience – the 'look and feel' of a design project is a common trope – but as a necessary philosophical method for political economy we can revive its true meaning:

> If anaesthetics befuddles and dulls us, causing us to not feel pain or pleasure, it would make sense to see aesthetics as the inverse of this: our lively sensitivity to stimulus from without and within; our sensate connectivity to a world of things and other people; our responsiveness to a world of feelings. (Highmore 2011)

Ben Highmore acknowledges that the aesthetic experience is vital to understanding everyday life, and that aesthetics can be social and political. The study of everyday life is essential to understanding politics, our social condition, economics and, ultimately, understanding the conditions in which we practise and implement design. Further to this idea, Highmore invokes Foucault's concept of governmentality, and uses Anna McCarthy's explanation that Foucauldian governmentality is an ideal model for comprehending the impact of market-driven neoliberalism, where 'state policies synchronize with cultural practices to apply market-based individualism as a governmental rationale across the institutions and practices of everyday life' (ibid.). Without fully acknowledging or comprehending a political economy of design, designers cater to the 'competitive individualism' (ibid.) of Western neoliberal governmentality through Mosco's three main concepts of political economy of communications – commodification, specialization and structuration (Mosco 2009). These three concepts equip designers with analogies that allow us to build a political/economic critique of the professional practice of design and to investigate what this critique might mean for advanced design education and research.

(Mis)understanding commodification

'Commodification is the process of transforming things valued for their use into marketable products that are valued for what they can bring in exchange' (Mosco 2009). There are two significant aspects of design and its relationship to commodification. The first is that design's 'reason for being' is historically built around producing commodities that contribute to economic health and the culture of everyday life. The second is that everyday life and its reliance on consumption in turn influences the practice and commodification processes in design (ibid.). Designers are well versed in producing products for profit, and the history of design is a roll-call of the efforts to commoditize everyday life. It runs parallel with the history of the Industrial Revolution, which runs parallel with the history of manufacturing and distribution, which in turn relies on the history of transportation. There is very little design that is not commodified through standard business practices of manufacturing and distribution within government guidelines and policies. Design's very existence is so intrinsic to capitalist ventures that it is difficult to imagine how to break free from this supply-and-demand paradigm.

Within this capitalist paradigm lies a sad truth for designers. While economic theory examines the production and manufacture of design, it does not account for 'the context of use, of the role played by products, communications, environments, services and systems in the lives of people beyond the point at which most economic theory halts: *the point-of-sale*' (Heskett 2009). For all the rhetoric built around the cultural, economic and social values of design, contemporary economics support the concept that products of design *depreciate with use*. Art is an appreciated asset, and therefore any design treated as art (such as a Marc Newson's chaise lounge[3]) can appreciate with age, but design, whose cultural value relies on planned obsolescence, creates things that are intended to depreciate. In earnest, designers attempt to affect the future by producing thoughtful, intentional and honest work, but the economic *value* of these products will always decline unless designers critique and confront the economical, political and social infrastructure in which they live, work and attempt to affect.

Recent rhetoric developed around design practice posits design's ability to democratize – through the use of technology, the availability or prolific-ness of designed goods, or new methods in the design process, such as crowd sourcing or co-creation – to achieve social and economic equality. This notion of democratization does not take away the bottom line for design, however. Designers continue to make things for people to consume. The challenge here is that as it goes unexamined, designers working under the guise of democratization don't often question the capitalist paradigm of production and consumption within which they continue to work. Democratization in design usually means faster, more accessible, cheaper and more plentiful things for consumers. And while websites such as Kickstarter are exalted for their democratizing effect on manufacturing, distribution and crowd-sourced funding (Karabell 2013), these models maintain a commodified presence within consumer culture, using gifts and early product purchases as motivation to participate.

The practice of design has also led us to the commodification of the designer him/herself. Within the political economy framework of control and survival, designers continue to assign iconic status to individual designers, recreating design histories that often go unchallenged. The pursuit of iconic status, in fact, often becomes a preoccupation for many designers looking for ways to avoid cultural and/or economic depreciation of their work, knowing that 'knowledge of technology and experience can appreciate into human capital' (Heskett 2009). Philippe Starck's BBC television production in 2009, 'Design for Life', is a prime example of this. This TV show was a televised design competition where twelve product designers competed to win a six-month internship at Starck's Paris-based design agency. Not only did this increase the iconic status (as an appreciating asset) of Phillipe Starck, it used the medium of television as a way to transform the labour of the twelve young designers into commoditized entertainment.

Most of these examples of commoditization have been public-facing work, commoditizing the products, labour and human resources in design. Arguments exist that work designed and produced in the private realm, and not mass-manufactured, begins to chip away at the commodification model of consumer culture. This approach to design, often working in the guise of democratization, is easily relegated to the classification of D.I.Y. and hobbies or craft. It becomes an outlier of design: un-designed in the sense that it does not follow conventional practices and methods, unacknowledged publically in the canon of design work, and therefore unappreciated on a wider scale culturally.

Designers do engage in positive, engaging, and culture-shifting work. The optimism and impetus to 'do good' in this world emanates from most designers. However, the working structure of government bureaucrats, policy-makers, economists, politicians and law-makers is upheld by the status quo of consumer culture – a powerful cultural force that must be addressed politically and econom-ically if design expects to affect change in the future.

Spatialization and design's contribution to ecological concerns

Spatialization refers to 'the growing power of capitalism to use and improve on the means of transportation and communication, to shrink the time it takes to move goods, people, and messages over space, thereby diminishing the signifi-cance of spatial distance as a constraint on the expansion of capital' (Mosco 2009). The spatialization and commodification of design that has occurred during the twentieth century has had a massive impact on the manufacturing processes, supply chain of materials and labour, and ultimately our global ecology. The lack of spatial constraints on designers has led to a continuation of the exploitation of global resources. Most designers will argue that while these changes have benefited the economic wealth and health of design, and have had far-reaching consequences in terms of democratizing design, the impact of the globalization of manufacturing and distribution of designed products has been ecologically devastating. Most significantly, design's embrace of plastic as a favoured material has caused irreparable damage to our oceans and landscapes. Seduced by the ever-availability of plastic – its longevity and its ability to be manipulated into any shape – design has been slow to address the sustainable use of resources, and negligent in its ability to measure long-term impact as an initial consideration in the design process.

The challenge, now, is for designers to develop knowledge of full systems – to examine processes beyond acquisition of materials, manufacturing processes, and distribution networks. Designers must understand the social and political impacts of their work – not from the perspective of their clients or 'end-users'' experiences but from the impact to the entire supply side of design. In order to effect change in the ecological impacts of design, designers must develop a political economical *accounting* of their work: *socially,* by asking how we really know our design changes the way people interact with each other; *empirically,* by acknowledging the real cost of making things when taking ecological damage and reparation into account;[4] and *culturally,* by asking how we measure or observe cultural shifts or changes from all points in the sourcing of material and development of design.

Structuration: Identifying hegemonic concepts and practices within design

Structuration as it applies to design, addresses the social constructs developed as we practise design, and the hegemonic views – how we view ideas or concepts as simply common sense – that go unchallenged and unidentified. Designers have attempted to address structuration, although not explicitly naming it as such, in pronouncements such as the First Things First manifesto. Ken Garland's original 1963/64 manifesto (Garland 1963), Émigre Magazine's 1999/2000 revival (Émigre 1999) and First Things First 2014 (Peters 2014) have all attempted to turn a mirror towards practising designers in order to effect change in the practices and expectations of designers. These attempts are optimistic in spirit; however, a discourse analysis of these three related documents would reveal problematic hegemonic concepts underwriting current design practice, as statements like 'we do not want to take the fun out of life'[5] continue completely unquestioned in the context of both practising and implementing design.

Revealing hegemony is difficult and complex, and building responses to the identification of problematic issues requires systematic and transitional approaches to redesigning practices in design. An incomplete list of unexamined and hegemonic statements might include:

- design is meant to be consumed;
- design is meant to be mass-produced;
- design 'responds' to industry and marketing needs;
- designers are 'problem solvers';

- skills and conceptual knowledge in design education are opposing forces;
- Design educators should defer to the practice of design rather than critique it;
- new knowledge about design practice comes from business models or technology;
- design practice is led by 'icons', whose practices and accomplishments are measures of success;
- design products and ideas are proprietary.

These statements address a variety of issues that affect designers socially: how to share knowledge and work professionally and academically, and provide collegial critique in the spirit of improving the field as opposed to competing and devaluing our colleagues; how to question 'common-sense' designs (including the swiping, tapping and pinching gestures dominated by mobile devices) that are replicated and reproduced by designers without question; how to truly contribute to democratization, to build on a creative commons model; how to educate future designers who have become increasingly affected by tuition debt and the ability to attain a salary that will allow them to address this debt.

Moving forward

This chapter is intended to sort through some of the messiness of online chatter and academic discussion and to provide clarity and support for these discussions by locating the work of political economy in design. It is not intended to turn designers away from the possibilities of their field or to foreclose on the positive effects of design. It is a call to action to designers and design students to examine deeper systems at play that affect design and its influence in the world. It is meant to encourage designers to develop new knowledge and to break hegemonic paradigms. Already, there exist many approaches and responses to the volatility and flux of design practices, yet there is very little centralized discussion on its overall political economy. Have we only 'trained' designers to implement design solutions without understanding the larger cultural and political issues? Must designers and design academics conform to models and theories from other disciplines on the periphery of design – political, economic, sociological and so on – in order to develop a better understanding of what we do, or can we develop our own specific and particular epistemologies?

'Calls for collaboration both within and between disciplines require knowledge of the knowledge and practices that are being brought together, or such calls will remain more rhetoric than reality' (Carvalho, Dong and Maton 2009). It is one thing to acknowledge the influence of the knowledge other disciplines outside design can contribute to design fields, but designers must also synthesize the heterogeneous and often inconsistent work between educational institutes, various practices and professional bodies. Designers can work towards redefining their practice with the best intentions; however, if the conditions under which design education and practice don't change, and the cultural, social, political and economic contexts for design don't change, then design will not be effective, and its products will not appreciate in value over time.

While the focus on political economy provides new opportunities for designers researching at a PhD level, possessing the ability to create and disseminate new knowledge, learning about the true efficacy and political economy of design should and could occur at all levels of study in design. As a start in identifying this nascent work, and keeping in mind that commodification, spatialization and structuration remain as influential forces, I propose a focus on four points of investigation: acknowledging our limits, studying our own habits, understanding aesthetic politics, and foregrounding political economy in a non-commercial practice in design.

Designers are interdisciplinary and collaborative by nature, but they cannot be designers *and* engineers, designers *and* economists, or designers *and* sociologists. Establishing the limitations in understanding the knowledge and contribution of other disciplines is essential to locating design's own knowledge. Because 'ontology distinguishes seeing things as structures or as processes' (Mosco 2009), designers have an opportunity to uncover, organize, and discuss ontologies as a means to making the practice of political economy of design visible. New knowledges in design and new practices in the political economy of design possess the potential to redirect policies, business practices, aspects of commodification and consumption in order to make room for effective change.

One of the ways of understanding our limitations is acknowledging and speaking the truth about design's habits in practising, educating and otherwise replicating ourselves as a mode of survival. If we establish our habits on 'how things are experienced', then we have built a habitual culture, and culture is governmentalized. 'Ideas about the ordinary, about habit and about everyday life are often mobilised in the name of governmentality' (Highmore 2011). The potential for changing our habits directly conflicts with the economic and political forces that provide infrastructure and context for the work that designers do. Design, for the most part, is conventional by definition. It works within the confines of conventions based on beliefs about what design accomplishes and contributes towards culture. As designers, we cannot change if conventional infrastructure remains unchallenged.

There is no such thing as benign design. Even design relegated to the superficial and simply 'aesthetic' works on a political level. Acknowledging this politics of aesthetics means connecting the aesthetic values of society to the political and economic structures that construct society. The design of systems and processes, generally seen as 'immaterial', are also susceptible to politics. Where designers expect to change behaviour or habits in their 'audiences' or 'users', they must accept that changing habits requires a change in sensory experience.

Designers determined to focus on the political economy of design will need to foreground political economy in their practice, rather than having it as a condition of other, dominant, forms of design practice. Leading out with social processes and relations as a condition of political economy, which sets all contexts for design, has the potential to change design practices. Coming to terms with an honest critique of design processes and consequences is the first step in developing a richer, and responsive, discipline.

Notes

1   In the online article 'RGD and GDC at Odds Over Certification', http://designedgecanada.com/news/rgd-and-gdc-at-odds-over-certification/, the comments following the news item are just as revealing as the article itself about the confusion of the goals and mission of professional organizations.
2   Online discussion and arguments demonstrating the dynamic between practitioners and educators erupted in the summer of 2014 after Carnegie Mellon University began publishing and discussing their updated curriculum, much to the dismay of some of their alumni. This online forum is an example of the dynamic between practitioners and educators, and their expectations of each other, https://groups.google.com/forum/#!topic/overlap/5IpWQOQV5xI
3   Newson's Lockheed Lounge sold for a record price of two million pounds sterling in early 2015, retaining its title as the world's most expensive design item (De Zeen Magazine 2015).
4   Issues of sustainability in design are vast and complex, however it is generally agreed that very little design acknowledges throughput – 'the flow of raw materials and energy from the global ecosystem's sources of low entropy (mines, wells, fisheries, croplands) through the economy, and back to the global ecosystem's sinks for high entropy wastes (atmosphere, oceans, dumps)' (Throughput definition, 2010) – when financially accounting for the cost of design and manufacturing of any given product.
5   Both the 1963 and 2014 versions of the First Things First Manifesto use these words, indicating that design rooted in ethics may be less 'fun' than the typical design practice.

References

Carvalho, Lucila, Dong, Andy and Maton, Karl (2009), 'Legitimating Design: A Sociology of Knowledge Account of the Field'. *Design Studies* (Elsevier Ltd) 30, no. 5 (2009): 483–502.

De Zeen Magazine. *Marc Newson's Lockheed Lounge sets new record at auction.* 29 April, 2015. http://www.dezeen.com/2015/04/29/marc-newson-lockheed-lounge-new-auction-record-design-object-phillips/ (accessed 8 August 2015).

Design Edge Canada. *RGD and GDC at odds over certification.* 22 March, 2013. http://designedgecanada.com/news/rgd-and-gdc-at-odds-over-certification/ (accessed 15 July 2015).

Eames, Charles. *Charles Eames Design Process Diagram.* 1 January, 2015. http://www.eamesoffice.com/the-work/charles-eames-design-process-diagram/ (accessed 25 July, 2015).

Emigre. *First Things First Manifesto 2000.* 1999. http://emigre.com/Editorial.php?sect=1&id=14 (accessed 8 August, 2015).

Garland, Ken. *First Things First Manifesto.* 1963. http://www.designishistory.com/1960/first-things-first/ (accessed August 8, 2015).

Google Groups. *Design culture is a frozen sh*thole' by_Cole_Peters*. 5 August, 2014. https://groups.google.com/forum/#!topic/overlap/5IpWQOQV5xI (accessed 27 July, 2015).

Heskett, John (2009), 'Creating Economic Value by Design'. *International Journal of Design* 3, no. 1.

Highmore, Ben (2011), *Ordinary Lives: Studies in the Everyday*. London: Routledge.

Karabell, Zachary. *The Atlantic*. 13 February, 2013. http://www.theatlantic.com/business/archive/2013/02/the-kickstarter-economy-how-technology-turns-us-all-into-bankers/272841/ (accessed 8 August, 2015).

Mosco, Vincent (2009), *The Political Economy of Communication*. 2nd edn. London: SAGE Publications Ltd.

Norman, Donald and Scott Klemmer. 'State of Design: How Design Education Must Change'. *Don Norman: Designing For People*. 25 March, 2014. http://www.jnd.org/dn.mss/state_of_design_how.html (accessed 23 July, 2015).

Peters, Cole. *First Things First 2014*. 2014. http://firstthingsfirst2014.org/ (accessed 8 August, 2015).

Throughput definition. *Vocabulary & Concepts*. 5 January, 2010. www.sustainableeconomics.org/vocabulary.htm#throughput (accessed 16 October, 2015).

Chapter 4

POST-NORMAL DESIGN RESEARCH: THE ROLE OF PRACTICE-BASED RESEARCH IN THE ERA OF NEOLIBERAL RISK

Cameron Tonkinwise

When something new fights for recognition, it tends to be self-obsessed. As its own identity is exactly what is at stake, it is natural for it to be exaggeratedly assertive about its own qualities and agency. It is not strategic to foreground other forces that are in fact at play. Practice-based design research often had this defensive insularity as it tried to shore up its epistemological claims throughout the 2000s. The maturity that practice-based design research has now attained should allow a more honest history.

While not up there with other great revolutions on behalf of oppressed peoples, the establishment of practice-based design research at universities, especially within doctoral programmes, was nevertheless a struggle. As with many successful empowerments, those who later enjoy such accomplishments are often unaware of how hard won it all was. Forgetting how the current state of affairs came to be can entail misplacing why it came to be. There are legacy responsibilities that come with the creation of new opportunities that should not be forgotten. In the following, in order to point out its wider task in our contemporary societies, I want to recall some of the contexts in which practice-based design research arose.

There are perhaps three levels to the history of practice-based design research becoming a 'thing' over the last few decades. I will call these: Disciplinary, Institutional and Paradigmatic.

Disciplinary

One understanding of design sees it as present from the very start of human history. To be human is to design (Fry 2012).

In its modern incarnation – as visually planning the mass production of useful things for mass consumption – design is however a relatively recent profession and an even more recent discipline. Wide-view surveys of modern design, such as Richard Buchanan's notion of the Four Orders of Design (2001a), which is not really a historical schema, would suggest that, nevertheless, the practice of design has matured quickly over its century-and-a-bit:

Table 4.1 Design's increasing complexity/influence.

	Design of	Design as
First Order	Communications	Marketing-led Styling
Second Order	Products	Use-context Research-based Form-giving
Third Order	Services	Human-centred Design-driven Innovation of Experiences
Fourth Order	Organizations	Social-change-oriented Systems Interventions

Although the conceptual birth of Design, according to Christopher Alexander's fable (1964), involves Design differentiating itself from Craft as a more self-conscious approach to making, one that can be formally taught rather than only-ever-tacitly derived from imitation of the practice, Design as a professional practice was in fact established at the beginning of the 20th century for the most part outside the university. In the USA, the first product designers (as opposed to some of the applied or decorative arts) are self-made consultants – I am thinking of the Streamliners (Meikle 2001) – outside Schools. In Europe, Design is established as Schools – the various incarnations of the Bauhaus (Findeli 1989, 1991) – but ones that explicitly attempt to combine the atelier with the apprenticeship. History for instance, as something essential to a developmental discipline, is proscribed from the Bauhaus.

It is not until the world in which Design operates is cast as something more complex after the Second World War that Design truly becomes self-conscious about the legitimacy of its processes. As Design begins to confront larger-scale initiatives with more networked technologies in contexts of increasingly non-homogenous cultures, designers look for more reliable methods (the 'Design Methods' movement – Cross 1984; Evans et al. 1982). At that time, the dominant faith lay in the enhanced power afforded rationality by developments in computation. Design's first formal forays into university theorizing and research therefore take place in the contexts of computer science and cognitive science, largely under the guidance of the existing discipline of architecture.

Shortly into this project, its inadequacies became apparent, and a series of para-rationalist pathways opened for design processes and research that created its first authentic disciplinary form:

Table 4.2 Post design methods conceptual directions

Planning	Social Design	Human Computer Interaction
Wicked Problems	Reflective Practitioner	Contextual Inquiry
Dialogue Mapping	Pattern Languages	User-centred Design Personas
	Systems Thinking	Design Thinking

These realigned Design with the Humanities (Buchanan 2001b), or at least the Social Sciences, rather than the techno-scientific disciplines. The principles underlying this shift were multifaceted:

Researching Social Problems

Designing differentiates itself from others of the creative industries by having a problem solving imperative. But the problems with which it engages have to do with social practices and so require comprehensive understandings of people as they go about their distinct everyday lives. In other words, practising Design now demands comprehensive Social Research. This Research for Design is looking for interventions, changeability, innovations. There is a desired immediacy of action that further differentiates this Research for Design from more objective, understanding-focused Social Research, which may or may not have extrapolated Recommendations in its Conclusion (see Fallman's distinction (2007) between 'Research-oriented Design' and 'Design-oriented Research'). Part of the emerging Discipline of Design will therefore be the development of its own forms of Social Research, something evident in the shift from User-centred Design through Human-centred Design to Generative Design (Sanders and Stappers 2012) and more recently the sub-discipline of 'Design Ethnography'.

Reflective Creative Practice

Although problem based, Designing is nevertheless a creative act. The idea-generating aspect of Designing involves, it is claimed, non-rationalizable abductions or creative leaps (Cross 2006). At best, these conjectures about promising solutions are based on a not-readily-explicable expertise that involves precedent-banks of similar cases and pattern recognition in relation to the outcomes of Social Research for Design (Lawson 2012). What gives validity to these solution-oriented conjectures are, according to Donald Schön's influential work (1983, 1987), tight cycles of evaluative Action-Research with regard to each design 'move'. This means that the practice of expert designing involves precisely the sorts of meta-cognitive, processual knowledges that characterize a discipline. Reflective Practitioners are scholar-makers, and Research of Design also takes place in, and as, Research by Design.

Design as *'Interessement'* *(Akrich et al. 2002a, 2002b)*

Because the problems with which designers engage concern everyday social practices ('how should we live?', 'how to enhance our quality of life?'), design will not only involve understanding a problem through social research, then ideating responses through reflectively creative leaps, but also always involve convincing others of those proposed responses given those framings of the problem. The practice of designing must therefore be legible to (e.g. Requirements Specification, Dialogue Mapping), if not directly involving (e.g. Participatory Design, Co-Design), non-designers. The Practice of Designing increasingly depends on the Discipline of Design (and Design Studies) to increase Design Literacy.

In this narrative, Design becomes a Discipline because of the expanded field of its Practice. Design's entrance into the University is not epiphenomenal to its commercial application but a consequence of its needing to be more sophisticated and comprehensive when negotiating the complexity of technologizing multi-cultural societies. As a result, Design enters the academy with distinct needs that cannot be serviced merely by adding other disciplines to designing. Design demands new forms of social research, new accounts of creative cognition and new modes of communication, persuasion and alliance building.

These more designerly versions of the Discipline of Design did not appear immediately. While Design started to become this sort of a distinct university discipline in the 1970s, it was not till the 2000s that Research by Design was substantial enough to assert itself (I am taking as exemplary the biennial *Research into Practice* Conferences at the University of Hertfordshire from 2000–2008, convened for the most part by Michael Biggs, with proceedings published in the *Working Papers in Art and Design* online journal). The claim of this history, of Design's maturation into a higher order process, is that Design entered the academy because of a need for these more designerly modes of research even though they took some decades to be articulated. And this history is not yet at an end. These developments were not merely about Design taking its place alongside other disciplines in the University, they also entailed claims about designerly approaches to research and action being more valid than other existing disciplines, at least for the kinds of social problems to which Design was now seeking to respond. These even more assertive arguments are only just now being made, and this chapter arrogates that it is part of that next phase in Discipline of Design.

I will come back to this in 'Paradigmatic', so want now only to register one aspect of the practice-based nature of the Discipline of Design. The debate about practice-based design research that has characterized Design's becoming a Discipline has involved debates primarily about two related aspects of design research.

The first is, I believe, mistaken. This is the claim that designs speak for themselves, that designed artefacts manifest research without the need for verbal apparatuses. While there are ways in which experiencing designed products can demonstrate material and interactional phenomena more directly than verbal descriptions (Tonkinwise and Kasunic 2005), such descriptions are not incompatible with design practice. The issue is not verbal versus non-verbal, but rather the extrapolatibility of what is being articulated – the second debate about design research. Design tends to discover new things in the process of making new things, but these findings remain context specific. Only certain aspects of any design response can be extended beyond the situation to which those designs respond. This means that design research must remain case-based, a kind of phronesis (Flyvbjerg 2001).

Institutional

The narrative of Design maturing into its disciplinary place within the university gives all the credit to Design. The situation was of course more complex, with changes to the nature of the university allowing, and in fact in some cases requiring, Design to take a place in the academy.

To explain, note that doctoral degree programmes in Design are more prevalent in nations with government-funded higher education systems (Europe, Scandinavia, Australia and New Zealand) than in nations with private higher education systems (North America). This suggests that design research is implicated in neoliberalism.

In the second half of the twentieth century, nations with government-funded university systems started making more proactive use of universities as economic development mechanisms. Post-secondary educational institutions were encouraged to significantly increase enrolment numbers in order to train the labour force for economies restructuring from industrial bases to information- and knowledge-based employment. The financial fluctuations of the 1980s, with recessions and high inflation and unemployment, prompted governments to rationalize their higher education systems along with all government spending. Two versions of these rationalizations collided to afford design entry to the university as a research-active discipline. Firstly, various kinds of post-secondary institutions were amalgamated with universities to streamline management and expenditure. In many countries, this saw institutions teaching design in technical colleges or art schools relocated into universities. Secondly, governments introduced measures to better ensure return-on-investment for funding university research. These were primarily Quality Assurance measures, such as 'number of PhD completions' as a measure of research productivity.

Together, these meant that Design was required to enter the academy and immediately become research active through the formal mechanism of the PhD. Design educators became university employees, but with the stipulation that they add to, or convert, any professional practice they might also carry out into peer-reviewable research. Given the maturity of higher order Designing, as described in the previous section, Design educators were able to comply with these demands for research activity by proposing some epistemological innovations. Rather than merely adopting the research models of the social sciences, Design educators advocated for practice-based forms of research.

Design was not alone in resisting assimilation into existing forms of research, succeeding instead in getting university research to accommodate to its particular ways of working. Design was just one of the Creative Industries that were also subject to amalgamation or to the edict to formalize their research practices (Haseman 2006). But perhaps more significant is the wider politics behind these rationalizations of higher education productivity. This was the era of neoliberalism. The 'liberal' aspect to neoliberalism was to free markets from government regulation. This demanded paradoxical government interventions that were intended to facilitate systems of self-regulatory continuous improvement. The content agnostic nature of research quality assurance measures, for instance, benefited new entrants like Design and the other creative industries. But, conversely, the applied nature of these new creative research disciplines like Design fitted perfectly the productivity objectives of neoliberalism. It was therefore in the interest of neoliberal reforms of universities that space be made for exemplars of more 'impactful' research like Design.

It is worth recalling that this argument is precisely the one that Jean-Francois Lyotard made in his famous *The Postmodern Condition* (1984), a booklet written as a report for the Québécois Conseil des Universités. Since legitimation of knowledge required increasingly expensive scientific equipment, having access to funding (from the state or private enterprise) became a proxy for having legitimacy. But access to funding is measured according to 'performativity – that is, the best possible input/output equation [...] [the] State and/or company must abandon the idealist and humanist narratives of legitimation in order to justify the new goal: in the discourse of today's financial backers of research, the only credible goal is power' (p. 46). Lyotard's late 1970s argument proceeds by way of the technoscience of The Information Economy. But in retrospect it is apparent that performative power lies more in practices like Design, the discipline that makes the interfaces for those technologies and then makes communicable sense of the data they collect and store. Consider the designerliness of the following questions: 'The question (overt or implied) now asked by the professionalist student, the State or institutions of higher education is no longer "Is it true?" but "What use is it?" [...] In the context of the mercantilization of knowledge, more often than not this question is the equivalent to: "Is it saleable?" And in the context of power-growth: "Is it efficient?"' (p. 51). Or note Lyotard's deprecation of the interdisciplinarity that Design often claims as its own 'super power': 'The idea of an interdisciplinary approach is specific to the age of delegitimation and its hurried empiricism. The relation to knowledge is not articulated in terms of the realization of the life of the spirit or the emancipation of humanity, but in terms of the users of a complex conceptual and material machinery and those who benefit from its performance capabilities. They have at their disposal no metalanguage or metanarrative in which to formulate the final goal or correct use of that machinery. But they do have brainstorming to improve its performance' (p. 52). All this recasts the narrative of design research entering the university; from one of the now mature expert practices deserving a place in the university for the ways in which it engages with wide-ranging social challenges, to the more pragmatic, if not cynical, inclusion of a higher-performing approach to research in the era of competing knowledge economies.

What I am arguing, by way of Lyotard, also repositions Donald Schön's ideas about Reflective Practice which are so central to the epistemology of practice-based design research. Schön's account of studio learning describes a highly performative process of make-it-to-see. Schön promotes Design as exemplary of professional ways of knowing because it proceeds, contrary to other forms of technocractic expertise, without the need for rationally formulated theories to structure its hypotheses; Designing, rather, develops its understandings of situations by making things that can be immediately put into those situations. From the perspective of the kind of neoliberal performativity that Lyotard is arguing was structuring universities at the time, design therefore has the added advantage of getting on with the job of producing things. It moves faster – something that has now been emphasized by recent trends relating to Design Thinking Innovation techniques – and is more responsive – or, in the more contemporary parlance of UX Design, Agile and Lean.

This 'many quick iterations' way of working demands that the designer maintain constant reflectivity about their process. This is what gives the practice-based researching of design its validity. But, again, from the perspective of neoliberal management of creative industries, this reflectivity suggests a very convenient form of self-regulation. In this light, Schön's Reflective Practitioner looks a lot like Michel Foucault's self-disciplining modern individual (1988). Much like the prisoners in Bentham's Panopticon, who learn to police themselves after living in a complex of constant surveillance, so the designers learns to crit themselves after living with studio crit throughout their education (Webster 2006). Such graduates have an exemplary work ethic as a result of their drive for innovation yet commitment to craft.

That practice-based design research may have established itself because of its compatibility with a wider neoliberal ideology is not inherently damning. The point of Lyotard's report is that it should be noted that the regime of performativity depends on acts of creation that can force consideration of what 'rules' currently constrain those acts and even promote the creation of new 'rules'. This suggests that Designing should always also entail redesigning designing (Jones 1991). The responsibility that comes with being an agent of neoliberalism is not merely to innovate within existing economies but also to propose alternative economies. Or to put it more pointedly, Designing must involve Critical Design; not where the latter is merely another source of innovation, but, rather, where what is being criticized, through the creation of things that do not make sense within existing accounts, are current modes of Designing. The 'flection' or the Reflective Practitioner must involve bending away, not just self-monitoring (Bleakley 1999).

Paradigmatic

Lyotard's account of the arrival of the postmodern movement in universities depends, ironically (Lingis 1994), on a fairly modern narrative of progressively increasing technological intensity against the background of a consistent capitalist system. Although the most remembered tagline of Lyotard's report is 'incredulity toward metanarratives', his argument explains more a pragmatic shift in what counts as legitimacy than some crisis of faith: 'This incredulity is undoubtedly a product of progress in the sciences ... [an] obsolescence of the metanarrative apparatus of legitimation [...] [which] is losing its functors [...] being dispersed in clouds of narrative language elements' (p. xxiv). However, I believe that there is a wider context for the transitions that Lyotard describes, one that explains better the university's 'Design Turn' and one that increases the responsibilities that design research should be attending to.

While Lyotard was describing, philosophically, the shift from the modern to the postmodern, Ulrich Beck, the German Sociologist (who shared with Lyotard a common enemy in Jurgen Habermas) was noting the shift from modernization to reflexive modernization (1994). For Beck, modern society (in North Atlantic economies) was the result of a process of modernization, or what Anthony Giddens termed 'detraditionalization'. Existing systems of knowledge and their sustaining organizations were actively replaced with modern institutions structured around rational technoscientific principles. This process required uninstalling people's existing beliefs and values and reinstalling more 'modern' ones.

At a certain point in the latter half of the twentieth century, this process of modernization begins to turn on itself, undermining the legitimacy of the modern institutions that initially benefited from this programme of social epistemology change. For Beck, the turning point concerns ecological politics (1995). Ecosystems involve interdependencies at microscopic levels (e.g. toxins moving through food chains, nuclear radiation damaging DNA) and macroscopic levels (e.g. climatic systems, depletion of rare earth metals from the planet's crust). These relations traverse modern boundaries between what is considered 'natural' and 'artificial' (Latour 1993). The complexity involved means that phenomena are more probabilistic than factual. Yet what is at stake is the well-being if not viability of anybody; there is no clear 'proletariat' for the 'bads' of unsustainability associated with the manufacture and distribution of modern goods (Beck 1995). For all these reasons, the technoscientifically rational institutions that built, and operate, modern society start to seem inadequate. The postmodern Risk Society is therefore characterized by a very pointed incredulity towards modern expert institutions like universities.

Consider for instance a relatively recent incident near where I currently live. Extreme cold (resulting from 'wobbles' in the Arctic Jetstream that have been associated with Climate Change) caused some storage tanks containing a solvent used in coal processing to rupture. The resulting chemical leak – the tanks were on the banks of a river – entered the drinking water of nearby towns in West

Virginia. People became ill from the liquorice-smelling water and so were told to stop all water usage. Towns further down the river halted intake to prevent contamination of their water systems. One of the main problems was that almost no one understood anything about the proprietary chemical in question – about its toxicity or longevity for instance. The only people who could advise populations about the risks associated with this chemical were the industrial chemists who created it in the first place. Scepticism about the information provided by the very people who caused the problem in the first place seemed justified. In Beck's account, incidents such as this, occurring all the time around the world, result in growing anti-science sentiment – the sort of thing that is evident with 'climate-denialists' and 'anti-vaxxers'.

Beck's historical account better explains the 'incredulity' that Lyotard uses to account for changes in the nature of the university at about the time that Design enters as a Discipline. For Beck, the reflexive modernization of a Risk Society contains the danger of Barbarism – a rejection of all modern institutions and a re-embracing of pre-modern forms of society: ethnically non-diverse communities, religious beliefs and so on. Beck's prescription, and one that he does also see taking place in some parts of our societies as they negotiate these transitions, is a productive embracing of doubt rather than a cynical rejection of what is being doubted. The former demands that the production of knowledge become much more participatory.

Details of what this could entail have been elaborated by Silvio Functowicz and Jerome Ravetz (1993). In their schema, as the uncertainties of a situation increase along with the amount at stake in any decision in relation to that situation, what is required shifts from routine applied science through contextually specific expert consultancy to the more negotiated processes of Post-normal Science. Functowicz and Ravetz still place science at the centre of these situations: determinations of the quality and quantity of risk are technically possible and so necessary. But the meaning of those determinations will vary depending on the stakeholders, and can in turn be varied by deciding on different courses of action. These are then very precisely Wicked Problems that demand the involvement of both expert scientists and lay people in ongoing manipulations of the situation – what Functowicz and Ravetz promote with their ideas of 'extended peer communities' (Healey 1999). By adopting more open and flexible processes for negotiating the relationships between facts and values, risks and options, experiments and decisions, Post-normal Science also restores the credibility of scientific institutions.

On the one hand, this trajectory from Lyotard through Beck to Functowicz and Ravetz should seem very foreign to Design Research, especially since it is so embedded in the kind of technoscience that the Discipline of Design avoided after the Design Methods movement. On the other hand, the iteratively constructivist process of Post-normal Science should seem very familiar to designers, especially those favouring Co-design.

The point here is that Design did not merely mature into a research active university discipline; nor did it cynically take advantage of the neoliberal effort to increase the productivity of university research, or become appropriated by it. Rather, Design also enters the Academy as part of a legitimate response to a legitimation crisis manifesting as societal unsustainability.

This means that practice-based design research at universities should not just be a higher order form of conventional design practices. Nor should practice-based design research be a more strategically applied form of research. Practice-based design research is part of a larger project to create knowledge about preferable futures in an era of complex risks. This demands that the reflectively abductive outcomes of practice-based design research be comprehensively negotiated with a range of stakeholders.

Professing (not Professional) Practice-based Design Research

To put it the other way round, the difference between practice-based design research and a mature research-based design practice in a neoliberal era is its location in the university. This institution exists to legitimate knowledge about preferable futures. Its legitimacy has been undergoing a postmodern or reflexively modernizing crisis. The participatory constructivism of practice-based design research is part of the Post-normal response to that crisis, a way of reconstructing trust in processes for determining future directions for our society.

In short, this means that practice-based design research must always also involve articulating its experiments to a wide range of people and not speaking only to other expert practitioners.

References

Akrich, Madeleine, Callon, Michel, Latour, Bruno and Monaghan, Adrian (2002a), 'The Key to Success in Innovation Part I: The Art of *Interessement*'. *International Journal of Innovation Management* 6 (2).

Akrich, Madeleine, Callon, Michel, Latour, Bruno and Monaghan, Adrian (2002b), 'The Key to Success in Innovation Part II: The Art of Choosing Good Spokespersons'. *International Journal of Innovation Management* 6 (2).

Alexander, Christopher (1964), *Notes on the Synthesis of Form*. Cambridge, MA: Harvard University Press.

Beck, Ulrich (1995a), *Ecological Politics in an Age of Risk*. Oxford: Polity Press.

Beck, Ulrich (1995b), *Ecological Enlightenment: Essays on the Politics of the Risk Society*. Atlantic Highland, NJ: Humanities Press International.

Beck, Ulrich, Giddens, Anthony and Lash, Scott (1994), *Reflexive Modernization: Politics, Tradition and Aesthetics in the Modern Social Order*. Stanford: Stanford University Press.

Bleakley, Alan (1999), 'From Reflective Practice to Holistic Reflexivity'. *Studies in Higher Education* 24 (3).

Buchanan, Richard (2001a), 'Design Research and the New Learning'. *Design Issues*. 17 (4).

Buchanan, Richard (2001b), 'The Problem of Character in Design Education: Liberal Arts and Professional Specialization'. *International Journal of Technology and Design Education* 11 (1).

Cross, Nigel, (ed.) (1984), *Developments in Design Methodology*. New York: John Wiley and Sons.

Cross, Nigel (2006), *Designerly Ways of Knowing*. London: Springer.

Evans, Barrie, Powell, James A. and Talbot, Reg, (eds) (1982), *Changing Design*. New York, John Wiley and Sons.

Fallman, Daniel (2007), 'Why Research-oriented Design isn't Design-oriented Research: On the Tensions between Design and Research in an Implicit Design Discipline'. *Knowledge, Technology and Policy* 20 (3).

Findeli, Alain (1989), 'The Bauhaus: Avant-Garde or Tradition?'. *The Structurist* 29.

Findeli, Alain (1991), 'Bauhaus Education and After: Some Critical Reflections'. *The Structurist* 31.

Flyvbjerg, Bent (2001), *Making Social Science Matter: Why Social Inquiry Fails and How It Can Succeed Again*. Cambridge: Cambridge University Press.

Foucault, Michel, Martin, Luther H., Gutman, Huck and Hutton, Patrick H. (1988), *Technologies of the Self: A Seminar with Michel Foucault*. Amherst: University of Massachusetts Press, 1988.

Fry, Tony (2012), *Becoming Human by Design*. New York: Berg.

Functowicz, Silvio and Ravetz, Jerome (1993), 'The Emergence of Post-normal Science'. In von Schomberg, Rene (ed.) *Science, Politics and Morality*. Dordrecht: Springer.

Haseman, Brad (2006), 'A Manifesto for Performative Research'. *Media International Australia* 118.

Healy, Stephen (1999), 'Extended Peer Communities and the Ascendance of Post-Normal Politics'. *Futures* 31 (7).

Jones, John Chris (1991), *Designing Designing*. London, Architecture Design and Technology Press.

Latour, Bruno (1993), *We Have Never Been Modern*. Cambridge MA: Harvard University Press.

Lawson, Bryan (2012), *What Designers Know*. New York: Routledge.

Lingis, Alphonso (1994), 'Some Questions about Lyotard's Postmodern Legitimation Narrative'. *Philosophy Social Criticism* 20 (1).

Lyotard, Jean-François (1984), *The Postmodern Condition: A Report on Knowledge*. Minneapolis: University of Minnesota Press.

Meikle, Jeffrey (2001), *Twentieth Century Limited: Industrial Design in America 1925–1939*. Philadelphia: Temple University Press.

Sanders, Liz and Stappers, Pieter Jan (2012), *Convivial Design Toolbox: Generative Research for the Front End of Design*. Amsterdam: BIS.

Schön, Donald (1983), *The Reflective Practitioner: How Professionals Think in Action*. New York: Basic Books.

Schön, Donald (1987), *Educating the Reflective Practitioner*. San Francisco: Josey-Bass Publishers.

Tonkinwise, Cameron and Lorber-Kasunic, Jacqueline (2006), 'What Things Know: Exhibiting Animism as Artefact-based Design Research'. *Working Papers in Art and Design* 4.

Webster, Helena (2006), 'A Foucauldian Look at the Design Jury'. *Art, Design and Communication in Higher Education* 5 (1).

Part 2

SOCIO-CULTURAL IMPACTS OF THE DESIGN PHD
IN PRACTICE

Chapter 5

DESIGNING THE PHD CURRICULUM IN THE DESIGN DISCIPLINES

Henry Mainsah, Andrew Morrison, Jonny Aspen and Cheryl E. Ball

Introduction

Graduate, and especially doctoral, education in the design-related disciplines is growing fast internationally. This is the case pedagogically and as a topic of research. The diverse and interdisciplinary nature of the design disciplines and their corresponding professional practices pose a considerable challenge in regard to the design of curricula. Added to an already complex scenario of diverse, inter-secting and contrasting disciplines and relationships to professional practice is a tendency for doctoral design programmes to under-articulate the educational frameworks on which their curricula are based. Such programmes typically do not include, project or promote explicit learning theories, or articulate their design and enactment by way of expressed pedagogical practices.

In this chapter we focus on the challenges and potential in the design of a curriculum for doctoral education in design-related disciplines in increasingly interdisciplinary contexts, and where the PhD is located within a wider research project or strategic research area. We do so with reference to the implications for the growth of pedagogies that support doctoral students' professional devel-opment as researchers beyond formal taught courses in the confines of a PhD school, and the role of participation in wider research project-based inquiry and the role of supervisory support.

The trans-disciplinary nature of doctoral-level design research requires collab-orative and distributed forms of teaching and learning, where an integral link between context, social environment and learning is created. The authors offer their approach to a curriculum design *for* design PhDs at The Oslo School of Architecture and Design (AHO) that is flexible and responsive in relation to the current changes within professional practice and research within products, services, interactions and systems design. The content of the curricula draws strongly on the portfolio of practice-led design research projects across different institutes in the university. This approach reflects a shared commitment to building a doctoral education for training an engaged and able future community of practitioner-researchers capable of thinking and acting across disciplinary contexts and primed to face contemporary global challenges.

The four domains of research in AHO's design institute – Product Design, Interaction Design, Service Design and Systems-oriented Design – join together a wide variety of fields, such as computing, engineering, visual communication, art, Science and Technology Studies, anthropology and Cultural Studies. In partnerships with a diversity of designers, artists, businesses, research collaborators and students, doctoral research at the institute has covered a variety of areas, spanning maritime ship bridge design, methods for service innovation, multimodal interfaces and disability, and social media and performativity in urban environments. The research context from which we draw our views is characterized by the strong presence of practice-based research in design, and the growing placement of doctoral studies in design within larger, interdisciplinary research projects and teams, extending to industry placements. In the past decade, the PhD curriculum at our institution has been through what we see as three main, interlinked phases: 1) architecturally centred with emphasis on the making professions with a lecture and seminar-based pedagogy; 2) increased attention to design in a socio-culturally inflected and task-based pedagogy; 3) a thematized, interdisciplinary approach with focus on contexts of inquiry and research methods with staged activities. We draw on these legacies from the interdisciplinary PhD school, but focus this chapter on curricular practices for design PhDs within the Design Institute at AHO.

Considering a curriculum for novice–experts

In the considerable body of research on the changing character of the design PhD (Dunin-Woyseth and Nilsson 2012; Michl and Nielsen, 2005; Morrison 2013; Tonkinwise and Vaughan 2013; Vaughan and Morrison 2014), there is an increasing need to identify the unique qualities of researching and supervising in design and the different strategies for achieving this (Allpress et al. 2012). Drawing on a socio-cultural approach to learning, which indicates that learning is developmental through social and cultural processes (Hakkarainen et al. 2004; Lave and Wenger 1991; Scardamelia and Bereiter 2006; Vygotsky 1986), we have found that each PhD thesis process and product represents an instance of this transformational and developmental approach.

For many doctoral research projects there is an iterative character between making and reflecting, between implicit and explicit practice. Here, practice processes, artefacts and performances can be described and interrogated using a diverse set of research literatures that over time form part of a more coherent apparatus, which goes through a series of drafts, formulations, presentations, internal reviews and professional peer reviews. Students come to understand their work through seeing other students' work in progress and at various points of completion and assessment. This provides them with a scaffolding for learning. However, close attention to writing as a generative activity is key. It is a type of writing geared towards critical interpretation, and representing the authorial voice of the designer.

Doctoral design students may begin to understand that there is a dynamic relationship between what they have made, earlier research and the voicing of their own analysis. It empowers design research to build up new concepts. The acts of new making are now infolded with an explicit twine of research. Over time, students come to see how interpretation can be built through dialogue with their peers and supervisors, in spelling out the relationship between how they know things through making and what they know analytically through critical reflection.

A coherent curriculum needs to identify the elements of knowledge that students will acquire. Much of a PhD in design concerns shifts from tacit to explicit knowledge. As Polanyi (1967) stated, in design practice much knowledge is tacit in status and in its development, being sensual and conceptual and embedded in acts of making. Such knowledge is internalized, and is the result of a developmental practice that leads to connoisseurship. But it can be difficult to pinpoint elements of knowledge within connoisseurship models of design curricula. Gilbert (2009), drawing on several previous studies (see for example, Ross 2000), suggested the following knowledge types in curricula:

1. abstract propositional knowledge – knowledge about facts, theories, and concepts;
2. abstract procedural knowledge involving conceptual skills and cognitive abilities of analysis and problem solving;
3. embodied knowledge that is action-oriented and likely to be only partly explicit – acquired by doing and rooted in specific contexts;
4. tacit knowledge involved in expert practice and professional judgement;
5. encultured knowledge related to the process of achieving shared understandings, embracing the perspectives and experiences of others;
6. embedded knowledge residing in systematic routines, technologies and practices or explicit procedures (p. 58).

In such a view, it is the developmental, reflexive and processual character of coming to know and the ability to work synthetically within and across a variety of concepts, materials and potential designs that mark an approach to deal with what have been called *wicked problems* (Buchanan 1992). These are challenges, needs and directions posed within the task at hand and the overall approach to designing. Tackling wicked problems requires a good measure of flexibility, and an ability to work towards not simply finding solutions to problems, although these are needed, but finding and better defining them, and ways to meet them. Here, context, activity and process are central to understanding how designing (as activity and practice) works – where knowing may be beyond what is immediately being designed, and where artefacts and agency are linked through multiple modes of mediation.

Vaughan and Morrison (2013) attempted to map out the key components of the pedagogies and research practices involved in undertaking a doctorate in design. They show the rich variations in structure, curriculum formats, teaching approaches, modes of publication, changing professional practices and modes of knowing that exist across different design schools and in different national contexts. They argue that professional design practice itself brings to doctoral education in design special ways of working, researching and knowing. Thus doctoral education in design has the potential to develop its own identity, developed from within but also connected with the wider world through its inter-disciplinary linkages with industry and practice.

Our university has seen a variety of doctoral research projects over the past two decades. They have varied in approach from theoretical and technical to poetic and performative. Projects have taken concepts of *myth* and *secret* to design innovative services for the tourism and sports industries, technical specifications of ship-building to design new interfaces for ship bridges, choreography to track dancers' movements for design visualization uses. Projects have also aligned with a number of different design professions or fields of practice, from architecture and engineering to communications and service design. For instance, a recent project coming out of the Service Design domain applied co-creation principles to collaboration in the engineering-focused field of shipbuilding. Another project borne out of Interaction Design draws on communication design and cinematography to show how invisible design materials such as RFID and GPS can be made visible for designers' use.

Research has also been conducted in a variety of contexts ranging from the laboratory and the studio to the company office and the street; it spans different modes of inquiry, including self-reflexive, collaborative, critique, exploration and experiential. Self-reflexive projects are often found in the Interaction Design domain, where designers work alone, or in small teams, gathering data, and then reflect on that data independently to critique a method or create concepts and approaches that are usable by future design-researchers. One example of this would be the project, mentioned above, which was concerned with making invisible technologies visible. In this project, the design researcher photographed thousands of instances of people using handheld technologies, and then reflected on and wrote about the pervasiveness of technological usage in a networked city environment. A different, collaborative project involved a design-researcher working closely with information communication technology (ICT) and insurance companies to design better services for their customers. Knowledge, in this setting, is produced in collaboration between designer and company in a research-by-design approach. To forward their research, each of these projects drew on a range of knowledge types, moving, for instance, from tacit and implicit knowledge of how customers interact with technology companies to explicit, embodied knowledge of customer interactions. Anyone who accesses the online portfolio of doctoral research projects at the Centre for Design Research at AHO is bound to see the wide variety of the themes, disciplines and modes of inquiry covered (www.designresearch.no).

Building designerly pedagogies

The curriculum model in the design institute at AHO has relied so far on individual supervision of students, and informal communities of practice that bring together PhD students and faculty in small clusters such as reading groups, hallway meetings and collaborative mentoring and sharing of resources and ideas across domains. There are challenges in this informal approach: some students fall through the cracks and lose traction on their degree completion, supervision models may differ among the faculties, and knowledge may be only sporadically exchanged. Despite these challenges, the design PhDs have been successful in producing top-quality research, individually and with their supervisors and colleagues, in ways that have allowed us to reflect on those processes to create the topological model above.

For example, strategies used by the supervisor to support a recent group of PhD design candidates included: spending a considerable amount of time working one-on-one with the PhDs to hone their domain knowledge; referring them to other researchers in the design institute to increase their knowledge of modes of inquiry, such as experimental methods that would be acceptable in academic research on interaction design; encouraging them to see a productive collaboration between their research and teaching, which required them to make their internal domain knowledge and modes of inquiry explicit through guest-teaching or teaching their own courses to undergraduate students; forming cohorts sharing in-progress research among students and with faculty so that academic writing could be critiqued and shared and learned collectively.

Faced with such a configuration, the principal challenge is to construct a combinatorial and transformative curriculum that is both general and specific, that is inclusive of diversity while differing, and demarcating how those different disciplines are constructed and related. This is an issue of scale, and questions whether such a curriculum *can* be formalized given the often-changing landscape of design. While, at AHO, such a curriculum has been formalized at the PhD school, allowing explicit academic knowledges to be taught across the four institutes in the university (namely, architecture, design, urban planning and landscape, and form/theory/history), there is nevertheless a need to apply our model specifically within the design institute and its subdomains, where there is a demand for the understanding of the pragmatics and changing texture of design work (new materials and tools, new means of production, changing marketing, etc.) and the impact of communication technologies. Attention needs to be given to new tools and their roles in the conduct and character of both design making and research interpretation and analysis; and the expectations and outcomes of this work in the design domain are different from those of the domains of architecture, urban planning, or form/theory/history.

The design curriculum at the PhD level needs to provide scope for working with the experimental, and in designerly ways, but also for shaping what the experiment means in design inquiry. For example, in a research through design PhD curriculum, Krogh et al. (2015) included a variety of designerly experiments (as being either accumulative, comparative, serial, expansive or probing). This needs to be connected also to the application of emerging tools from the creative and technology industries for mapping, documenting, annotating, archiving and publishing multimodal research.

Further challenges and implications of a design-specific curriculum for PhDs

Challenges are also about making space for a peer-to-peer exploration of, and interest in, processes and formal analysis. There is a need to build a curriculum that has room for the frequent presentation of work in progress, so that the level of activity of producing written research (students in design have a special need for ongoing support) exposes students to lateral levels of analysis in which they see a similar problem or a similar analysis that they can relate to their own study or writing. Institutionally, funding and publication-dissemination needs and requirements have a forceful bearing also on the developmental composition and enactment of the design curriculum. Students in a design PhD need collective modelling of these types of high-level research processes in ways that can be made explicit to them through a formal curriculum. Pedagogically, there is a need for a meta-view that addresses the complexities that have been revealed by the topological model we have presented above. These complexities would allow space for the multivariate design domains, types of knowledge and modes of inquiry that occur regularly, and often implicitly, in design curricula.

Towards a topological view of the doctoral curriculum

The interdisciplinary design curriculum is complex and difficult to construct. It needs to contain a focus on design domains related to a variety of academic disciplines (and subsets of them). These disciplines are connected to the types of knowledge that are being accessed and enacted through the modes of inquiry. In Figure 5.1, we provide a diagram illustrating some of these relational elements.

This we call *a sociocultural topological view* on PhD design pedagogy. It is a view that allows us to look at the activities, tools, and mediations, and research production involved in design curriculum and pedagogy from a socio-cultural framework on learning. It allows us to see the intricate relationships between intersecting, overlapping and divergent components that are central to the dialogical and mediated meaning-making of a sociocultural pedagogy for doctoral design research education. The illustration presents components that may be combined in different relationships that shift the focus from the concept of the topographical to the topological. In this regard, topological refers to a mapping approach, where the focus is on details of three-dimensional modelling and not the tradition of visual perspective and the predominance of an ideal

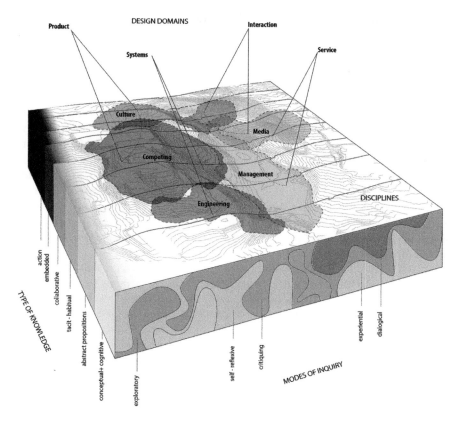

Figure 5.1 A topological view on sociocultural perspectives on doctoral design education. Courtesy the author.

image (Girot et al. 2014). The topological permits views that reveal more than features and elevations, as is the case with topographical mapping. Adopting a topological mode accentuates spatial relationships between places, components, and edges. It seeks to assemble and to communicate their 'physics' – the interplay of dynamic features, folds, structural parts and overlays – in a holistic mediation. The complexity of the landscape – learning, pedagogical and research – may be perceived through such a view.

Adopting such an orientation allows for a curriculum to be realized through actions of stretching, bending, curving and twisting, rather than separation, stitching or gluing. This allows for *transformational topological learning properties and dynamic elements* to be co-designed. *Learning properties* here refers to the identification and materialization of qualities of closeness, distinction and divergence. Through these relational properties, the curriculum, learning events and potential for learners' actions may be co-configured as resources within a transformational pedagogy. A master's or doctoral student in design working on their thesis project needs to be able to make more explicit the degrees of relationship in their own mapping or assemblage of a selected mode of inquiry, its relationship to identified and emergent types of knowledge and the situatedness of the project with respect to the various (overlapping) domains of design.

Here, the acts of stretching, bending, curving and twisting need to be made more apparent. First, this is to identify the actual complexity of the design inquiry and its learning character. Second, it is to engage in processes of enacting selected linkages. For example, a doctorate by Lise Hansen at AHO in interaction design recently drew together exploratory and collaborative software development of a tool for whole-body movement tracking (Hansen 2014). It linked this to conceptual analysis and the elaboration of a wider multimodal socio-semiotic analytical framing, with links to underlying expertise in performance, chore-ography and graphic design. The overall thesis by compilation drew together practice and analysis in iterative inquiry that included diverse publication, lab-based events and open source scripting as part of a wider move to make explicit movement as material for design.

In such a view, it is the *dynamics* of the topological perspective that also needs to be articulated. This is a dynamics that comes into being through a performative discursive curricular enactment of a number of intersections: of modes of inquiry and types of knowledge, related research concepts and methods and the design notions and techniques. These too need to be charted, related and placed in terms of their proximity, connectedness and continuity. In master's and doctoral thesis work, such as Hansen's, what is then needed is a complex set of actions that may involve students, co-authors and supervisors in negotiations about what is to be foregrounded and how this is to be achieved, through co-creation and collabo-rative interpretation.

There is also room in this model for movement between the course design for a PhD school or group and the design of the individual doctorate. Each individual doctoral project will highlight in one way or another selected aspects of this topological map. At the same time, it will be developed in relation to a wider doctoral educational programme also framed through such a charting.

Learning goals in a PhD design curriculum that faces such complexity need to:

- build analytical frames specific to design domains;
- theorize not only through available scholarly research but through the design practices they already use to build new theories and modes;
- address innovations in how we teach modes of inquiry through methodological experimentation and practice;
- teach students to communicate their research through academic writing in a way that honours, and is adapted from, the strengths of their practice as designers, filmmakers, engineers, dancers and artists.

We recommend that such curricula make these goals explicit when teaching PhDs in design, which will allow students to move more quickly from novice to expert researchers in design. Even in informal curricula, there is need for communities of design research practice with diverse and intersecting membership interests. Such a community should include senior researchers and students, in partnerships of co-authors who draw on, reflect on and learn from each other's research practice. These will be major undertakings to co-create and build rich landscapes for designerly ways of knowing that are equally synthetic and abductive, transformative and transgressive, developmental and novel. This topological model that expresses the ever-changing landscape of design may help schools and institutes build curricula specifically for design PhDs.

References

Allpress, B., Barnacle, R., Duxbury, L. and Grierson, E. (2012), *Supervising Practices for Postgraduate Research in Art, Architecture and Design*. Rotterdam: Sense Publishers.

Buchanan, R. (1992), 'Wicked problems in design thinking', *Design Issues* 8 (2): 5–21.

Dunin-Woyseth, H. and Nilsson, F. (2012), 'Doctorateness in design disciplines. Negotiating connoisseurship and criticism in practice-related fields', *FORMakademisk*, 5 (2): 1–11. Available from: http://www.FORMakademisk.org/ (accessed 1 September 2015).

Dunin-Woyseth, H. and Nilsson, F. (2013), 'Design Education, Practice and Research: On Building a Field of Inquiry', Keynote address at *DRS / CUMULUS 2013 Oslo: The 2nd International Conference for Design Education Researchers*. Oslo: 14.01.2013–17.05.2013. Retrieved from http://www.hioa.no/eng/About-HiOA/ The-Facultyof-Technology-Art-and-Design/DRS-CUMULUS-Oslo-2013 (accessed 1 September 2015).

Gilbert, R. (2009), 'The Doctorate as Curriculum: A Perspective on Goals and Outcomes of Doctoral Education', in D. Boud and A. Lee (eds) *Changing Practices of Doctoral Education*, 54–70. London: Routledge.

Girot, C., Freytag, A., Kirchengast, A. and Richter, D. (eds) (2014), *Topology*. Berlin: Jovis. (Kindle edition).

Hakkarainen, K., Palonen, T., Paavola, S. and Letninen, E. (2004), *Communities of Networked Expertise: Professional and Educational Perspectives*. Amsterdam: Elsevier.

Hansen, L. (2014). *Communicating Movement: Full-Body Movement as a Design Material for Digital Interaction*. PhD thesis. Oslo: Oslo School of Architecture and Design.

Krogh, P., Markussen, T. and Bang, A. (2015), 'Ways of Drifting – 5 Methods of Experimentation in Research Through Design'. In A. Chakrabarti, (ed.), *ICoRD'15 – Research into Design Across Boundaries. Vol. 1*, 39–50. New Delhi: Springer.

Lave, J. and Wenger, E. (1991), *Situated Learning: Legitimate Peripheral Practice*. New York: Cambridge University Press.

Michl, J. and Nielsen, L. V. (2005), *Building a Doctoral Programme in Architecture and Design. Research Magazine 7*. Oslo: The Oslo School of Architecture and Design.

Morrison, A. (2013), 'Becoming more Definite about the Article'. In J. Dehs, M. Esbensen and C. Pedersen (eds), *When Architects and Designers Write / Draw / Build /? Essays on Research in Architecture and Design*, 182–97. Aarhus: Arkitektskolens Forlag.

Polanyi, M. (1967), *The Tacit Dimension*. London: Routledge.

Ross, A. (2000). *Curriculum: Construction and Critique* (vol. 2). Cambridge: Psychology Press.

Scardamalia, M. and Bereiter, C. (2006), 'Knowledge Building: Theory, Pedagogy, and Technology'. In K. Sawyer (ed.), *The Cambridge Handbook of the Learning Sciences*, 97–115. Cambridge: Cambridge University Press.

Tonkinwise, C. and Vaughan, L. (2013). *Critiquing the North American Design PhD: An International Symposium at Carnegie Mellon University,School of Design*. 5 October, Retrieved from http://phddesigncrit.info/ (accessed 5 September 2015).

Vaughan, L. and Morrison, A. (2013), 'Form, Fit and Flair: Considering the Design Doctorate'. In J. Reitan, P. Lloyd, E. Bohemia, M. Nielsen, I. Digranes and E. Lutnæs (eds), *Design Learning for Tomorrow – Design Education from Kindergarten to PhD: Proceedings of the 2nd International Conference for Design Education Researchers*, vol. 4, 1819–31. Oslo: ABmedia.

Vaughan, L. and Morrison, A. (2014), 'Unpacking models, approaches and materializations of the design PhD', *Studies in Material Thinking* 11, 1–19. Available from: http://www.materialthinking.org/papers/159 (accessed 1 September 2015).

Vygotsky, L. (1986), *Thought and Language*, A. Kozulin, trans. Cambridge, MA: MIT Press.

CHAPTER 6

DOCTORAL TRAINING FOR PRACTITIONERS: ADAPTR (ARCHITECTURE, DESIGN AND ART PRACTICE RESEARCH) A EUROPEAN COMMISSION MARIE CURIE INITIAL TRAINING NETWORK

Richard Blythe and Marcelo Stamm

This project has received funding from the European Union's Seventh Programme for Research, Technological Development and Demonstration. Funding provided under Grant Agreement No 317325. www.ADAPT-r.eu
The aim of the European Union Marie Curie Initial Training Network Grant 'Architecture Design and Art Practice research' (ADAPTr) is to mobilize the adoption of a practice approach to doctoral research training, and enable seven European universities to: explore its applicability to their contexts; adopt this proven approach to doctoral training through the establishment of an open supervisory network; develop allied support resources; achieve substantial engagement of SMEs (small and medium enterprises) in doctoral training; conduct research into this innovative approach (Blythe et al. 2013). The core feature of this approach to doctoral training is the premise that new knowledges are developed through certain kinds of creative practice (identified as 'venturous') from which research can be 'extracted'.[1] ADAPTr provides a model that fills an internationally identified gap in postgraduate training. It involves reflection on an existing body of peer-acknowledged work and reflection during the production of new works produced concurrently with, and informing, the doctoral research. The works, processes and methods of the practice are placed in a broader disciplinary context which allows the research to be theorized from within the practice discipline and to clearly identify contributions to disciplinary knowledge. Thus, the research work of the PhD examines, and is also transformative of, the practice within which it is situated. This chapter will provide an overview of this approach to doctoral training, with specific reference to ADAPTr and the grant's key research work packages.

ADAPTr draws on recent work at RMIT University in developing a design practice research PhD. Although the first PhD graduation in this mode was in 2002, the model was originally based on a post-professional master's degree that developed over a twenty-year period with significant international input under the guidance of Professor Leon van Schaik.[2] In 2011 Professor Richard Blythe further developed the model as the successful basis for ADAPTr and the approach has continued to be refined through the expanded ADAPTr and RMIT teams.[3]

The new paradigm is the result of a careful evaluation of the experimentation undertaken at RMIT University; it is essentially a carefully constructed and curated social learning model which franchises both SME practices and academic institutions. In it, candidates are not treated as isolated individual practitioners but integrated into a research community made up of academics and venturous practitioners. The organization and choreography of significant events are key to the successful open supervisory model in which, while candidates work with a primary supervisor, all supervisors and candidates are continually exposed to and engaged with the work of one another.

The grant activities are focused on RMIT's two annual *Practice Research Symposia* (PRS). The practice research symposium is set up as a semi-public event, including the examination sessions. The examinations are by viva, and take place within a PhD exhibition. The structure of the symposia sessions and examination process promotes immediate dissemination and contextualization of the work, among a community of scholars. The examinations, coupled with the symposia make it possible to see the entire doctoral process from end to end in one event, an excellent training opportunity for researchers. Further training components use these various activities as an immersive learning platform. A web portal is currently under development that will provide training resources, open courses and a community platform to augment the training aspects of the PRS.[4]

The examinations immediately precede in-progress review sessions which take place over the PRS weekend. Each candidate has one hour divided into two 25 minute sessions (with a 10 minute set up and transition time). During the first 25 minutes, the candidate provides an update and overview of the research as it is progressing, including accounts of key findings and problems. The second session is devoted to discussion with the appointed panel and the wider audience of peers. The panel is appointed by the supervisor and includes the supervisor and other attendees of the PRS event (including examiners) who the supervisor feels will be of benefit to the research. Panels of about four members are the most effective. An important variation on this model occurs with candidates who are partners in a practice jointly undertaking the PhD. In these cases more than one candidate presents in a combined session with an extended time frame. The decision to present separately or jointly is made between the supervisors and candidates. For the examination, multiple approaches have been formulated. In some cases (Kalinina and McAdam) two candidates make independent presentations based on a common exhibition. In the case of fashion designers S!X (Sprynskyj and Boyd), each partner participated in the presentation of the exhibition as a silent assistant, which provided the audience with a view of crucial non-verbal interactions between partners of a creative practice.

Candidates are selected into the programme through a pre-application process. Applicants are invited to attend a PRS and to make a 20 minute pre-application presentation in which the applicant has 15 minutes to provide an overview of their practice and insight into its key motivations, with a 5 minute window for discussion with a panel of experienced supervisors. The purpose of the presentation is to establish whether the practice is substantial enough to sustain a PhD enquiry using this particular methodology.

In addition to the examinations and in-progress reviews, the PRS offers an opening keynote lecture which is intended to offer insights into wider research contexts. Invitees have included recently completed candidates, examiners and key researchers. The least successful lectures have been from people with no previous engagement with the PRS ecosystem. The weekend concludes with a plenary session in an informal setting in which participants are invited to offer reflections on the PRS, used both in the PRS generally and in ADAPTr as an important quality feedback mechanism and as part of the ongoing review and refinement process.

The PRS is punctuated with informal social activities – morning and afternoon tea, lunches, dinners and so on, and including one formal PRS dinner – all critical to the learning model. Many completing candidates report key conversations from these social activities in which colleagues have offered important insights into the research. The PRS model has found resonance with key industry sectors and has been described by one prominent journal as a 'world-leading PhD program for practitioners', in an article in which many of these aspects of the PRS are explained (Rattenbury 2015).

The four-million-euro ADAPTr programme is based on forty fellowships, thirty-three for 'Early Stage Researchers' (ESR), and seven for 'Experienced Researchers' (ER). The ESR fellowships vary between three and eighteen months, and the ER fellowships between twelve and twenty. While the ESRs are practitioners researching into their own practices, the ERs conduct research across the programme at post-doctoral level, researching practice-based research and researching into the research of the ERs. One of the challenging aspects of ADAPTr is that the ESRs are generally more senior disciplinary figures than the ERs, even though the ERs are more experienced in research conventions, thus inverting the experience and authority more common to these roles. Early results show that the work of the ESRs has provided rich material for researching, and that the research of the ERs has been beneficial to the ESR practitioners in both research and practice terms.

There are four main work packages: Primary Research, Training, Dissemination and Management. The fellows are responsible for the Primary Research deliverables and are active participants in the Training and Dissemination activities. This chapter will focus on the Primary Research work package deliverables.

The Primary Research package is divided into six elements: Case Studies, Communities of Practice, Transformative Triggers, Public Behaviours, Tacit Knowledge and Methods. The development of these elements was based on close observation of the PhD process at RMIT, and while they are significant to practice-based research, and effective as supervisory cues for assisting candidates throughout their creative practice research trajectory, they also provide a set of perspectives useful for the examination of practice-based research across a collection of individual practitioners. Within ADAPTr, the elements are used as *scaffolding* to guide the PhD work of ESRs, who are invited to respond to them in their PRS presentations, and are used also by the ERs who have been researching into them, collecting data from the ESRs and other researchers in the PRS ecosystem through interviews, workshops, observing PRS presentations and reviewing documents and work produced by the ERs.

The scaffolding terms of the ADAPTr framework have emerged organically from the practice-based research paradigm; they were either in current use (Public Behaviours, Community of Practice), or were coined specifically for ADAPTr (Transformative Triggers, Case Studies, Explication of Tacit Knowledge and of Methods). Either way, such scaffolding terms have grown from observations of practice-based design research in action, for the purpose of exposing gaps in the researcher's description of a practice and the practice itself, for situating the research in relation to its domain, and for identifying ascension moments in a practice. The set of terms is neither absolute nor closed. The domain of practice-based design research is thus not unified by generic and objectified methods of investigation, but rather defined by highly context-dependent, situated, singular and concrete approaches which nonetheless benefit from forms of scaffolding that also provide common points of reference.

Case studies in practice-based design research

The term 'case study' in practice-based design research refers to an individual practitioner's comprehensive research into his practice: each practitioner as such represents a singular case study. The specificity and singularity of the case study in question must not be misinterpreted as suggesting a purely subjective nature of the case under scrutiny. It is by virtue of the situated, concrete, embodied and materialized nature of practice that observations are made that can be shared, as they can be shown and used as communal points of reference by different researchers.

The notion of the practitioner's individual case study can be related to the idea of three orders of knowledge to be distinguished with regard to the way a practitioner contextualizes his work: specific select projects, potentially grouped under certain research- relevant perspectives (1st order of knowledge) can be contextualized within the full body of the work of the practitioner, so that, for example, transformations and shifts in the practice may become apparent (2nd order of knowledge). In a transversal perspective, the individual case study of one practitioner may then be differentiated, and positioned within a field of other, parallel, adjacent or contrasting, case studies (3rd order of knowledge) (Blythe 2014b).

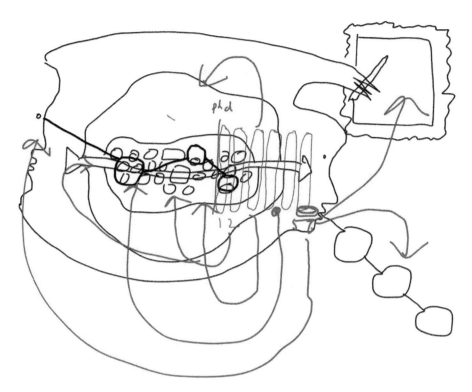

Figure 6.1 See https://vimeo.com/112465233. The practitioner reflects on a body of work (the cluster of small circles identifies the series of projects that make up the practice) and works in progress within the context of a wider community of practice (disciplinary context identified by the middle enclosing ring) noting key intentions and ascension moments in the research (identified by the three circles linked to the eye of the researcher). The researcher practitioner then makes an account of this which is communicated through exhibition (picture frame on the top right), verbal presentation (three linked circles falling from the mouth) and exegesis. The PhD is structured round a three-year programme comprising six PRS events. The numbered lozenges identify each PRS and the arrows point to the foci of each PRS. (Blythe 2014c). Courtesy the author.

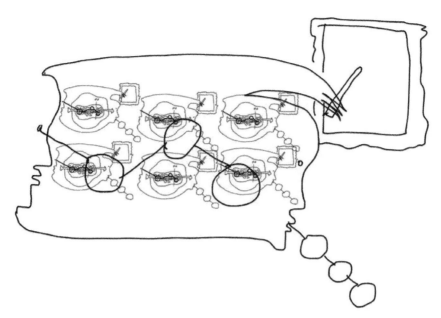

Figure 6.2 See https://vimeo.com/112465233. This diagram shows a researcher making observations across a range of practices, noting key incidents (three circles linked to the eye of the researcher) and explicating them to a wider audience (same three linked circles now falling from the mouth and through exhibition indicated by the picture frame top right). When viewed en masse each PhD provides a case study in a wider disciplinary field. This perspective allows for disciplinary, or '3rd order', insights in which key characteristics can be identified and explicated (Blythe 2014b). Supervisors and the ADAPTr ER fellows have undertaken this kind of research, but each PhD candidate also, to some extent, operates at this order in locating their research/practice within the disciplinary field (Blythe 2014c). Courtesy the author.

Communities of practice

The investigations of a practitioner's community of practice serves a two-fold purpose: to contextualize and position an individual research case study within a realm of practices for which the findings and outcomes of the research in question may have relevance and impact, but also in order to reference the practice into adjacent practices that may exhibit different degrees of influence on the practice under scrutiny. Due to the critical nature of situating the research in the field, the notion of 'community of practice' is an instrumental term with the potential to allow the researcher to differentiate their own research from that of seemingly neighbouring peers: divergence and dissent become as important as possible confluence and resonance. The practice which is conducted in research mode may conceive of a community of practice as also a critical 'community of inquiry'.

Rather than communities of practice being perceived as a static stock of backdrop practices, they can be seen to be highly dynamic, and varied to the point where the researcher may attribute variable communities of practice to different individual projects within the body of work. Communities of practice may also be understood in a narrow sense to be the aggregation of contributors who play a role in the production of a piece of work by way of direct collaboration with the practitioner undertaking the research.

Further, a community of practice can be understood as the choir of voices that operate as self-talk during the creative process. This self-talk, although an individual phenomenon, is an internal conversation with peers and collaborators (and sometimes challengers) extending the social aspects of community also to individual thinking.

Transformative triggers in practice-based design research

The concept 'transformative triggers' serves to induce reflection both into the dynamic and possible transformation of a practice and into the roots and causes of potential shifts and changes observed in a practice. A specific explanatory gap identified during the research process can 'trigger' a new project that interrogates the bespoke issue in order to close the particular research gap through a transformed practice in response to such gaps.

Some researchers make a distinction between tranches of work reflecting transformations of the practice and respective phases triggered by shifts in perspective, approach, attitude, intended design outcome. Practice-based design research thus uses the term 'transformative triggers' to sensitize the researcher towards detecting and analysing both transformations and transformational stimuli, at different levels and phases of the practice and in different orders of knowledge under scrutiny.

Public behaviours in practice-based design research

The term 'Public Behaviours' stems from close observation of the 'natural history' of the creative individual in general, who seeks rhapsodic exposure to public scrutiny and validation of the quality and innovative nature of the practice, but then retreats again into the non-public sphere of the individual practice laboratory where new observations and discoveries are made which may innovate and transform the practice afresh.

Such public behaviour follows a repeated pattern and a propensity to seek recognition in a public realm of the claims and perceived achievements of a venturous practice. Public 'practice behaviour' platforms include actual and concrete realms of exposure, such as client relationships, exhibitions, competition and award forums. It can also exist in virtual forums such as new social media or communities 'at a distance'. Specific platforms for public 'research behaviour' include the two-yearly Practice Research Symposium (PRS), but also the standard peer review process associated with research publication outlets.

A specific sense of 'public' behaviour is linked to the idea of the practitioner's enchainments: creative and innovative achievements can be traced back to specific forms of constellational engagement of the practitioner with other individuals and external positions; such engagement in turn depends on the practitioner's capacity to constellate – that is, to be able to operate in public modes beyond the stereotype of the notoriously secluded and solitary endeavour of the creative individual.

Tacit knowledge in practice-based design research

The notion of tacit knowledge points towards dimensions of something 'known' but not articulated, as well as to specific modes of 'knowing' akin to 'experiential knowledge' and 'operational knowledge', which can be shown, exhibited and demonstrated rather than made explicit in discursive and conceptual ways. The practitioner, thus, may also explore individual forms of explicating modes of 'knowing how' rather than 'knowing that'. The practitioner observes him- or herself as operating on the basis of knowledge dimensions and resources that are not – or cannot be – all at the same level of articulation. The sister notion of 'embodied knowledge' also points at 'material knowledge' and materiality, and the body as 'sites of knowledge', in the wake of understanding thinking as potentially material and intelligence embodied in morphology and materiality rather than being dependent on, and residing in, a conceptual realm.

Practice-based design research understands that there is no singular realm of 'tacit knowledge', but that the 'tacit' relates to diverse layers and dimensions of the unspoken, including that which the practitioner takes for granted or regards as trivial. To foreground, uncover, expose, unfold and extract what is otherwise neglected, covered up, avoided or compacted can take the form of (self-)critical engagement with what is wrongly assumed, with unreflected presuppositions and pre-conceptions, hidden premises, (cognitive) biases operational routines and 'thinking styles'. Under the critical lens, the tacit points towards a disjunction between what the practitioner (sometimes mistakenly) perceives as prima facie central to the practice and what may be operative in the background; tacit knowledge analysis may thus help to debunk myths regarding the principles of operation in a practice.

Methods in practice-based design research

Practice-based design research cannot draw upon a received and sanctioned set of research 'methods': the term, while it suggests that some such repertoire of methods may be available, is therefore contested: practitioners sometimes prefer to talk about individual research strategies and specific research tactics on the intentional side (e.g. 'mapping', 'categorizing') and to particular research techniques on the operative side (e.g. 'drawing', 'diagramming', 'videoing' etc.).

It is a basic premise of practice-based design research that each practitioner has to develop and test a distinctive individual range of ways to conduct the research. While there may be common and shared perspectives and useful lenses (or temporary scaffolding) that suggest themselves within the practice-based paradigm, each researcher will have to develop and explore an individual methodological take on how to investigate these possible research perspectives. Different directions and foci of reflection warrant different ways of conducting such diverse reflections.

Methodological approaches are individualized through the application of techniques that have been developed within the ecology of the specific practice and are specific to the discipline. The advancement of the discipline through the explanation of methods depends not on imitation, repetition and literal transfer of methods in formulaic patterns, but on ongoing adaptation, mutation and recasting of approaches as they are explained and explicated in their dependency on new research contexts and projects. The specific adequacy of a method, its relevance and yield, are then understood by the fellow practitioner as belonging to a specific practice and interrogation. It is only by virtue of methodological explicitness at this level of specificity that 'methods' in practice-based design research can claim a second order transferability and objectivity.

In the same way as a case study may mature to the point where the practitioner's highly individual and authentic voice emerges, and generic jargon and abstract discourse recede, an authentic mode of researching emerges as a genuine research achievement in its own right.

Conclusion

The ADAPTr work package concepts have been developed, and continue to develop, based on close observation of the ways in which creative practitioners have gone about the extraction of a PhD from their design practice, adapting and refining design practice approaches and methods to research. This kind of research is founded in, and continually 'sheeted' back to, practice through careful observation. As Marcelo Stamm has observed (2015), this specific research paradigm is rooted in material and practice knowledge. Stamm is cautious of concepts external to design disciplines. For example, at the ADAPTr Making Research Researching Making 2015 conference, keynote speaker, Albena Yaneva, described how in her recent collaboration with Alejandro Zaera Polo she had applied a philosophical concept – cosmopolitical – to a reading of architecture and its practice. While Yaneva's work may provide some insight into the condition of architecture from an external view point (a sometimes useful perspective), it is questionable whether such a perspective provides substantial insight into the practice of architecture itself; a philosophical concept can easily misdirect in research terms, also, and force you to look for something that is not there at all (Stamm 2015).

This condition has also been described by Blythe, as a 'topological error' in design research (Blythe 2012). Blythe points to the ways in which different knowledge realms hinge at a certain point, reflect into each other and yet need to be understood as autonomous – meaning that it is common but highly problematic to seek to establish research authority for design disciplines from within other disciplines such as philosophy, even though each may reflect usefully into the other in the creation of knowledge. To illustrate this point the position seems almost absurd if expressed in the reverse direction: that philosophy might seek to authenticate itself through art practice – even though art practice may be a productive muse for philosophy.

The ADAPTr work package terms are used in an instrumental supervisory sense to assist design practitioner-researchers to find valid means of examining their own practice while avoiding this kind of common research pitfall, and to provide an open structure (in the sense of both not a closed set and open to continual adaptations) to assist in the PhD process for candidates and for supervisors. The PRS structure, the joint supervisory model and the continual invention and refinement of terms through the PRS process shared between candidates and supervisors facilitates an effective way to extract a PhD from an existing practice, allowing the practitioner to remain primarily focused on practice which is positively transformed through the process. The net result is the formation of a researcherly network of PhD trained practitioners, who are enabled to operate in new ways across both academia and industry.

Notes

1 'Venturous' was originally adapted by Richard Blythe from Terry Cutler's Venturous Australia report on research and innovation and has become part of the language of the programme distinguishing practices which undertake 'researcherly' practice from those practices that deliver a professional service.

2 See *Three Orders of Design Knowledge* (2014b). Directed by BLYTHE, R. Vimeo. https://vimeo.com/116316562 (accessed 10 September 2015); and *Framework for a Practice Based PhD*, 2014a. Directed by BLYTHE, R. Vimeo. https://vimeo.com/90515214 (accessed 10 September 2015) (2014a). Blythe's simple RMIT model video, designed for candidates and supervisors, has had over 10 000 loads in more than 100 countries since it was posted publicly on Vimeo in 2014.

3 For further information on the RMIT program see: Schaik, Leon van (2009); Schaik, Leon van et al. (eds) (2012); Blythe, R. et al., (2013); Stamm, M. (2013); Schaik, Leon van et al. (2014); Stamm, M. (2015).

4 The site can be accessed at creativepracticeresearch.info (accessed 5 October 2015).

References

Blythe, R. (2012). 'Topological Errors in Creative Practice Research: Understanding the Reflective Hinge and the Reflective Gap'. In Boutsen, D. (ed.) *Good Practices Best Practices*. Antwerp: EPO.

Blythe, Richard Johan Verbeke, Clause Peder Pedersen, Katherine Heron, Tadeja Zupančič, Veronika Valk and Sally Stuart (2013). ADAPTr: Architecture, Design and Art Practice Research. Ghent, Barcelona: European Union's Seventh Programme for Research, Technological Development and Demonstration. European Commission, http://cordis.europa.eu/projects/rcn/106609_en.html. www.ADAPT_r.eu (accessed 15 August 2015).

Blythe, R. and Schaik, L. V. (2013), 'What if Design Practice Matters?' In M. Frazer, (ed.) *Design Research in Architecture*. Surrey: Ashgate Publishing Limited.

Framework for a Practice Based PhD, 2014a. Directed by R. Blythe, Vimeo. https://vimeo.com/90515214

Hatleskog, Eli and Holder, Anna (2015), 'Transformative Triggers: 10 Individual Accounts of Transformative Practice Triggers'. ADAPT_r European Union's Seventh Programme for Research, Technological Development and Demonstration. European Commission.

How to do a Practice Based PhD in Three Minutes, 2014c. Directed by R. Blythe, Vimeo. https://vimeo.com/112465233

Rattenbury, K. (2015), 'The Imitation Game: the best crit system in the world?' International PhD programme PRS lets architects develop their work as research. RIBA Journal.

Schaik, Leon van (2009), 'Design Practice Research, the Method'. In Verbeke, J. (ed.) *Reflections*. Brussels: St Lucas.

Schaik, Leon van and Spooner, Michael (2010), 'The Practice of Practice 2: Research in the Medium of Design'. Melbourne: School of Architecture and Design, RMIT University.

Schaik, Leon van, Ware, S. A., Fudge, C. and London, G. (2014), *The Practice of Spatial Thinking: Differentiation Processes*. Melbourne: Onepointsixone.

Schaik, Leon van and Johnson, A. (eds) (2012), *The Pink Book. By Practice By Invitation*. Melbourne: Onepointsixone.

Stamm, Marcelo (2013), *Reflecting Reflection(s): Epistemologies of Creative Practice Research*. Brussels: St Lucas, University of Leuven.

Stamm, Marcelo (2015), 'Conditions of Creativity. Researching Creation Through Creation: Nothing is Hidden'. Aarhus: ADAPT_r European Union's Seventh Programme for Research, Technological Development and Demonstration. European Commission.

Three Orders of Design Knowledge, 2014b. Directed by R. Blythe, Vimeo. https://vimeo.com/116316562. Keynote address, Melbourne PRS, 22–26 October 2014.

Chapter 7

KNOWLEDGE EXCHANGE THROUGH THE DESIGN PHD

Ben Dalton, Tom Simmons and Teal Triggs

Follow the hum of enlivened voices, and the buzz of activity gradually comes into focus as you round the stairwell to the 5th floor studio in the School of Communication, Royal College of Art (RCA). Enter the studio space, and 3D printed shapes, yellow post-it notes, exposed electronics, measured lengths of string, experiments with silk and card pinned to the studio walls all denote research in progress. In one network structure visualization we see a method of identifying keyword searches, in another tactile representation of digital networked relationships. The white-topped desks, laptops and anglepoise lamps give a sense of a working design studio, even supplied with suitably designed upholstered chairs. However, the biotech equipment on one shelf, theatre maquette on another, smart sensor prototype on a third suggest a design studio that has been complicated by less familiar practices and collaborations. This interdisciplinary studio is shared among the School's postgraduate research degrees students and six of the twenty-one students registered to the Creative Exchange Hub (CX) – an Arts and Humanities Research Council (AHRC) funded consortia of three UK universities led by Lancaster University with Newcastle University and the RCA.[1] The CX Hub emphasizes ongoing academic development and university research cultures by placing a substantial cohort of PhD researchers at the core of each step of the knowledge exchange process – from partnership building to proposal development and funding bid formulation, to research, prototype development and evaluation, analysis and review.

The CX Hub emerged out of shifting contexts fuelled by new UK government policies and global economic drivers. It took the contested theme of 'digital public space' as its research focus, but is also shaped out of digital public spaces itself, out of affordances of digital connectivity, complex on-demand networked resources and their personal, social, cultural and political implications. In the CX Hub, the emphasis on digital public space(s) encompasses a breadth of initiatives, from supporting the development of online spaces to make the assets of national cultural associations more accessible, enhancing understanding of the open and/ or shared data protocols and practices of local authorities and government, raising awareness of the flow of social media and its implications for individuals and groups, and investigating the influences of digital public spaces on lived human experiences. The CX Hub is one of four AHRC funded Hubs that have each explored how a range of organizations including commercial, non-commercial and academic parties might better collaborate. In the CX model, established approaches to academic research and the relationship to fostering the creative industries while enhancing business innovation was reconsidered. This, in turn, became a catalyst for exploring a new and innovative research degree model in order to inform and shape future innovation and research within and between the UK's creative industries and academia. The CX Hub was launched in 2012, and set out to develop new thinking under the theme of digital public space, with the main aims being to develop new services, products, technologies and policy interventions, establish new forms of knowledge exchange between academia, industry and communities and, at the same time, develop individuals skilled in knowledge exchange through an innovative PhD programme focusing on design and knowledge exchange. A new PhD model for design has been developed where the PhD student is situated at the centre of a knowledge exchange context and process, which is underpinned by a series of short-term collaborative projects with academics and industry partners.

This chapter will introduce the CX PhD model and propose its value for design research through the relationships formed between academics, industry partners and PhD researchers. By emphasizing the development of expertise in generating ideas, engendering exchange, managing cross-sector relationships and developing collaborative design-based research, the PhD student is well equipped to contribute to informing and shaping future interrelationships between academia and the creative industries. The CX model has the potential to address how designers navigate an increasingly complex context of wicked problems and digital networks. The notion of a lone scholar is no longer viable as a means of addressing such 'real world' design challenges. This paper introduces the concept of 'inter-organizational' research as applied to the experiences of RCA CX PhD researchers and their supervisors based at the Royal College of Art, who have worked with academic and non-academic partners in order to build new knowledge in the design, production and use of digital public spaces.

Characterizing the CX PhD Model

The CX model operates through a series of collaborative projects focusing on the theme of digital public space, in which the PhD student's own research is situated (see Figure 7.1). The centrality of the PhD in the Creative Exchange structure, process and scale (with a cohort of twenty-one researchers) provides a unique opportunity to examine the role of doctoral researchers in inter-organizational research. We can begin to identify features that characterize research across numerous short-term funded projects and their partnerships, and elements that might even distinguish this type of student research as a new form of knowledge

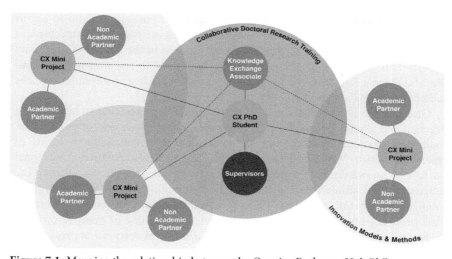

Figure 7.1 Mapping the relationship between the Creative Exchange Hub PhD researcher, academic and non-academic partners. Courtesy the author.

exchange *through* the design PhD. At the same time, this model suggests that while knowledge exchange is itself a focus for some of the CX doctoral researchers it is more commonly seen as a method for undertaking collaborative research in support of developing innovation: research *through* knowledge exchange.

The roots of inter-organizational research are found within the literature of marketing and management where the term often refers to firms who 'must seek cooperative relationships with other firms' especially within competitive environments. (e.g. Kumar, Stern and Anderson 1993) More recently, scholars have written about social network perspectives and applied this approach to inter-organizational models. This posits a move beyond a 'self-reliant view of organizational action and outcomes to one that is essentially relational'. (Zaheer, Remzi and Milanov 2010: 63). In technology research, head of MIT's Media Lab, Joi Ito (quoted in Copeland 2012) has called for inter-organizational research models that reflect the on-demand, digital, networked resources of Internet start-up, and free and open-source software cultures. In the case of the CX PhD, inter-organizational describes a series of research and innovation-orientated collaborative partnerships where short-term projects have been negotiated *through* the aims of the PhD research. The 'lens' through which the majority of the RCA's CX collaborative projects are developed is that of communication design. Here, the collaborative approach is facilitated through an act of making, and with this act of making the CX researcher is a participant in transferring and sharing knowledge between one (or more than one) organization and another.

Inter-organizational collaboration can be thought of as extending interdisciplinary research approaches. Interdisciplinary research emphasizes dialogue and exchange across university departments and fields of thought. The value of interdisciplinarity has been recognized in the richness of outputs, and in a shift from individual academics seeking out collaborations to institutional structures of collaboration (Blackwell et al. 2009). This can be seen in the history of university departments like the University of Cambridge Crucible research network and the MIT Media Lab, and the approach of large research and development labs including Xerox Parc and Bell Labs.

One of the main characteristics of the CX PhD is its position in both design practice and digital connectivity. The research approach is one of concurrent, multi-organizational projects that demand adaptable, collaborative forms of research practice. When collaborating with non-academic partners, traditional models of knowledge exchange have often drawn on multiple disciplines. The differences and similarities between fields of thought encourage, and require, interdisciplinary thinking. However, by extending a conventional collaborative PhD process from one to many research partners, and one to many knowledge exchange processes, the CX has established a doctoral research approach that is not only interdisciplinary but also inter-organizational. Inter-organizational research, then, is encouraged and required by the differences and similarities between organizational contexts of practice in the CX projects.

What is the experience of this inter-organizational research process, of concurrent, multi-organizational projects that demand adaptable, collaborative forms of research practice? We might think of it as a form of sampling and data collection through project-focused design practice. For example, two CX projects run by one of the doctoral researchers near the beginning of the CX Hub were connected to very different public events in the same month, but this led to common emerging themes on which to ground theoretical development. The first project used a week-long ethnographic and participatory design method to develop a workplace app for freelancers at a large media organization, and was driven by questions of fragmenting work routines and workplaces. The project was a collaboration with an architecture school and an office space consultancy company, and the design that emerged emphasized subtle, personal communication in small teams through the sharing of pictures of desks and workspaces. The second project was quite different, using a critical speculative design approach to launch an intentionally privacy-violating public space 'brand' and 'service' at an art festival, in collaboration with artists, computer programmers and festival organizers. It was driven by concerns relating to social media data harvesting, and the design involved a performance of conversation recording and web publishing in a fake café, and emphasized critical arts practice, communication design branding and public experiences of personal data. Taken together, these two projects, both products of multiple partner organizations and research cultures, have contributed rich insights to the doctoral research from which themes of personal identity design in the age of digital networked data have been developed.

Messiness of design research

Our research hub draws on models of design research to demonstrate and test *knowledge exchange* driven by approaches taken from creative practice. Each of the three university partners has a history of innovative applied design research. We can characterize creative practice in design as collaborative and adaptive, suited to 'messy' and uncertain challenges. Traditional academic knowledge exchange can have a tendency to be driven by structure and bureaucratic patterns. Design research scholarship has recognized this trend (Jones 1977), and pursued more adaptive and collaborative approaches – in part through the influence of the daily practice of designers and design studios. Research insight in design practice is often drawn from the intersection of multiple projects, clients or briefs. By using design research approaches, the Creative Exchange is therefore characterized by drawing on not only multiple disciplines but also multiple organizational contexts. This shift beyond interdisciplinary to inter-organizational thinking defines the CX PhD and emerges as a product of the applied design research expertise of the CX Hub co-investigators.

Our hub has focused on research questions concerning the theme of digital public space, a topic that is well suited to research methods that can meet demands of growing complexity and rapid connectivity. Inter-organizational research in digitally connected networks shapes doctoral researchers who are comfortable drawing dynamically on diverse organizational and intellectual resources. However, in addition, this research approach acts to shape the participating organizations, both universities and partners, to better suit digitally connected collaborative contexts. For example, in a project about personal data stores, a commercial partner speaking at a design workshop organised by the CX researcher saw a design idea about a solid stone memory store. The sketch idea triggered a conversation about the scales of a lifetime of data, which in turn led the partner to build a prototype app with 50 years of test data, where before they had tested with a year of data at most. In the same project, a partner university struggled to allocate an academic to such a short project using traditional Full Economic Costing and departmental approval process intended for much larger and longer projects. The CX student and academic had to develop a workshop series as an alternative collaborative process instead. Both organizations found their cultures and practices shifting, through the CX knowledge exchange hub and the PhD student involved.

Supervising the CX PhD

Inter-organizationality brings with it certain challenges for supervisors. The supervisors as well as the PhD researchers are on a journey in shaping and managing multiple projects and partners, the convention of what a PhD constitutes holding true – rigour, systematic approaches, and identifying a contribution to knowledge. But then whose knowledge and knowledge exchange, and how is this evidenced? A broader concern is also to articulate what the PhD might be as a result of operating within the CX Hub context – a process which has essentially informed and potentially enhanced the research and its outcomes.

In many traditional, established academic subjects doctoral supervisors are able to provide a subject overview. Their specialism allows them to develop a working mental model of the current research landscape, to suggest potential areas of fruitful investigation, to quickly assess claims of originality and to suggest appropriate research methods. Interdisciplinary academics, including those in fields such as new media, in which specialisms are less well defined, are often not able to provide such a succinct overview. Supervisors of interdisciplinary PhDs are not expected to have mapped each potential discipline in full. Instead, the approaches for navigating multiple perspectives and methods become key to what supervisors offer. In interdisciplinary PhDs, supervisors may also draw on an established project network to suggest appropriate collaborators and specialist resources.

We can think of an inter-organizational PhD as one in which the doctoral researchers cannot expect to look to the supervisor for an overview of all the available collaborators and resources. Instead the form of the PhD is characterized by the student's finding and maintaining connections directly. Here, not only is an emphasis on navigating multiple perspectives and methods vital but also having strategies for organizational collaboration. The supervisor's key expertise becomes guiding the student in approaches to working with many organizations effectively within overarching research objectives. As is the case with the Creative Exchange, supervisor involvement in setting research agendas and distributing organizational collaboration funding helps to drive inter-organizationality within the PhD programme and for individual doctoral researchers. Co-investigators and tutors with significant experience and expertise in managing inter-organizational research labs and projects formed the CX Hub. A process of network building, partner consultation, thematic scoping and project development 'sandpit' events were created by the CX Hub in advance of recruiting the doctoral researchers. The sandpit events were instrumental in informing and framing collaborative research, knowledge exchange and innovation opportunities, contexts and challenges, particularly for projects in the Hub's early stage of operation. More recently, and particularly at the RCA, these initiatives have been led more directly by CX PhD researchers working with their supervisors, and the CX Hub's core team of investigators, using a more varied set of approaches motivated by discrete research orientations and developing networks. Challenges for the supervisor reside also in the handling of what added value of the CX PhD context may provide to the student. This is in the form of supervisors and co-investigators 'managing' partnerships, so that the student is benefiting from first-hand knowledge of skills needed to project manage successfully and develop life-long learning skills in negotiation and listening. At the same time, the relational aspects of the CX PhD means having an understanding in the management of partnership agreements and keeping an eye on 'intellectual property' agreements, which may also require additional training and support from university research offices.

Towards inter-organizational PhDs

Inter-organizational processes and networks shape the CX PhD research journey and thesis outcomes (see Figure 7.2). We have outlined above a trend leading from traditional, field-specific PhDs, to interdisciplinary doctoral research, to a form of inter-organizational PhD. The trend describes a growing breadth of PhD approaches, with the space (and perhaps necessity) for all three forms of PhD to be found in a contemporary research context. Within the time limits of a UK PhD programme and word-count limits of a thesis, in each form of PhD differing emphasis must be placed on differing parts of the process and documentation.

A traditional single-discipline, single-organization PhD is generally focused on mapping a subject specialism within a strongly defined discipline in the context of a particular university institution. The approach is suited to reaching the edges of a single subject. It offers a deeper understanding in order to map, analyse and progress a theoretical position. Methodology must be articulated, but is often one of several well-established within a field.

An interdisciplinary PhD emphasizes mapping of methodologies and perspectives. A researcher must go deeper in finding ways of synthesizing points of view and identifying conflicting assumptions. The approach can reach areas of focus that fall outside or between disciplinary boundaries. Interdisciplinarity also lends itself to bringing methods of one field to bear on another, or appropriating resources. An example of technical resources would be the use of early computer science facilities at night to develop novel approaches in architecture (Negroponte 1996).

What, then, does an inter-organizational PhD concentrate on mapping? Following the trend, it would seem that mapping organizational resources and collaborative methods are important – finding ways to synthesize resources and perspectives across disparate research and practice cultures. An inter-organizational PhD might be expected to draw on multiple institutional frameworks,

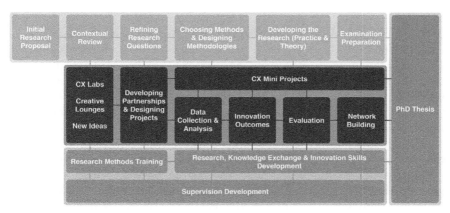

Figure 7.2 Mapping a model for the Creative Exchange Hub PhD research process. Courtesy the author.

and to use not only a multitude of methods and perspectives but also resources for carrying out all aspects of the practical process. Ito (quoted in Copeland, 2012) describes research methods that draw on (digitally) networked resources on-demand like this, in terms of networked software that 'pull' request resources from a network 'just-in-time'.

Risks in new forms of PhDs in design

If we look again at the example of the interdisciplinary PhD we can extrapolate some of the challenges faced by inter-organizational PhD researchers, supervisors and institutions. As the potential of interdisciplinarity has been explored through projects, university structures and PhD programme design, tensions have emerged between academic traditions and research innovation (Cross 2007). We can draw on these tensions to understand more of the potential challenges and opportunities facing inter-organizational doctoral programmes.

Academics approaching interdisciplinary collaboration from an established position within a field and institution are able to speak with a voice of an authoritative expert. The traditions of academic progression and structure signify trust, and aid confidence in collaborators unfamiliar with other disciplines. Newly graduated postdoctoral researchers from a traditional form of PhD have had time to build a close relationship with a department or school, and with a specialist subject research community. Conferences and publications are also largely organized around disciplines.

Interdisciplinary PhD researchers, on the other hand, are able to develop their experience of multiple disciplinary methodologies, and languages (or dialects) of research, but at the cost of strengthening their position within a single field. In the process of their PhD and viva examination, they will often face academics from several fields, who may see them as disciplinary outsiders, and they may have to overcome issues of domain expertise and trust in each new paper and project.

Inter-organizational PhD researchers not only position themselves across multiple disciplines, but also across several organizations. They gain a greater understanding of collaborative processes and a range of organizational research cultures, but at the cost of having less time to establish an intellectual and social position within a single institution. They will often encounter an outsider status in each organization and discipline they operate within, including their 'home' university and department. However, as with the benefits of interdisciplinary 'discipline multilingualism', the benefits of being a 'nomadic inter-organizational native' may outweigh the difficulties.

We have to acknowledge that an inter-organizational PhD may need to shift the focus of 'depth' from subjects and perspectives to systems. Where a traditional PhD might go deepest in theoretical analysis, and an inter-disciplinary PhD might place emphasis on evaluating differing methodological or technical approaches, an inter-organizational PhD may need to emphasize something of the organizational structures in the context of the research. However, there are institutional expectations within universities, such as the tacit narratives of traditional disciplinary research often found within research methods and supervision, and the wording and structure of annual processes and final assessment that researchers and supervisors must contend with.

The established traditions of doctoral process and assessment across academia also seem biased towards the traditional research model of single discipline and single organizational context. The Framework for Higher Education Qualifications in England, Wales and Northern Ireland describes the second of four criteria for the award of a doctorate as follows:

> a systematic acquisition and understanding of a substantial body of knowledge which is at the forefront of an academic discipline or area of professional practice. (QAA 2008: 24)

Placing the emphasis on a singular academic discipline or area here might still allow for an interdisciplinary and inter-organizational approach; either by describing the interdisciplinary context as a new disciplinary space, or by arguing that an area of professional practice demands an inter-organizational approach. However, this phrasing leaves little room for exploration of the interdisciplinary and inter-organizational contexts suggested by the new form of PhD we have highlighted thus far. Similarly, in the UK, the history of the Knowledge Transfer Partnership process – and other approaches in individual institutions – tends to focus on a single project established by a single supervisor and partner organization, often in advance of recruiting a PhD student (see, for example, Gov.UK 2015).

Traditionalism within the stages and expectations of the doctoral process help to ensure consistency of academic excellence, but also pose a challenge to shifting demands on the requirements of doctoral training. A research approach that places less weight on academic disciplines may be criticized as lacking discipline altogether. Supervisors, researchers and research communities like the CX PhD must therefore be explicit about intentions and critical position.

Learning from the arts

Despite some traditions of cautious and conservative disciplinary definitions of design research, design and the arts also have a long history of consideration for progressive approaches to doctoral structure and assessment (Koskinen et al. 2011). The RCA – as with many art schools – has predominantly fostered research *into* art and design with a single disciplinary focus of historical, aesthetic or theoretical depth (Frayling 1994). However, the design and art school context of the RCA also has a strong tradition of setting out the benefits of the PhD by practice, and research *through* art and design (Frayling 1994), as key drivers in producing successfully applicable research. The existing RCA models of PhD by practice have provided case studies of successful doctoral approaches to documentation and assessment of design-researchers, as well as modes of assessment and supervision that recognize the shifting role of the academic support and guidance required.

Co-investigators from the School of Communication and the Helen Hamlyn Centre for Design have shaped the Creative Exchange at the RCA – two overlapping design communities which are explicitly focused on collaborative design-research practice with networks of partners and participants. The School of Communication is characterized as a 'culturally connected and fluid environment [...] grounded in experience and expertise' motivated to 'help build a better world' (Brody quoted in Reeve 2015); and the Helen Hamlyn Centre for Design is exemplified by 'inclusive and interdisciplinary' design research with 'business, academic, government and voluntary sector partners' (HHCD n.d.). The designer-researcher and artist-researcher tutors at the College bring with them theoretical and methodological sensitivity (Bryant and Charmaz 2010) that is often interdisciplinary and inter-organizational in nature. Arts practice is nuanced and networked, taking into account complex interactions of social and organizational systems. Similarly, successful design is often measured by practical use, either as working (networked) prototype, or when tested within commercial or social systems.

The Creative Exchange provides a fertile context for exploring the form of an inter-organizational PhD, in part because of its synthesis of digital and arts perspectives. One RCA PhD CX researcher is exploring what we might be able to transfer from arts practice, for example, to better understand design and knowledge exchange. The focus on digital public space brings the agile, start-up, networked expectations of 'post-internet' inter-organizationality (Copeland 2012). It is not just that the Creative Exchange proposes new forms of PhD as part of its knowledge exchange process, but that it is vitally positioned to explore the new forms of PhD that are inevitably emerging from shifting demands of, and opportunities for, academic research and inter-organizationality in digital public spaces. The CX Hub has offered a valuable opportunity to extend the understanding and potential feasibility of this PhD model by positioning it within a history of creative practice, drawing from the insights and experience of arts and design research, and by advancing a cohort of twenty-one doctoral researchers simultaneously through the programme.

In his seminal text on research in art and design, Christopher Frayling (1994) set out three potential forms of research that he had observed in art education, and at the RCA in particular. Research *into* aspects of art and design, research *through* the process of art and design, and research *for* supporting the act of doing art and design. We might borrow and adapt his terms to describe the Creative Exchange design research process in the context of the RCA. Many previous art school knowledge exchange processes could be considered as being primarily knowledge exchange *into* or *for* the design PhD – straightforward exchange with an organization to provide a theoretical position or process that the PhD looks *into,* or exchange with an organization that generates reference materials *for* the PhD. The Creative Exchange on the other hand, it could be argued, provides an emphasis on a form of knowledge exchange *through* the design PhD. The process of the doctoral researcher's initiating, coordinating, developing and documenting inter-organizational projects and networks throughout the duration of the PhD drives novel and valuable knowledge exchange between the networks of organizations and individuals involved.

Note

1   Professor Rachel Cooper OBE at Lancaster University is Principal Investigator and Director of the Creative Exchange Hub with co-investigators Professors Neville Brody and Jeremy Myerson based at the RCA. For full details of all three universities and the 21 CX PhD researchers and their projects, please see http://www.thecreativeexchange. org/ (accessed 22 September 2015).

References

Blackwell, A. F., Wilson, L., Street, A., Boulton, C. and Knell, J. (2009), 'Radical innovation: crossing knowledge boundaries with interdisciplinary teams', *University of Cambridge/NESTA Report*, Cambridge: University of Cambridge Computer Laboratory.

Bryant, A., and Charmaz, K., (eds) (2010), *The Sage Handbook of Grounded Theory*. London: Sage Publications Ltd.

Copeland, M. V. (2012), 'Resiliency, Risk, and a Good Compass: Tools for the Coming Chaos', *Wired*, June 11. Available online: http://www.wired.com/2012/06/resiliency-risk-and-a-good-compass-how-to-survive-the-coming-chaos/ (accessed 27 July 2014).

Cross, N. (2007), 'From a design science to a design discipline: Understanding designerly ways of knowing and thinking', *Design Research Now*: 41–54.

Frayling, C. (1994), *Research in Art and Design* (Royal College of Art Research Papers, vol. 1, no. 1, 14) (Other). London: Royal College of Art. Available online: http://researchonline.rca.ac.uk/384/ (accessed 22 December 2015).

Gov.UK (2015), *Guidance Knowledge Transfer Partnerships: What they are and how to apply*. Available online: https://www.gov.uk/guidance/knowledge-transfer-partnerships-what-they-are-and-how-to-apply (accessed 29 December 2015).

HHCD. (n.d.), 'About', Royal College of Art. Available online: http://www.rca.ac.uk/research-innovation/helen-hamlyn-centre/about/ (accessed 22 December 2015).

Jones, J. C. (1977), 'How my thoughts about design methods have changed during the years', *Design Methods and Theories* 11(1): 48–62.

Koskinen, I., Zimmerman, J., Binder, T., Redstrom, J. and Wensveen, S. (2011), 'Research Programs', in *Design Research Through Practice: From the Lab, Field, and Showroom* 39–50, Waltham, MA: Morgan Kaufmann.

Kumar, N., Stern, L. and Anderson, J. (1993), 'Conducting Inter-organizational Research Using Key Informants', *Academy of Management Journal*, vol. 36 (6): 1633–51.

Negroponte, N. (1996), *Being Digital*, New York: Vintage.

QAA (2008), *Frameworks for Higher Education Qualifications – England, Wales and Northern Ireland*. The Quality Assurance Agency for Higher Education. Retrieved from http://www.qaa.ac.uk/publications/information-and-guidance/publication?PubID=2718 (accessed 6 September 2015).

Reeve, O. (2015), 'Professor Neville Brody Trans-forms the School of Communication', Royal College of Art. Available online: http://www.rca.ac.uk/news-and-events/news/ professor-neville-brody-trans-forms-school-communication/ (accessed 22 December 2015).

Zaheer, A., Gözübüyük, R. and Milanov, H. (2010), 'It's the Connections: The Network Perspective in Inter-organizational Research', *Academy of Management Perspectives*, 24 (1): 62–77.

Chapter 8

EDUCATING THE REFLECTIVE DESIGN RESEARCHER

Pelle Ehn and Peter Ullmark

The role of design in society is changing, and traditional design research and research education are challenged. What kind of research practice would be useful? How should the education of PhD students be organized? The tentative answers we give in this essay are based on our experiences as supervisors for a number of PhD students in Design (altogether about twenty) and organizers of design PhD education. We have both, from the start of 2008 until the end of 2014, been deeply involved in setting up and running the national research school for design in Sweden, with over eighty students involved. So far, twenty-six of these PhD students have been examined, and there is a continuous influx of new students. Their educational and professional backgrounds have varied. They have been trained as industrial designers, interaction designers, architects, fashion designers, artists, engineers and social scientists. Their ages and earlier careers have also been diverse. Some students have come to the PhD programme relatively inexperienced, but many have had significant experience of professional design work.

To situate the design PhD programme we look first at the potential for design research in relation to societal challenges, then we briefly sketch and reflect on the transdisciplinary dilemmas, challenges and controversies that design research has been confronted with during the last decades (at least in Sweden); finally we move towards an understanding of research education as co-design, and the specific challenges of supervising and organizing such education.

The potential of design research

Design research, nowadays, often meets with high expectations. Politicians and people in industry hope that it will help in developing breakthroughs in science and other areas of discovery in innovative products and systems. At the same time, there are people asking for another kind of contribution from design research, a creative input to the strategic discussions of our time, relating to, for example, urban development and climate change. They ask for scenarios that present a meaningful, coherent and visionary whole, in the manner that design and art often can, by combining elements in an ingenious way, avoiding simplifications and clichés.

These expectations of design research and design researchers are of course difficult to live up to. Still, there is a specific quality in the designerly way of handling complexity that has the potential to become a useful complement to other kinds of knowledge development. Ideally, design typically avoids early identification of the problems presenting in a given situation. Different perspectives and approaches are tried, tentatively, with no way of predicting if, or what, they will deliver. In this way, and by remaining patient and confident, the established and apparently self-evident strategies and solutions that would otherwise more or less automatically dominate can be put to one side, and new possibilities actualized. The fundamental gain is, however, the very special, continuous learning and insight into a situation that comes from this kind of experimental approach.

As we have argued before (Telier 2011), this kind of experimentation and inquiry can be understood as pragmatic knowledge production in the tradition of the philosopher John Dewey. It is a general epistemology of creative and investigative processes, where *experience*, as growing out of encounters with real-life situations, is fundamental to understanding. In his theory of inquiry, as outlined in his main work on research philosophy (Dewey 1938) and his specific work on aesthetics (Dewey 1934/10), creative processes include everyday practical reflections as well as artistic production and scientific research. According to Dewey, all these creative activities show a pattern of controlled inquiry: framing situations, searching, experimenting, and experiencing, where both the development of hypothesis and judgement of experienced aesthetic qualities are important components in the process, the main difference between scientific research and art work being that the former aims at the production of theories whereas the latter concerns inquiries into materials in producing works of art.

Accordingly, to Dewey, aesthetics is not limited to fine art theory, and his concept of *aesthetic experience* is not limited to art work but to a more general human ability to attain the skill to make judgements. This includes an organizing energy, and generates a degree of felt wholeness and aesthetic quality that makes it possible for the individual to participate in creative democratic practices.

Since the 1980's, the pre-eminent doctrine teaching such design (research) skills has been Donald Schön's 'conversational' design approach to 'educating the reflective practitioner' (Schön 1983, 1987). He gives classical descriptions of how designers learn and conduct professional artistry through processes of *reflection-in-action*, in which knowing and doing are inseparable, and of how this is carried out as *on the spot experiments*, where the materials available to the situation (models, sketches, drawings, etc.) *talk back*, often in a surprising way. Of special relevance to our discussion are his studies of the architectural studio as an educational model for this kind of reflection-in-action, and the perception of such a *reflective practicum* as being characterized by learning-by-doing, coaching rather than teaching, and as a dialogue of reciprocal reflection-in-action between teacher and student.

How can we move towards such a *reflective practicum* for design research education? What can be learnt from the Swedish design PhD programme?

Design research in flux: Design, interaction design and the humanities

The diversity of the academic and professional backgrounds of PhD students in the Swedish programme demonstrates that design research is no longer an activity only for design schools. Such schools were even, for a long time, ambivalent towards research, and reacted quite slowly to the demands from university authorities to introduce research perspectives and results from research in the education programmes, and to start PhD education in accordance with the Bologna process. There was concern in the traditional design schools that the artistic perspective would be set aside and that more rational and engineering-style agendas might become dominant.

Much of the work towards developing design research has instead been carried through in university departments working with applications of new information and communication technology. After the first period of technical development, where the work was focused on very basic functions, and the 'users' just had to accept what they were offered, many different directions for the continued development work became evident. The researchers and developers understood that a design approach including an inclusive dialogue with those affected by the technical possibilities focusing on their practice and experiences was necessary to make proper choices. Interaction design as a discipline emerged.

This more process-oriented perspective did not, however, meet the expected interest from designers and design theory where the products and systems still were in focus. Interaction design had to find complementary kinds of support from different academic disciplines. An advantage in that search was a familiarity with the Social Sciences and the Humanities among the actual researchers. Much inspiration came from Philosophy, Social Psychology, Organization Theory and Pedagogy.

An important theoretical and methodological input came from earlier research taking place in industry within the tradition of Scandinavian participatory design. In contrast to conversational design, *participatory design* emphasized power relations. The ambition of the projects was not only to get better concrete results in the design work but also to contribute to the development of industrial democracy. As a result of the projects, employees and unions became prepared for an active involvement when new technologies and modes of production were to be introduced.

For a period, these projects were quite extensive, with researchers coming from many different fields. We were both deeply engaged in this work. After a while, however, the political support for this kind of research became weaker, and this resulted in difficulties with finance and the ability to carry through the projects.

Design for design and co-design

In the years just before and after the millennium it became obvious that design was no longer a process that would always result in finished products, programmes or environments. Design had become a question of 'design for design', where 'users' regarded the results as more or less prototypes and continued to develop the solutions over time. They learned from their experiences, while also actively looking for new ways to adapt to the dynamics of the operations and the surrounding environment.

This continuous design process may take place with or without support from the designers initially involved. The responsibility of the designer becoming less clear cut has changed the demand for qualifications. The earlier focus on understanding the use by 'user studies' to attain specific functional qualities is no longer automatic. It has become much more accepted for the members of a successful practice to be able to work together with different stakeholders in quite complex social situations. In such *co-design*, professional designers should no longer automatically be in charge, with other participants merely offering support. The aim should be rather to create a situation where all stakeholders have a role in the analytical and creative work as far as possible on equal terms, and sharing the responsibility.

These social qualifications have opened up for new fields of practice. Service design has in a short time become a strong practice and an important application domain of design research. The starting point has often been the physical design of service points, and of systems to present and agree on commissions; but the conditions for the social interplay between customer and provider have become more and more important as a design issue.

This more dynamic perspective has also resulted in a new kind of interest value for the outcome of the design processes. Transparency and flexibility have both become more important. The ambition is to find more open technical solutions where the components can be easily replaced by new ones to improve the functionality, and to make it easy to introduce the new generations of technology already in the pipeline.

In addition, the focus of many researchers has moved from the realization of single design processes to the development of a widespread ability to take part in different change processes in society, a creation of a democratic infrastructure. This programme is however still far from realization. In many sectors of society there is a regressive tendency when it comes to influence.

At the same time that design research has been developing, as a consequence of the new roles and practices, another body of project initiatives has been actualized. These projects focus on controversial and global issues relating to climate, migration, urban development and democracy. Especially for young people, research has become a way out of participation in the commercial practices that to a large extent remain focused on satisfying highly questionable human desires, not least from an environmental point of view. Universities seem to offer the potential for living more in accordance with strong ethical and political principles.

The problem is that the universities are meeting with increasing difficulty in living up to these expectations of intellectual independence. Both industry and society are actively engaged in trying to increase their influence at the expense of the research society. A well-thought-out strategy will be necessary if use is to be made of the freedom that still exists. This would include a proactive discussion of the meaning of scientific quality and the role and obligations of academia. This is a general need for all disciplines, but of particular importance for new fields such as design research. It is a question not only of paradigms that are taken for granted, and a resistance to tradition-bound senior researchers and research administrators, but also a way to explore new ways of working within research.

To identify and develop these new possibilities, very basic questions about knowledge and knowledge production have to be put forward. To all practitioners it is obvious that established traditional cause-and-effect relationships are not in themselves adequate for real-life action. When these single-knowledge elements are combined and put in new contexts, unexpected effects appear and have to be managed. Although, often, professionals are able to carry through this design-oriented aspect of their work in an entirely satisfactory way, they are frequently left to themselves to develop this ability, and the knowledge that lies behind it. They receive little support from research, either from relevant and well-thought-out case studies to compare with their own experience, or from more comprehensive theoretical work.

The young researchers, with their broad perspectives and local, strong engagement, could be of help in finding new ways to manage this problem. There are, however, two traps. The first is that the reflective and theoretical work is given insufficient time: it becomes subordinated to the object of generating concrete proposals to help people in actual situations. The second is that the conclusions become too simplified and superficial. This has happened before in design research, when much of the work was directed towards concrete recommendations to designers concerning their ways of working. Such efforts resulted in a number of models of the design process having formalized methods and distinct working steps, thus disregarding the principle that sensitive adaption to the specific situation and the people involved are what really matters.

Integrated basic and applied research

So, how to carry through this complex mission, and be useful both in the actual context and for development of the general understanding of design? It is a question of balance. With too much emphasis placed on theoretical ambition there is a risk of inadvertently leaving the design field and moving into other disciplines such as philosophy, psychology, anthropology and sociology, without really having the qualifications to do so. With too strong a focus on the design elements in the research work, the result may not be useful for other design researchers, or in the long run.

There are basically two types of involvement of practice in design research. The first, for a long time predominating, is the study of real-life design processes. At a very basic level, such case studies could in themselves be very useful for design practice as examples of both typical situations and of different ways to approach specific problems. They could complement the narratives that have such an important role in the dissemination of new knowledge in practice.

To obtain these qualities, the situation and the circumstances have to be described in sufficient detail as to be able to be understood from a basic human, social and political perspective. At the same time, the whole has to be kept alive. In most cases, this is impossible to achieve without the use of both textual and visual material. This is a matter of artistic talent and training often encountered by designers. Encouragement should be given to the development of this competence, which is often neglected in the research context, which traditionally tends to give priority to strictly formalized texts.

A serious scientific contribution, however, will also include an analysis of the studied process and the results. To achieve this in a way that makes it possible for the study to contribute to a more general knowledge development, it has to build on comparisons with other studies, and established insights into actual situations. There has to be an articulated, theoretical pre-understanding to refer to, question and develop.

This is easier to talk about than to carry through. An extremely meticulous investigation is needed to discover deviations. As all studies of paradigms show, established understanding is extremely resistant to change. As designer in the role of an observer, it is also difficult to avoid every sort of intervention and retain independence.

Another approach is to accept that, in practice, attaining independence and objectivity is impossible, and to instead make conscious interventions to improve the situation being observed – following the action-research agenda initially developed by Kurt Lewin and later adopted and developed within pragmatic conversational as well as participatory design research. In this case, it is necessary to make a continuous identification and articulation of any observed shortcomings, and the effects of the interventions. (For an overview of the broad – participatory – actions-research tradition since Lewin, see Coghlan and Brydon-Miller 2014).

Still another method is to carry out design-based experiments. These differ from most other scientific experiments in not aiming for the confirmation or rejection of a given hypothesis. They correspond to design practice in having the same aim and direction: pragmatic experimentation. They start from an idea, rather than focusing on a specific problem, and continue until there seems to be nothing further productive to be achieved. Consequently, there is no automatic end to the study, with validated conclusions, but, instead, a series of attempts to open up the actual situation and demonstrate new possibilities. It is important, nevertheless, to make an analysis of the outcome of each step, in order to learn more about the situation in hand and to clarify the motives for a change of direction.

This approach must include reflection on the sources of inspiration. These may be very different. Some are the result of systematic academic studies that have been carried through to 'the edge'. Others may still be academic but used more pragmatically, meaning that the line of thinking has not been followed back to the basic thought traditions and ambitions of the authors. This way of taking advantage of scientific sources in design research has often been criticized, but may nonetheless play an important role in the development of new ideas. It should not, however, be accepted without explicit reflections on such use.

An important consequence of a higher theoretical ambition in design research is that the design-based parts of the work cannot be very extensive. Both the number of engagements and the commitments to stakeholders in the actual situation have to be reduced to leave enough time for reflection and re-considering.

Research education as co-design

How should research education be organized to meet all these needs? According to Donald Schön, design education is a question of creating a *reflective practicum*. The ideas behind this concept are still relevant, and also applicable to research education. The practicum cannot, however, be reduced to just the design studio, as in the studies of Schön. It is necessary to learn from the development leading from conversational and participatory design to design for design and co-design, and to include all kinds of stakeholder and the controversies of everyday life, and to seek opportunities for extended networks of collaboration.

This actualizes both the advising/supervising and the research environment for the PhD students. Generally, universities reflect quite low ambitions for this area of education, which is extraordinary given the sum of money invested in each PhD student, and the impact on the quality of future research. Apart from a set of courses that the students are expected to follow, the responsibility is left to the supervisor alone, and to his or her ability to provide advice and at the same time direct the work to follow the confirmed study plan. This mixture of support and control can sometimes lead to very destructive conflicts.

Often, as many of the senior researchers are overloaded with project work and management, much of the practical supervising is left to relatively young and inexperienced researchers. They are offered courses to become authorized supervisors, but these courses are often focused on rights and obligations, and the practical supervision work receives insufficient attention. The part of the courses appreciated most is usually the opportunity to meet with colleagues from other fields. Very often, however, there is no follow-up providing new meetings to discuss different ways of working and potential difficulties.

These problems with research education were beginning to emerge within design research almost ten years ago. There was an obvious risk that without a strong joint effort an internationally interesting research development would come to an end. This led to a group of senior researchers from design schools, but also from technical universities and business schools, to initiate D!, the Swedish

National Research School in Design. After a while – and a lot of arguing – by a special decision of the Swedish Parliament the consortium was granted generous funding for a period of five years. Even though this period has come to an end, D! is still working, but with fewer resources.

D! has developed a programme consisting of a basic two-year course, based on meetings lasting between two and three days and taking place four times a year at different universities. The courses are thematic, but are not carried through in exactly the same way each time. During these meetings there are also seminars and workshops. Each student is expected to present his or her work and have it discussed at least once during such a period. A number of senior researchers are present throughout, to support the discussions and be available for more private consultations.

Through collaboration between Denmark, Finland, Norway and Sweden a separate organization called *Nordes* has also been created. Every second year, *Nordes* organizes an international research conference to take place in one of the four countries, with a doctoral consortium, and even an opportunity for PhD students to submit papers. In the years when there is no conference, a week-long summer school for PhD students is arranged.

These meetings at the national and the Nordic level have resulted in a unique community of practice, where not only PhD students but also senior researchers have established close contacts and started up collaborative projects. The community of practice has opened up the whole field of design research in a way that makes it possible for each PhD student to contextualize her or his own work in a much more interesting and effective way. The opportunity to invite interesting international guests to the courses has also been important for the widening of perspectives. Smaller special interest groups are another interesting possibility, possibly leading to new collaborative research programmes in the future.

Nevertheless, all the problems are not solved. In many of the university departments involved, design research is a small component, and many PhD students are not included in the research groups of colleagues and research leaders with similar interests that are formed for everyday conversations about their work. Individual supervision, also, remains unsatisfactory in many cases. The available supervisors are too few, and overloaded. Quite often, also, their experience lies in other fields, which makes it difficult for them to understand, or advise on, the specific issues of design research.

Our own experience shows that these issues dominate the situation. Without experience, it is difficult to approach a series of decisions on how to proceed. At the same time, an important part of the education is to learn how to manage these decision-making processes. Simple advice does not work. This means that much time has to be spent on discussion of the possible consequences of different decisions. Quite often, this discussion leads the PhD student to engage in extensive reading, and this results in a need for new discussions. Sometimes, it may become necessary for the supervisor him- or herself to research more deeply into given fields of knowledge, which can be time-consuming. Supervising PhD students in design is not something that can be achieved with ease.

We often regard this work as travelling *with* the PhD student. We are not deciding where to go, but are expected to guide the tour so that important places and experiences are not missed, and also to point to the experiences of other people who have made corresponding tours, or more reflected on this kind of experience in a more general way.

At the same time, we have to remind the student of the limited time available, and actively ask for priorities to be considered. Some interesting places will have to be passed by very quickly and just noted. Others will have to be investigated so deeply that there is nothing left to extract. The trace has to be followed to the edge. These choices are decisive for the quality of the thesis. Hence, to maintain mutual confidence, the guidance has to be carried out with considerable sensitivity. Altogether, it is an experience that comes close to what happens in co-design.

But research competence is not a question only of individual knowledge and judgement. It is equally important, particularly in design research, to be able to relate to a complex environment and be part of a collaboration with people from a different background. The concrete design experiments are, of course, the principal source for this experience and ability. It is necessary, however, also to meet researchers with other interests and from other disciplines and to become accustomed to establishing joint platforms for collaboration without reaching a full consensus. All this is fundamentally a question of applying a co-design perspective on research education. A research school and a larger group of collaborating supervisors is a good basis for such an organization.

A school of design research

A school of design research, a contemporary Bauhaus, as suggested, cannot be reduced to 'conversational design', just as the early Bauhaus could not be reduced to creative meetings between art and technology. There is more at stake than interdisciplinary and designerly ways of working. Donald Schön, himself, in his later research (Schön 1994) acknowledged this challenge and suggested that design could play an important role in major social and political issues by providing implicated actors with a creative 'frame analysis' of their possibly contradictory basic assumptions and values. A further step has been taken by several of the PhD students that have participated in the Swedish design PhD school. They have not only analysed frameworks but engaged in co-design of alternative possible futures by hacking and re-framing the fashion system, by challenging market-oriented modes of product design through forming co-operatives, by suggesting modest but radical ways for design to engage in the global environmental crises far beyond the sustainability agenda, by vitalizing democracy through exploring new forms of public engagements – and so on. The repertoire of such controversial democratic design experiments (in microcosm), co-designed by educated reflective design researchers, should be at the core of emerging school of design research and evolving networks of educated design researchers.

References

Coghlan, David and Brydon-Miller, Mary (2014), *The SAGE Encyclopedia of Action Research*. Thousand Oaks: London: SAGE Publications Ltd.

Dewey, John (1934/80), *Art as Experience*. New York: Berkeley Publishing Group.

Dewey, John (1938), *Logic: The Theory of Inquiry*. New York: Henry Holt and Company.

Schön, Donald A. (1983), *The Reflective Practitioner*. New York: Basic Books.

Schön, Donald A. (1987), *Educating the Reflective Practitioner*. San Francisco, CA: Jossey-Bass.

Schön, Donald A. and Rein, Martin (1994), *Frame Reflection: Toward the Resolution of Intractable Policy Controversies*. New York: Basic Books.

Telier, A. and Binder, Thomas, De Michelis, Giorgio, Ehn, Pelle, Jacucci, Giulio, Linde, Per, Wagner, Ina (2011), *Design Things*. Cambridge, MA: MIT Press.

Chapter 9

BUILDING THEORY THROUGH DESIGN

Thomas Markussen

Research through design has established itself as a maturing research discipline with a proliferation of conferences and a growing list of publications dealing with foundational issues and controversies. In particular there is one fundamental matter of concern that is dividing design researchers and to which increasing attention has been dedicated: can design work lead to theory? And, if so, what is the balance, in practice-based design research, between conceptual work and design work? How do we account for artefacts as vehicles for theory construction? (see, e.g. Beck et al. 2013; Bowers 2012; Carroll and Kellogg 1989; Friedman 2003; Gaver 2012; Haynes and Carroll 2007; Markussen et al. 2012; Markussen et al. 2011; Zimmerman and Forlizzi 2008; Zimmerman et al. 2010).

It is valuable for the future development of the research through design approach to examine some of the recent answers that have been given to these questions. Zimmerman et al. (2010: 314) have emphasized that there is a need 'for serious development of research through design into a proper research methodology that can produce relevant and rigorous theory'. Progress in the field is hindered, in their view, by a lack of 'agreed upon methods' for evaluating theory as a knowledge outcome in research through design. In contrast, Gaver (2012: 941) argues that artefacts and design work should be conceived of as the fundamental achievement of research through design, while theory comes in second. Its primary role is to inspire new designs, or to annotate design examples in a portfolio, 'rather than to replace them' (Gaver 2012: 938; cf. Bowers 2012). It would be damaging for the field, he says, if standardization and disciplinary rigour get prioritized over the diverse methods for working with theory characteristic of the field.

In this chapter, I will argue for appreciating both views rather than seeing them as representing a deep and unresolvable controversy. On one hand, there is, as Zimmerman et al. correctly point out, a lack of understanding of how design work can lead to the construction of new theory, but we do not have to submit to their ideals of conforming to traditional scientific standards and processes. Inevitably, this would result in unproductive discussions of which standards should be considered most valid, with scientism having from the outset an upper hand in relation to artistic criteria. On the other hand, Gaver is right in warning against design work and artefacts becoming mere illustrations of theory while being fundamentally constitutive for the approach. However, by reducing the role of theory to a matter of annotating portfolios or inspiring new successful designs, there is a risk of overlooking the many exciting ways in which research through design can contribute to novel theory, not only for design but for other disciplines as well.

The aim of this paper is to provide doctoral students, their supervisors and design researchers, with a better understanding of how design work can lead to new theory. To set the scene, I start out by briefly examining ideas on this issue presented in existing research literature. Thereafter, a general characterization of how theory can be built through design will be given, alongside an exemplification of three ways in which it is manifested in recent doctoral work published at Aarhus School of Architecture and Kolding School of Design in Denmark. More specifically, I shall refer to these ways as, 1) *extending theories*, 2) *scaffolding theories* and 3) *blending theories*. Finally, I conclude on how the contribution of the paper fits into a broader view on the role of theory in practice-based design research.

Related work

The idea that processes of designing and making artefacts can lead to theory has been introduced by Carroll and Kellogg (1989). More specifically, Carroll and Kellogg argue that computational artefacts implicitly embody a set of psychological claims, and rationales of how the user shall interact with them. Working in HCI in the late 1980s, their analytical focus is evidently biased towards interfaces supporting usability and task efficiency, but their proposal is interesting, and appreciates conceptual work as an outcome in itself. Furthermore, they argue that cognitive psychology offers the accurate heuristic terminology and concepts for articulating theoretical contributions embedded in artefacts.

In a more recent publication, Haynes and Carroll (2007) elaborate on this original idea, arguing for establishing a 'theoretical design science' able to evaluate 'designs as embodied hypotheses that could lead to theories'. To found the discipline and the validity of research outcomes, they suggest a set of evaluation criteria derived to a large extent from the philosophy of science. For example, theoretical design science should be *purposeful*, because an artefact is 'defined by the function and purpose it is intended to serve in support of humanity at work'. It should be *illuminating* in the sense that it 'clearly identifies operationalizable constructs, research questions, and hypotheses that are subject to empirical evaluation'. It should be '*grounded* clearly describing how conjectures were derived to address the gaps between what is already known from prior work'. It should also be appropriate, meaning that 'theoretical design research that emerges from ethnography and other immersive fieldwork, for example, might be judged as inherently more appropriate than technological solutions dreamed up in a laboratory' (ibid.: 165–6).

While I sympathize with the attempt of Haynes and Carroll to establish some evaluation criteria, I find their account too restrictive for a number of reasons. First of all, there is an underlying functionalism in Haynes and Carroll that is reflected, for instance, in the criterion 'purposeful'. Today, artefacts and computers are designed for many purposes other than 'humanity at work'. This has put pressure on HCI to include a series of novel theories from the human and social sciences which cannot always be assessed according to the same set of criteria. Even more critically, design researchers need to be aware of how functions and purposes limit people's everyday life. As Dunne and Raby (1999, 2001) have made abundantly clear, what are deemed 'functional' and 'optimal' are not reliable evaluation criteria. Indeed, by introducing terms such as 'in-human factors', 'parafunctionality' and 'post-optimal objects' as design ideals, Dunne and Raby encourage us to reflect on the unspoken norms, politics, ideologies and cultures that permeate any act of designing and design research, but which are rarely highlighted. Design objects may embody not only propositions and theory but also critical questions and discourse (Seago and Dunne 1999).

Secondly, the valorization by Haynes and Carroll of ethnographic field work and user-involvement as being most appropriate is excluding from the arena of research through design those design-oriented approaches that are either being conducted in lab settings (e.g. Frens 2006; Ross 2008) or are artistically inclined in the sense of exploring, for instance, expressive qualities of new materials (e.g. Worbin 2010). As research through design has shown a promising potential for theory development in all these areas, it seems more appropriate, like Koskinen et al. (2009, 2011), to view contributions of the approach in the light of at least three research contexts and cultures of evaluation referred to as the *lab, field and showroom* (see also Koskinen 2015).

Thirdly, the criteria of being able to 'clearly identify research questions and hypotheses that are subject to empirical evaluation' reflects a scientism in Haynes and Carroll that is challenged by some doctoral work considered exemplary of research through design. Consider, for instance, von Busch (2008), who is interested in democratizing the fashion system by making it possible for ordinary people and professional amateurs (so-called *proams*) to have a say in the shaping of fashion. His central assumption is that, for this to happen, a new activist approach to fashion design has to be invented, inspired by theories on hacker culture, art activism and DIY. None of this is testable or subject to empirical evaluation in the ordinary sense. This does not mean, however, that evaluation is absent from Busch's work. It just follows principles and criteria that are not accounted for by the philosophy of science (on this issue see, e.g. Markussen, Krogh and Bang 2015).

My critique is in line with Gaver (2012) and Bowers (2012), who provide further clarification on why scientism is unwarranted in justifying theory produced by research through design. For Gaver, the goal of theory is essentially different in research through design and in science. Unlike scientific theories, he says (2012: 940), 'theories produced by RtD are not falsifiable in principle'. They are not to be evaluated according to whether they hold true (as in the natural sciences) or provide meaningful interpretations of existing reality (as in the human and social sciences). This is because design theories are not confined to descriptions, explanations or predictions of existing reality. Instead, they should deliver creative 'propositions' (Zimmerman et al. 2010) or 'generative statements' (Gaver 2012: 941) for investigating a potential future through the process of designing and making of artefacts. For the same reason they take on a totally different form from scientific theories. They tend to *be provisional, contingent and aspirational* – or what Zimmerman et al. (2010: 312) refer to as 'nascent theory'.

To illustrate this, it can be useful to give some examples of the several forms theory may take. In research through design, it is common to distinguish between *guiding philosophies, conceptual frameworks and ideas borrowed from other disciplines, manifestos, annotated portfolios and design implications.*

Guiding philosophies take the form of sensitizing concepts to help direct designers and researchers in reframing design problems (cf. Zimmerman et al. 2010: 313). An example of this can be found in *Where the Action Is* (2004), in which Paul Dourish reframes embodied interaction so as to embrace two approaches that, until then, were considered separate: tangible computing and social computing.

Conceptual frameworks are commonly considered to be another form of theory where design researchers borrow ideas and concepts from other disciplines and apply them to design. This can be for the sake of inspiring new designs or articulating existing designs (Gaver 2012). For instance, Desmet (2002) borrows a conceptual perspective on emotions from psychology and has inspired many designs, from pleasurable products to products evoking the dark side of emotions (e.g. Fokkinga et al. 2010). Another example would be Petersen et al. (2004), who borrow ideas from pragmatist aesthetics (notably Dewey and Schusterman) to inspire new designs that are capable of evoking experiences that are sensuously rich as well as poetic and imaginative.

Manifestos are a third form of theory that differs from conceptual frameworks and guiding philosophies in that they are overtly political and ideological 'suggesting approaches to design as both desirable and productive of future practice'. (Gaver 2012: 938) Two examples of this would be the PhD theses by von Busch (2008), which can be read as a hacktivist manifesto for fashion design, or Trotto (Trotto 2011), whose grandiose vision is to found a new revolutionary design practice based on human rights, ethics and social justice in order to 'create a new civilisation through design'.

Annotated portfolios may serve, says Bowers (2012: 70), 'as an alternative to more formalised theory in conceptual development and practical guidance for design'. An artefact is typically the result of multiple considerations (functional, aesthetic, practical, ideological, etc.) which annotations can be used to make explicit. In this way, rationales underlying a designer's work may stand out more clearly, or a theme or an approach that conceptually ties together a collection of designs by associated designers can be communicated. Gaver mentions Dieter Rams' ten theses on Good design as an example of the first, while Bowers demonstrates how work from the Interaction Research Studio at Goldsmiths can be understood as a collection constituted 'in terms of the annotation *multiple outcomes through minimal methods*' (Bowers 2012: 71).

Design implications are a fifth form of theory produced by research through design (Zimmerman et al. 2010). It occurs when conceptual statements are articulated in general terms on the basis of an analysis of a series of designed artefacts or reflections on practice. An example would be Lynggaard (2012), who constructs a set of so-called *tactics for making home* derived from her ethno-methodological studies and design for highly mobile people.

In most treatments of the topic, design theory is looked on as something which is used to inform or inspire the design of new artefacts. Only rarely is attention paid to how resulting artefacts or design activities may refine or challenge theory – either by pushing it so as to reconfigure basic premises or by inventing novel concepts. In his account, Gaver mentions how Overbeeke and Wensveen (2003) originally borrow the concept of affordance from Gibson's ecological theory of perception, but later 'adapted this to focus on emotional appeal under the new name of "irresistibles"'. According to Gaver, this should be seen as an example of design researchers borrowing ideas from other disciplines, but actually this misses a central point. The concept of affordance is not able to accommodate emotional appeal in its semantic core. Gibson (1977) uses it to signify how we are able to perceive things and objects in the world in terms of their potential use-value: a chair is perceived as sit-on-able, a stone as throw-able, and so on. What Overbeeke and Wensveen did must instead be seen as an instance of novel theory construction. Although originating from affordance, irresistibles is an entirely new theoretical concept for design.

In the following section I will focus on three occurrences of theory construction in research through design and provide a more elaborate explanation of how they can be distinguished from one another.

Three forms of theory construction in research through design

Programmes are used in design research to frame what are to be considered the most central topics, questions and knowledge interests at a given time for the discipline (cf. Brandt and Binder 2007; Redström 2011). Usually, a programme is grounded in kernel theories as well as definitions, hypotheses or core assumptions helping understanding of a certain phenomenon. For instance, 'emotional design' is a programme that offers theoretical notions of how designers should conceive of emotions, their various forms, how they are elicited, measured, and so on. 'Embodied Interaction' is another programme, which takes its point of departure from the core assumption that bodily functions and skills are fundamental for how we as humans think and act (see, e.g. Dourish 2004; Hurtienne and Israel 2007; Klemmer et al. 2006).

When design work leads to new theory it usually touches on the knowledge base of existing programmes. This can occur in several ways, but in this section I shall focus specifically on three basic forms of theory construction, which will be exemplified by three PhD theses.

Extending theories

The first instance of theory construction is what I refer to as *extending theories*. It occurs when the process of designing an artefact leads to the expansion of a programme's kernel theories. This can take the form of inventing supplementary concepts or 'stretching' a whole theory to embrace novel aspects hitherto unaccounted for.

A vivid example is Kinch (2014), who, in her doctoral work, sets out to explore how she is able to design interactive furniture that evokes atmospheric experiences. Kinch's work falls under the programme in interaction design known as User Experience (UX). To be more precise, User Experience originated out of dissatisfaction with usability, and is generally understood as an approach that seeks to go beyond cognitive and functional aspects (see, e.g. Battarbee 2004; Blythe et al. 2003). Over the last decade, the UX programme has been progressively extended by researchers working on, for instance, 'pleasurable products' (Jordan 2002), 'playful experiences' (Arrasvuori et al. 2010; Gaver et al. 2004), 'affective interaction' (Boehner, DePaula et al. 2005; Fritsch 2009) and 'aesthetics of interaction' (Locher et al. 2010; Petersen et al. 2004).

The contribution of Kinch to this program consists in expanding UX to include atmospheric experiences. Based on her work on interactive furniture for airports and music halls, Kinch critically reflects on how she can use existing UX theories to describe her design work. By comparison, she shows that atmospheric experiences are similar to emotional, affective and aesthetic experiences, without being equal. For instance, unlike emotions and affects, atmospheric experiences involve spatial or architectural aspects. Moreover, emotions are a form of experience elicited when a person appraises certain sensuous stimuli as either negative or positive. Atmospheric experiences are not as articulate as appraisals of a subjective level of experience. Like affects, they emerge on a pre-subjective level, emanating from an existential domain where object and subject cannot be clearly separated (Fritsch et al. 2012). Yet, at the same time, atmospheres involve a spatial dimension, which is not covered by theories of affective interaction. To account for such differences, Kinch needs to stretch the existing kernel theories of UX so that atmospheric experiences can be properly understood and designed for. This can be depicted as 'the egg of theories' in Figure 9.1 (see below).

Scaffolding theories

Scaffolding theories is a second instance of theory construction. While extending theories consist in integrating novel aspects of design work into an existing theoretical body, scaffolding theories is about constructing a more comprehensive theory out of theories that are normally considered as separate, or existing side-by-side within a programme. Ebdrup's doctoral thesis is exemplary in this sense. Taking a participatory design approach, the overall goal for Ebdrup is to develop techniques and methods for involving people in the design of aesthetic qualities in educational environments. On the basis of results from her field studies, and feedback from a series of co-design workshops with multiple stakeholders, Ebdrup argues that aesthetic qualities can be integral for a variety of means and purposes: optimizing functionality, perceptual unity and harmony, expressing meaning, or re-configuring social relationships between people.

However, in her examination of existing theories of aesthetics, Ebdrup finds that these qualities are treated as if they were separate and not pertaining to the same phenomenon. For instance, Tractinsky (1997) and Norman (2004) treat aesthetics primarily in functional terms, while they offer no insights into how aesthetics can be a means for socially binding people together. While Bourriaud (2002) has a great deal to say about this, he's silent on how aesthetics qualities are responsible for establishing unity and harmony in perception, which is the central idea in Hekkert and Leder's (2008) account of product aesthetics.

The contribution of Ebdrup's (2012) doctoral work lies in convincingly binding together a number of these separate theories – design theories as well as art theories – into a coherent conceptual framework. More precisely, she offers architects, designers and stakeholders a 'ladder of aesthetic qualities' ranging from functional to social. I call this 'scaffolding theories', because a network of similarities, principles, and relationships are joined, and built into a more elaborate and fine-grained theoretical apparatus.

Blending theories

A third form of theory construction is what I shall call *blending theories*. It is characterized by design work resulting in two or more concepts becoming fused with one another to produce a new understanding that cannot be derived from either concept on its own. While extending theory is adding novel concepts to an existing knowledge base, and scaffolding theories is about integrating different theoretical concepts of the same phenomena, in blending theories concepts of different phenomena are merged. Blending theories is at stake in Knutz' (2013) work insofar as she merges concepts from psychological theories of emotion with narrative theory.

The aim of Knutz was to design a computer game to help hospitalized children cope with the negative emotions they experience during treatment in hospital. For this purpose she designed the Child-Patient Game, which once installed was played and tested over a period of three months by children aged four to six in the waiting room of the paediatric department at a Danish hospital. The Child-Patient Game offers a comical game-play, which allows children to attach emotions to an animated character which experiences situations similar to their own: blood taking, medical examination and so on.

There were two important aspects that Knutz had to take into consideration. First of all, it was necessary for her to be able to distinguish the emotions of the animated character from the emotions experienced by the child him- or herself in the waiting room. Often, the child tried out emotions in the game that were the reverse of the emotions that the child was actually experiencing and which were documented through observations and video. Secondly, it was clear that over time emotions evolve and are modulated during the sequence of actions taken in the game. In order to fathom this process of emotion modulation, Knutz constructed the hybrid concept of 'fictional emotions' (Knutz and Markussen 2010). In so doing, she merges the concept of emotions from cognitive psychology with a conception of how fictional experience evolves over time through narrative sequences of action.

To sum up, the three forms of theory construction in research through design can be depicted as in Figure 9.1, where the diagrams are designed to capture the basic principles and characteristics of each form. Starting from the left, the lying 'egg' represents the landscape of UX theories, which is extended through Kinch's adding of the new interactional category of 'atmospheric experiences'. In the middle, the 'ladder' represents Ebdrup's scaffolding of aesthetic theories, which used to exist as separate theories (the scattered lines). To the right, the Venn-diagram shows how Knutz blends two concepts from two different disciplines into a third, hybrid, concept: 'fictional emotions'.

Concluding remarks

In what way does this add to our knowledge of the role of theory in research through design? A large number of studies have already been made of how theory can be integrated into practice-based design research. Theory is often applied in a research process to help articulate a precise research question, or set up a working hypothesis; or it can serve as a systematic set of concepts enabling the researcher to group her observations, findings or discoveries under general categories. Given these functions, according to Friedman (2003), theory is capable of 'providing principles of analysis and explanation of a given subject matter'. This could be termed 'theory application'.

Other scholars have focused on how theory can be used instrumentally as a toolbox of concepts able to inform the shaping and design of artefacts. Such a view – which could be labelled 'theory information' – is defended by, among others, Carroll and Kellogg (1987, 1989), Barnard (1991), Haynes and Carroll (2007) and Hurtienne and Israel (2007). Even though this instrumentalist account looks on theory as an integrated part of practice, it is too limited, inasmuch as it depicts the theory-practice nexus as a one-way information process, while the question of how practice feeds back into and changes theory is left out of the picture.

What I have attempted here is to specifically shed more light on this question: how design work may lead to the building of new theory. In so doing, I wish to emphasize design work and theory as two equally important achievements in research through design. To be sure, what is needed, in my view, in order to account for this is not a theoretical design science shaped by ideals foreign to design practice. Rather, I have argued for looking more closely into the 'engine room' of how theory is actually produced in current doctoral work and design research. In fact, as outlined above, it is possible to detect at least three basic forms

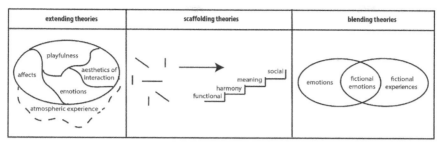

Figure 9.1 Three forms of theory construction through design. Courtesy the author.

of theory construction: extending, scaffolding and blending theories. These forms can be seen as underlying principles of theory formation that is supplementary to the list of knowledge outcomes suggested by Zimmerman et al. (2010), Gaver (2012) and Bowers (2012). Thus, extending, scaffolding and blending theories may lead to guiding philosophies, conceptual frameworks, manifestos, annotated portfolios or design implications. However, more research is required to work out further characteristics of how such theory formation may appear through processes of design.

This chapter is the product of a collaboration and discussion with PhD students during a series of workshops and seminars focusing on the theory-practice nexus in design research. These were arranged as part of the PhD education at Kolding School of Design between 2011 and 2013. Due to this contextual setting there is a preponderance of references to doctoral work conducted in Scandinavia and Northern Europe, while other regions and countries are unfortunately not represented. Hence, the contribution of the chapter should not be overestimated, but taken for what it is: a limited study shaped by a certain research culture. Nevertheless, I hope with this discussion to have dispatched useful ideas and models of theory construction, which can perhaps be valuable for doctoral students in accounting for their knowledge outcomes and discussing them with their supervisors, and for the examining researchers assessing and evaluating their work.

References

Arrasvuori, J., Boberg, M. and Korhonen, H. (2010), 'Framework'. In *Proc. of Design and Emotion 2010 Conference, Design and Emotion Society*.

Barnard, P. (1991), 'Bridging between Basic Theories and the Artifacts of Human-Computer Interaction Phil Barnard'. *Designing Interaction: Psychology at the Human-Computer Interface*, 103.

Battarbee, K. (2004), *Co-experience: Understanding User Experiences in Interaction*. Aalto University.

Beck, R., Weber, S. and Gregory, R. W. (2013), 'Theory-generating design science research'. *Information Systems Frontiers* 15 (4), 637–51.

Blythe, M. A., Overbeeke, K. and Monk, A. F. (2003), *Funology: From Usability to Enjoyment*. Dordrecht: Kluwer Academic Pub.

Boehner, K., DePaula, R., Dourish, P. and Sengers, P. (2005), 'Affect: From Information to Interaction'. In *Proceedings of the 4th decennial conference on Critical computing: Between sense and sensibility*, pp. 59–68. ACM.

Bourriaud, N. (2002), *Relational Aesthetics*. (trans. Pleasance, S., Woods, F. and Copeland M.) Dijon: Les Presses du réel.

Bowers, J. (2012), 'The Logic of Annotated Portfolios: Communicating the Value of "research through design"'. In *Proceedings of the Designing Interactive Systems Conference*, pp. 68–77. ACM.

Brandt, E. and Binder, T. (2007), 'Experimental Design Research: Genealogy, Intervention, Argument'. *International Association of Societies of Design Research, Hong Kong*.

Carroll, J. M. (1987), *Interfacing Thought*. Cambridge MA: MIT Press.

Carroll, J. M. and Kellogg, W. A. (1989), 'Artifact as Theory-nexus: Hermeneutics Meets Theory-based Design'. In *Proceedings of the SIGCHI conference on Human factors in computing systems: Wings for the mind*, pp. 7–14. ACM.

Desmet, P. M. (2002), Designing emotion. PhD thesis, Delft: Delft University of Technology. Delft: Netherlands.

Dourish, P. (2004), *Where the Action is: The Foundations of Embodied Interaction*. Cambridge MA: MIT Press.

Dunne, A. (1999), *Hertzian Tales: Electronic Products, Aesthetic Experience, and Critical Design*. London: RCA CRD Research Publications.

Dunne, A. and Raby, F. (2001), *Design Noir: The Secret Life of Electronic Objects*. Basel: Birkhäuser.

Ebdrup, T. (2012), 'Relational Aesthetics as a New Approach for Designing Spatial Aesthetic Expressions in Participatory Design'. In *Research: Uncertainty Contradiction Value*. Bangkok: Chulalongkorn University.

Fokkinga, S. F., Desmet, P. M. A. and Hoonhout, J. (2010), 'The dark side of enjoyment: Using negative emotions to design for rich user experiences'. In *Proceedings of the 7th International Conference of Design and Emotion Society*.

Frens, J. W. (2006), 'Designing for rich interaction: Integrating form, interaction, and function'. Retrieved from http://citeseerx.ist.psu.edu/viewdoc/summary?doi= 10.1.1.100.4299 (accessed 15 July 2015).

Friedman, K. (2003), 'Theory Construction in Design Research: Criteria, Approaches, and Methods' (24): 507–22.

Fritsch, J. (2009), 'Understanding Affective Engagement as a Resource in Interaction Design'. *Nordes*, (3). Conference paper – in the Proceedings of NORDES 2009. The Third Nordic Design Research Conference, Oslo. Norway: UIO.

Fritsch, J., Markussen, T. and Murphie, A. (2012), 'Exploring Affective Interaction: Special Issue of Fibreculture'. *Fibreculture Journal*, (21).

Gaver, W. (2012), 'What should we expect from research through design?' In *Proceedings of the SIGCHI conference on human factors in computing systems*, pp. 937–46. Austin Texas: ACM.

Gaver, W. W., Bowers, J., Boucher, A., Gellerson, H., Pennington, S., Schmidt, A., Steed, A., Villars, N. and Walker, B. (2004), 'The Drift Table: Designing for Ludic Engagement'. In *CHI* 4: 885–900. Citeseer.

Gibson, J. J. (1977), 'The Theory of Affordances'. *Perceiving, Acting, and Knowing: Toward an Ecological Psychology*, 67–82.

Haynes, S. and Carroll, J. (2007), 'Theoretical Design Science in Human-Computer Interaction: A Practical Concern?' *Artifact* 1 (3): 159.

Hekkert, P. and Leder, H. (2008), 'Product aesthetics'. *Product Experience*, 259–85.

Hurtienne, J. and Israel, J. H. (2007), 'Image schemas and their metaphorical extensions: intuitive patterns for tangible interaction'. In *Proceedings of the 1st international conference on Tangible and embedded interaction*, p. 134. ACM.

Jordan, P. W. (2002), *Designing Pleasurable Products: An Introduction to the New Human Factors*. Boca Raton, FL: CRC.

Kinch, S. (2014), *Designing for atmospheric experiences. Taking an architectural approach to interaction design* (Ph.D. Dissertation). Aarhus School of Architecture, Aarhus.

Klemmer, S. R., Hartmann, B. and Takayama, L. (2006), 'How bodies matter: Five themes for interaction design'. In *Proceedings of the 6th conference on Designing Interactive systems*, p. 149. ACM.

Knutz, E. (2013), *Fighting Fear of Blood Tests with Secret Powers – An Investigation of Fictional Emotions in Serious Game Design* (Ph.D. Dissertation). Kolding: Kolding School of Design.

Knutz, E. and Markussen, T. (2010), 'Measuring and Communicating Emotions Through Game Design'. In *Proceedings of the 7th International Conference on Design and Emotion*. Chicago: Illinois Institute of Technology.

Koskinen, I. (2015), 'Four Cultures of Analysis in Design Research'. In *The Routledge Companion to Design Research*, 217–24. Oxton: Routledge.

Koskinen, I., Binder, T. and Redström, J. (2009), 'Lab, Field, Gallery and Beyond'. *Artifact*, 2 (1).

Koskinen, I., Zimmerman, J., Binder, T., Redström, J. and Wensveen, S. (2011), *Design Research through Practice*. Amsterdam: Morgan Kaufmann.

Locher, P., Overbeeke, K. and Wensveen, S. (2010), 'Aesthetic Interaction: A Framework'. *Design Issues* 26 (2), 70–9.

Lynggaard, A. (2012), *Homing Interactions: Tactics and Concepts for Highly Mobile People*. Aarhus: Aarhus School of Architecture.

Markussen, T., Bang, A., Knutz, E. and Pedersen, P. (2012), 'Dynamic Research Sketching: A New Explanatory Tool for Understanding Theory Construction in Design Research'. In *Proceedings of the Design Research Society Conference 2012*. Bangkok: QUT.

Markussen, T., Knutz, E. and Christensen, P. (2011), *Making theory come alive through practice-based research*. Presented at the Practicing Theory or: Did Practice Kill Theory? Geneva: Geneva University of Art and Design.

Markussen, T., Krogh, P. G., and Bang, A. L. (2015), 'On what grounds? An intra-disciplinary Account of Evaluation in Research through Design'. In *Interplay – Proceedings of IASDR'15*. Brisbane, Australia.

Norman, D. A. (2004), *Emotional Design: Why We Love (or Hate) Everyday Things*. New York: Basic Civitas Books.

Overbeeke, K. C. and Wensveen, S. S. (2003), 'From perception to experience, from affordances to irresistibles'. In *Proceedings of the 2003 international conference on Designing pleasurable products and interfaces*, pp. 92–7. ACM.

Petersen, M. G., Iversen, O. S., Krogh, P. G. and Ludvigsen, M. (2004), 'Aesthetic Interaction: a pragmatist's aesthetics of interactive systems'. In *Proceedings of the 5th conference on Designing interactive systems: processes, practices, methods, and techniques* (pp. 269–76). New York: ACM.

Redström, J. (2011), 'Some notes on program/experiment dialects'. In *Nordic Design Research Conference*. Helsinki: Aalto University.

Ross, P. (2008), *Ethics and Aesthetics in Intelligent Product and System Design*. Eindhoven: Eindhoven University of Technology.

Seago, A. and Dunne, A. (1999), 'New Methodolgies in Art and Design Research: The Object as Discourse'. *Design Issues* 15: 11–17.

Tractinsky, N. (1997), 'Aesthetics and apparent usability: Empirically assessing cultural and methodological issues'. In *Proceedings of the ACM SIGCHI Conference on Human factors in computing systems*, 115–22. ACM.

Trotto, A. (2011), *Rights through Making – Skills for Pervasive Ethics*. Eindhoven: Eindhoven University of Technology.

Von Busch, O. (2008), *Fashion-able. Hacktivism and engaged fashion design [Elektronisk resurs]*. University of Gothenburg. Retrieved from http://hdl.handle.net/2077/17941 (accessed 20 October 2015).

Worbin, L. (2010), *Designing Dynamic Textile Patterns* (Studies in Artistic Research No. 1). Borås: University of Borås.

Zimmerman, J. and Forlizzi, J. (2008), 'The role of design artifacts in design theory construction'. *Artifact* 2 (1), 41–5.

Zimmerman, J., Stolterman, E. and Forlizzi, J. (2010), 'An analysis and critique of research through design: Towards a formalization of a research approach'. In *Proceedings of DIS 2010*. Aarhus: ACM.

Part 3

STRUCTURES FOR SUPPORTING DESIGN
PHD PROGRAMMES

Chapter 10

DESIGN (RESEARCH) PRACTICE

Thomas Binder and Eva Brandt

Design (research) practices as an inquiry of 'the possible'

Koskinen et al. (2011) have proposed a framework for what they call constructive design research which adheres to particular methodologies producing knowledge through prototyping new possibilities more consistently than do the broad notions of research through design (Fraylin 1993) or research through practice (Archer 1995). Thus the nexus of constructive design (research) is exploring the possible through making. Schön (1983) early on argued that design practices are based on different kinds of experimentation, and that this opens up a space of virtuality in which the questions of whatever is imagined can be done, where the experiment leads us and how we appreciate the outcome are raised simultaneously. For Schön, this leads to a conceptualization of the designer as a reflective practitioner, who, in an on-going dialogue with what he calls 'the materials of the design situation', establishes both problem and solution through iterations of naming and framing, re-naming and re-framing, the situation.

Designers typically work from a (design) brief, or a programme that sets goals for what is to be achieved by the design. The programme operates as the first framing of a design space within which possibilities can be explored through experimentation (Brandt and Binder 2007). Likewise, in relation to design research we have argued that 'the possible is always contingent and though research may convincingly provide arguments for certain possibilities both search and arguments have to be guided by programmes that set a direction' (Binder et al. 2011). Along these lines we see the programme as a provisional knowledge regime in the sense 'that it is not unquestionably presupposed but rather functions as a sort of hypothetical worldview that makes the particular inquiry relevant …[as] the design work unfolds, it will either substantiate or challenge this view and the dialectic between programme and probing is in our view central to any design practice' (Binder and Redström 2006: 4).

Our suggestion is to see design research practices as fundamentally homologous to any other design practices, both in terms of the way they are driven forward by a dialectic between programme and experiment and in how they actualize

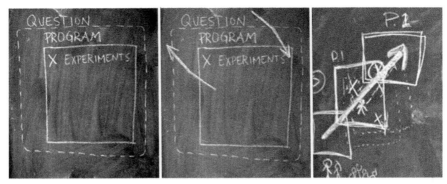

Figure 10.1 The original diagrams from the XLAB project. Left: The relationship between the overall research question, programme and experiments. Middle: What initiates a research project can come from the 'outside', or, conversely, a promising provisional experiment may let a more programmatic approach emerge that eventually shapes a research question. Right: The outcome of the experiments can result in the programme's drifting, or needing to be re-formulated (Brandt et al. 2011, pp. 24, 26 and 34). Courtesy the author.

potentialities through experientially manifesting 'the possible'. This does not mean that design practices are in themselves research practices. Research practices must be answerable to a research question or concern that resides outside the programme. Still, exploring the possible can only be pursued through adhering to a programme (Brandt and Binder 2007). Figure 10.1 shows our early attempts to visualize in various ways the relationship between the overall research question, design research programme and experiment. The main diagram to the left shows the overall research question as being larger than the actual research project, thus illustrating that whereas different research groups often focus on similar issues and questions they may, for example, apply varying research methodologies and relate to various contexts to investigate the research matter.

Design research as experimental

In our early writings, our hunch was that doctoral students in design would gain from stating more explicitly the design programmes they pursue and by embracing a more genuinely experimental methodology in their design (research) practice. The signposts that we wanted to navigate in between were, on one hand, the separation of design and research that we saw mainly in the UK in the system of dual evaluation of so called practice-based Ph.D.'s in design, and, on the other hand, the design-methods-centred doctoral projects that, although applying a case-based methodology, seemed to leave in the shadows the particularities of the design practices through which new methods were visualized. We carried out this work in our extended research environment in conversation with doctoral students, and we will give examples below of how these students picked up on the interplay between programme and experiment, but how they also took this work in new directions.

Flemming Tvede Hansen and Anne Louise Bang both entered design research with strong design profiles as practising designers of many years' standing: Hansen as a ceramic artist and Bang as a textile designer. The overall research question that Hansen shared with other researchers within his field concerned how to expand the practice of ceramic designers. Part of the research programme that framed his specific inquiry was the integration of 3D digital media into the process of creating form for ceramic design in natural materials. Combined with the repetition of practical experiments investigating themes like movement, transience and metamorphosis, Hansen explored the differences between arriving at finished designs (as designer) and artefacts that inform the design research. In relation to the latter he suggests the notion of 'epistemic artefacts', which are characterized by having the sole purpose, as tools, of providing knowledge. An epistemic artefact is good when it evokes new questions and inspires the making of new experiments. Thus epistemic artefacts support an open-ended design research inquiry based on the dialectic between research programmes and experiments (Hansen 2009, 2010).

As an example, Hansen's first experiment explores 'Dynamics' in the 3D digital software programme Real Flow, which can simulate effects related to physical reality, such as wind, gravity and liquids. Dynamics is animation-based, and typically used in the film industry. However, Hansen investigates themes like capturing transient phenomena by experimenting with various settings in Dynamics to produce various Real Flow animations, and then finding and freezing an interesting moment in the film and producing a 3D physical model by Rapid Prototyping. He then uses the 3D physical model to create a 'negative' model, in plaster, which becomes the plaster mould (Figure 10.2) used for slip casting in the next part of the experiment (Figure 10.3).

Here, Hansen decides to pour the liquid porcelain mass from a jug; this, he afterwards realizes, has implications for how the porcelain mass splashes and flows under the forming moment. The resulting artefact shows that both the traditional technique of slip casting and the use of digital media have made imprints on the artefact in the form of a soft curved edge and a 'conspicuous, organically growing and detailed formation in the middle' (Hansen 2009: 8).

According to Hansen, the resulting artefact works as an epistemic artefact, because, for instance, it produced a 'scale conflict', where the formation in the middle in the context of the whole artefact 'reflects a splash at a scale entirely at odds with the scale of the curved edge'. It is emphasized by the contours of the artefact, signalling Hansen's pouring of liquid porcelain, something that *actually happened in reality*. On the other hand, he argues that the central formation can be interpreted as a naturalistic, yet fictitious and very dynamic narrative, which suggests a dramatic event that *never happened in reality*. Hansen stresses that epistemic artefacts express the possibilities of what can actually be achieved, and that the unpredictable relationships that can result from various experiments are

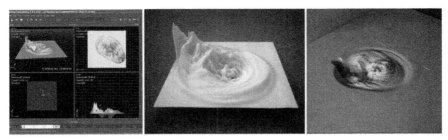

Figure 10.2 Left: Screen shot from the 3D digital software programme Real Flow. Middle: Rapid Prototyping of 3D physical model. Right: The plaster mould – the negative form of the Rapid Prototyping model (Hansen 2010: 99, 118, 119). Courtesy the author.

very valuable, in sparking new research questions and thus pushing forward the research.

The fact that Anne Louise Bang conducted her PhD project in collaboration with the textile company Gabriel A/S influenced research questions, the research programme and the nature of the experiments. The research objective 'is to operationalize the strategic term "emotional value" in relation to design of applied textiles by developing participatory procedures that the textile designer can apply to the design process' (Bang 2010: 51). This definition is the product of several attempts at formulating and reformulating the research programme and research questions, based on initiating, conducting and reflecting on the outcome of various experiments. The first experiment investigates everyday challenges experienced by the textile designers at Gabriel due to developments in Gabriel's

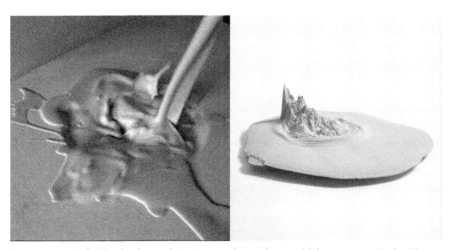

Figure 10.3 Left: The fluid porcelain is poured into the mould from a mug. Right: The resulting artefact showing the relationship between digital formgiving and slip casting in the artefact 'Splash' (Hansen 2010: 119, 120, photograph by Dorte Krogh). Courtesy the author.

overall business strategy. It was conducted as a pilot study, while framing the initial research programme in an application for research funding.

Gabriel is operating within a highly competitive international market, and thus has to find a position for itself within it. Analysis of Gabriel's annual reports show they repeatedly highlight innovation and value-adding co-operation. More specifically, the aim of the part of the strategy that Bang works with is to develop new market opportunities through juxtaposing emotional appeal and functionality for the end-user. Although not intended at the outset, it turned out that all her experiments developed into exploring possible transformations of the 'Repertory Grid' interview technique – originally used in psychology – to a collaborative tool for design (research). In the first experiment, it was used to establish a joint investigation based on the sensory perception of a number of material swatches, treating them as if they were upholstered. In the following experiment, it was embedded in the use of a probe kit investigating end-users' perception of upholstery fabrics in

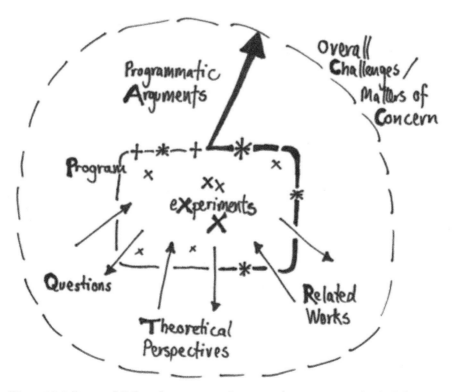

Figure 10.4 Bang and Eriksen have suggested merging their previous individual diagram modifications (of Figure 10.1) from their respective PhD theses with the new addition to distinguish between the different characteristics and roles of experiments (+ or x /X or *) throughout design research driven by research programmes and experiments. (Bang and Eriksen 2014: 49) Courtesy the author.

relation to the participant's own chair. In two further experiments, the technique became part of the guiding principles of two different design games, which also experimented with the application of Jordan's pleasure-based framework. In short, the Home Office Game explored the potential of home offices, and the Stakeholder Game explored how various stakeholders could jointly conceptualize potential approaches to the future design of applied textiles. With this short introduction to Bang's doctoral work, we hope to have illustrated that there is a definite interweaving of design research practice with possible design practices. However, Bang's PhD dissertation also suggests possible changes, both to description and the diagram, (in Figure 10.1, left) as a way to put into operation the experimental design research approach per se. Instead of going into detail about these changes, we will point to a more recent publication, where Bang and Mette Agger Eriksen (2014) take a more radical stance concerning the role of the experiment in design research driven by programmes and experiments. Bang and Eriksen extend the notion of conducting experiments to include, for instance, the design researchers' work with theories, concepts and the production of texts. They suggest that experiments play different roles throughout the research process in relation to the research programme, with some as 'initiating and driving experiments' assisting in describing research interests and thus a programmatic positioning, others as 'drifting or maturing experiments' and yet others as 'finalizing experiments' (see Figure 10.4).

Design research as collaborative encounters

To view design research practice as genuinely experimental, as proposed by Bang and Eriksen, would obviate the separation of research and design that allowed design experiments to be a means towards research (in design research), or research to be a means towards design (in design). Instead we are provided with imagery that lets us see the unfolding design (research) practice as a coherent series of experiments that explores iteratively the terrain of a particular programmatic drive. The increasing number of dissertations that consequently interweave theoretical and conceptual exploration with the documentation and reflection of empirical work also indicates that this move towards an experimental methodology is gaining a wider following.

However, the status of the design object and the characteristics of the design research practice as knowledge production remain unclear. Coming from the tradition of participatory design and co-design, where issues of representation and mutual learning have been pivotal concerns for more than four decades, we have been sensitized to think of outcomes, agency and knowledge as closely intertwined. In co-design, a network is engaged to explore and perform evolving practices; and through prototyping or infrastructuring participants rehearse new configurations of people and things (Halse et al. 2010). In particular, the concept of 'things' has attracted considerable attention in an interpretation of what is produced by such networks as assemblies understood as groupings around matters of concern (Telier 2011). We have suggested that in the broader context of design research these engagements should be seen as design laboratories that simultaneously configure both knowledge and agency in relation to evolving objects of design (Binder et al. 2011). This offers, for an unfolding of the status of the design object and the characteristics of knowledge production, an emphasis on relations and practices that, following the STS tradition of such scholars as Latour (see, e.g. Latour 2005), makes the object the *figure* of a networked *ground* of interwoven knowledge and agency. But what does this entail when we get closer to, for example, a specific doctoral work in design? Taking examples from three relatively recent dissertations, we will use the remaining part of this chapter to answer this question.

For Mette Agger Eriksen (2012) (who was also one of our initial collaborators), the central concern is the material engagements that are performed in co-design, but, unlike Hansen and Bang, she is not drawing a distinction between the professional work of designer and design researcher in terms of what is striven for in design experiments. Using a wide range of examples from her practice as design researcher, she presents and discusses an inventive array of formats and scores for collaboratively drawing things together which, with an emphasis on the mapping of landscapes and the staging and enactment of scenarios, perform a recognizable but also distinct attitude in co-design practices. These formats and scores are examined and conceptually unfolded successively to produce an evolving programme captured in a number of programmatic challenges. In the different projects that the examples are drawing on, the formats and scores produce outcomes such as service design blueprints or experience prototypes which are at the same time vehicles for collaborative exploration and possible end-points for this exploration. The object of design is here, by and large, the research, or rather the researching of, re-configuring networks, and design experimentation as it reveals itself across the project examples becomes the application of a particular toolbox invoking various landscapes of possibilities.

With approaches that in our view represent a new generation of design researchers, Sissel Olander (2014) and Li Jönsson (2014) have turned to recent developments in the social sciences and in anthropology in their appropriation of the programmatic turn in design research. For Olander and Jönsson methods are not universal strategies but particular tactics that in specific constellations provide a horizon for the research practice that defines both what can be known and how knowledge can be obtained. They are drawing on constructivist impulses from the social sciences, where issues raised and agency performed in social studies are seen as implicated in the work of the social scientist, and accountability is closely related to the particularity of the methodology. Lury and Wakeford (2012) suggest that this implicatedness must be embraced, and met with an inventiveness of method that promotes what they call 'the happening of the social'. The social sciences must engage in establishing a quality of openness towards the social that can reveal difference and potentiality. This opens the way for an interesting correspondence with design and design research in the orientation towards 'the possible'.

In Olander's work, these impulses are used to make a displacement towards method in her appraisal of the programme-experiment dialectic of the design laboratory. Her doctoral work sought to translate and install a co-design practice in a network laboratory, bringing together cultural workers and local citizens. The employment of a toolbox, similar to that of Eriksen, above, led cultural workers to stage conversations on the neighbourhood every day and have these materialized through a set of flexible formats that opened up for an exploration of how this every day may be different. Her work is programmatic in the sense that it pursues a particular movement of cultural centres and libraries towards co-production with citizens, in which this co-production enacts the issues it addresses. It is experimental in iteratively staging encounters for co-production with openness towards what this will lead to. What makes it stand out, here, is however not that it substantiates a particular programme or provides an extended collection of tools for collaboration. Instead, Olander's contribution is that she demonstrates a coherent experimental practice that revolves round the same relatively narrow set of tools and fixed temporal scores. With reference to Rheinberger (1994), she argues that this becomes a methodology as it produces difference and controls time yet stays the same from iteration to iteration. This 'difference' is, according to Olander, the actualization of potentialities, whatever these potentialities may be: the possible re-opening of the neighbourhood cinema, or the understanding reached between a local cultural manager and a circus director on having a local circus school for kids.

This final example illustrates a design research practice that simultaneously encompasses and transcends the interweaving of objects and processes of design. Li Jönsson (2014) has both been strongly influenced by the traditions of speculative and critical design and concerned with how to move beyond the human-centredness of contemporary design. Even if this indicates an already strong programmatic orientation, it is worth noting that she is simultaneously questioning the relevance of the conventional orientation in design towards particular problems or issues. As an example, we will highlight a few characteristics of her main case: urban animals and us. Here Jönsson and her collaborators prepare and engage in an extended encounter with the residents at a retirement home and the surrounding wildlife of urban birds. They craft three artefacts as centrepieces for these encounters: the BirdFlute, which enables the residents to make birdcalls to the birds outside the retirement home; the Birdcam, intended to be carried up by the birds to provide an aerial view of the area from the birds' perspective; the Phototwin, which takes digital photos inside and outside the home when triggered by a bird pecking at food on the artefact. The artefacts are all carefully constructed objects, well in line with designs made by others working in the tradition of speculative design (see Figure 10.5).

In the context of this chapter it is interesting, however, that Jönsson does not put any particular effort into motivating, or accounting for, the making of these particular things. Instead, she presents and discusses the sessions where the residents and researchers together prepare the bird-food to be attached to the Birdcam, the anxious waiting for the birds to pick up the Birdcams, and

Figure 10.5 Left: Jørn is testing the BirdFlute and the different birdcalls at department B1 at Grønnehaven. Right: The outdoor speaker is placed on the balcony (Jönsson 2014). Courtesy the author.

the moments where the resulting footage is uploaded to digital display. The artefacts are not in any way absent from these accounts, nor are the struggles and worries of the researchers during preparation, but the object of design here is, as Jönsson convincingly argues, the unfolding of an event in which materiality and temporality cannot be separated. As design research practice, these events encapsulate a becoming of the possible that does not separate the experiment either from its conceptual apprehension or from its experiential unfolding. The design research practice of Jönsson is not what leads to the design artefacts or the design events or the knowledge produced. The design research practice *is* the constellation of material artefacts unfolded as events as they make us grasp and grab the possible.

References

Archer, B. (1995), 'The Nature of Research'. *CoDesign*, Interdisciplinary Journal of Design, January: 6–13.

Bang, A. L. (2010), 'Emotional Value of Applied Textiles – Dialogue-oriented and participatory approaches to textile design', PhD thesis, Kolding Design School. Denmark.

Bang, A. L. and Eriksen, M. A. (2014), 'Experiments all the way in programmatic design research', *Artifact*, III (2): 4.1–4.14.

Binder, T. and Redström, J. (2006), 'Exemplary Design Research', *Proceedings of Design Research Society Wonderground International Conference*.

Binder, T., Brandt, E., Halse, J., Foverskov, M., Olander, S. and Yndigegn, S. (2011), 'Living the (co-design) Lab'. *Proceedings of the Nordic Design Research Conference*, Helsinki.

Brandt, E. and Binder, T. (2007), 'Experimental Design Research: Genealogy – Intervention – Argument', *Proceedings of International Association of Societies of Design Research Conference*, Hong Kong.

Brandt, E., Redström, J., Eriksen, M. A., and Binder, T. (2011), *XLAB,* The Danish Design School Press, Denmark.

Eriksen, M. A. (2012), *Material Matters in Co-designing: Formatting & Staging with Participating Materials in Co-design Projects, Events & Situations*, PhD thesis, Malmö University.

Frayling, C. (1993), 'Research in arts and design', Royal College of Art Research Papers 1: 1–5.

Halse, J., Brandt, E., Clark, B., and Binder, T. (2010), *Rehearsing the Future*, The Danish Design School Press.

Hansen, F. T. (2009), 'Epistemis artefacts: The potential of artefacts in design research', Proceedings of conference *Communicating (by) design*, Brussels, Sint-Lucas, School of Architecture. Belgium, April, 3–11.

Hansen, F. T. (2010), *Materialedreven 3d digital formgivning: Eksperimenterende brug og integration af det digitale medie i det keramiske fagområde*. (English title: Integration of the 3d Graphic Digital Media in the shaping process of ceramic craft), PhD thesis, The Danish Design School Press.

Jönsson, Li (2014), *Design events: on explorations of a non-anthropocentric framework in design*, PhD thesis, Royal Danish Academy of Fine Arts, School of Design.

Koskinen, I., Zimmerman, J., Binder, T. Redström, J. and Wensveen, S. (eds) (2011), *Design Research Through Practice – From the Lab, Field and Showroom*, Waltham: Imprint: Morgan Kaufmann.

Latour, B. (2005), *Reassembling the Social. An Introduction to Actor-Network-Theory*, Oxford: Oxford University Press.

Lury, C. and Wakeford, N. (eds) (2012), *Inventive Methods: The Happening of the Social London*, Abingdon and New York: Routledge.

Olander, Sissel (2014), *The Network Lab: A Proposal for Design-Anthropological Experimental Set-ups in Cultural Work and Social Research*, PhD thesis, Royal Danish Academy of Fine Arts, School of Design.

Reinberger, H. J. (1994), 'Experimental systems: Historiality, Narration, and Deconstruction', *Science in Context* 7 (01): 65–81.

Schön, D. (1983), *The Reflective Practitioner: How Professionals Think in Action*, Basic Books.

Telier, A., Binder, T., De Michelis, G., Ehn, P., Jacussi, G., Linde, P. and Wagner, I. (2011), *Design Things*, Cambridge, MA: MIT Press.

Chapter 11

EMBRACING THE LITERACIES OF DESIGN AS MEANS AND MODE OF DISSEMINATION

Laurene Vaughan

As evidenced by the chapters in this book, and the numerous other publications and examples of completed design PhDs, there is no one 'form' of a design PhD submission. There are numerous approaches to how PhDs are written, how research is documented, and how projects are presented, archived or exhibited. Different degree contexts, both institutional and national, have different requirements and expectations of what a doctoral submission should constitute. In 2013, Andrew Morrison and I (2014) undertook a reflective mapping exercise to identify the different models we had encountered, supervised, or examined in the course of our careers; and through this process we identified that despite the various programme structures there are typically three components to a submission – project work, a text (which has many names) and an oral presentation. This observation was shared with Haseman and Mafe (2009), who also noted these as consistent elements of practice-based submissions. Together, these components present the design artefacts of the research, situate the research into contemporary discourse, and critique the research and the discourse, thereby making a claim for the successful contribution of new knowledge. This is a process that fulfils the expectations of doctoral submissions in any disciplinary domain.

Despite this noted consistency of expectations, there continues to be a level of uncertainty regarding what constitutes an appropriate outcome and submission for examination from design research degrees, especially in relation to design PhDs. In this chapter, I will discuss what it means to embrace the literacies of practice in the form and articulation of design research, and how, in fact, it can be argued that it is the boundary-challenging practices of design researchers in the academy who are leading the way in the establishment of the twenty-first century doctorate in all disciplinary domains.

Being in the practice

Typically publications and discussions about practice-based research and all the variations related to this term focus on the form of the final submission. Much of the discussion becomes framed as practice-based, practice-led, or even creative practice or arts-based research. This has resulted in edited collections, themed conferences, special interest groups and events, all exploring ways to validate and articulate the relevance of such submissions, usually in relation to THE thesis. There are far too many to list them here as citations, but an attempt to position this was included in Vaughan and Morrison (2013, 2014). One of the key problems with much of this discourse is practice-based research being positioned in relation to humanities or social science academic theses, and the need for the creative domains to justify themselves or legitimate the language and method-ologies of these other disciplinary domains. Within this there is an assumption that all theses are the same, and that what is the norm in social science will be the same for a philosophy submission. However, in the course of reading, supervising and examining submissions from across disciplinary domains, it has become apparent to me that this is not the case. For some, a literature review and clearly stated methodology outlining lists of methods and samples sizes is a necessity; for others, an evolving argument through a series of intersecting essays to a thematic concern that draws on the literature is more acceptable. Put simply, there is no one form of acceptable academic thesis, just as there is no one language of research, discipline, or practice present in them all. What is consistent is the expectation that a doctoral thesis will evidence a well-thought-out body of research, that it will evidence a link to the field, an awareness of key discourses in relation to the research topic, and that it will be accessible and articulate. What matters is not the form of thesis but the contribution of research to the field – the new knowledge – which may be at a variety of scales and form, depending on the discipline, that the submission articulates.

It seems logical that a research submission for examination will be aligned to the academic forms and norms of the disciplinary field within which the study has been undertaken. In this way, the research makes an informed and novel contribution to the specific field, and thereby enables the research to make a vital and informed contribution to the discipline and society. Such an alignment enables academic research to make an important contribution to innovation by supporting disciplinary practices while challenging them. This needs to be our focus within the academy: developing frameworks that enable society and the academy to benefit from the years of critical enquiry that a research degree entails, rather than debating the need for design and creative practice to align to the norms of our peers across the other disciplinary domains in the academy.

Over recent years there has been a marked increase in the number of academic and professional domains keen to engage with, and learn from, design. This has been particularly evident in the rise of design thinking and its application to business, anthropology and computer sciences. The combination of enabling and embracing the possibilities of research through the practices of design and articulating through the literacies of these fields is a vital next step in academic research and the innovation discourses both within and outside the university.

Language of practice ~ multi-literacy

In 1999, Howard Gardner argued that there is a direct connection between our intelligence and the domain of culture and the field – with the field being a sociological construct – which will also form the basis for how we judge the performance of others in relation to that field. In this way, Gardner highlights that what is an appropriate type or level of performance for one field may be different for another, and, with this, each person will have greater or lesser strengths in skills or expertise aligned to one field or another. Gardner argues for the recognition that people have diverse ways of engaging with the world, and creating and communicating new knowledge. These modes of engagement he clusters as 'multi-literacies'.

Masny (2009) also argues that the concept of literacy 'has become inherently plural'. How and what we name a literacy is by its very nature a social construct. 'Literacies take on multiple meanings conveyed through words, gestures, attitudes, ways of speaking and writing, and valuing [...] Literacies are texts that take on multiple meanings and manifested as visual, oral, written, and tactile' (2009: 14). In this way, Masny is arguing that there is an inherent link between individual and collective professional, social, and cultural contexts and the texts that we produce. These texts, and their literacies 'constitute ways of *becoming* with the world' (2009: 14). The meaning of literacies is actualized according to the particular context in time and in space within which it operates (p. 15).

This idea of *becoming with the world* through a contextual language aligned with a series of cultural practices has a particular importance when we are discussing modes of communicating design research within a design PhD. This is true both for the language of communication that is used when undertaking the research, and for articulating the outcomes of the research at its completion. In the course of the research study, a student 'becomes' a design researcher; as a practitioner researcher the student is also learning to straddle two contexts for practice – the field of the design practice, and the field of the academy. The aim within a practice-based design research degree is that the researcher will become a design practitioner researcher who is literate within the domain of the academy *and* in their field of design practice. Building this bridge is essential – the aim for the sustainable benefit and contribution of the research is that there should be no artificial separation between the two contexts or fields of practice. There is a need for those of us in the academy to acknowledge that design practitioners work in diverse ways, which relate to their fields of practice and evidence their expertise in a manner appropriate to the field. This is what a practitioner researcher brings to the academy at the beginning of their research degree, and it should have the potential to grow, through the undertaking of the study. This includes students' capacity to engage with the written textual language of a field as well as with other modes of intelligence.

Cross (2007) argues for the addition of design as a natural intelligence that should be considered in relation to Gardner's (1999) list of intelligences. He maintains that design can be seen in the six intelligences identified by Gardner – linguistic, logical-mathematical, spatial, musical, bodily kinaesthetic and intra-personal. Although Cross does not argue for design to be a separate mode of intelligence he does state that 'I think that viewing designing as a "form of intelligence" is productive, it helps to identify and clarify features of the nature of design ability and it offers a framework for understanding and developing the culture of design' (p. 43). In this way, Cross is arguing that there is a diversity of modes of design; these manifest in different types of intelligence, and consequently they are aligned to different socio-cultural and professional fields of practice. For this reason, these different modes of design intelligence demand different types of literacy, as is appropriate to the context, field and audience of the practice; and for many designers this will vary project to project. Design is a deeply situated domain; it is practised in the world and it works to make the world. One of the significant ongoing benefits for a designer in undertaking a research degree is the deepening of their understanding of what their practice is and developing a meta understanding of their current and future contributions through the practice. This is the deep design practice capacity that is needed for us to design our way into the future. As Kellner states, 'we need multiple literacies for our multicultural society, that we need to develop new literacies to meet the challenge of the new technologies, and that literacy of diverse sorts […] is of crucial importance to restructuring education for a high tech society' (1998: 107). Rapidly changing technologies are just one of the many influences on future practice, there are also great social, cultural, economic and environmental shifts that equally demand an ever-expanding notion and enactment of design literacy.

Language of research – doing and disseminating

If we frame the PhD as a research training degree, we shift the focus away from the content of the research enquiry to the skills and expertise that emerge through undertaking the enquiry and the degree. It is this capacity to undertake research in a rigorous way and to communicate the outcomes in an informed and accessible manner that is the transferable learning that will form the basis for future research work. This has been the basis of the doctorate being the required qualification for future academic and research employment – the graduate not only has a deep understanding of a topic area but is able also to apply his or her capacity as an advanced researcher for future topics, and to teach others how to do this as well. Such is the expectation in the traditional areas of science, social science and humanities. A number of important changes have occurred within the academy over recent years, which challenge this traditional expectation of the doctorate. Notably within this has been the inclusion of art and design schools within the university system. This has had two important impacts for both the academy and the fields of art and design. The first is that the practices and processes for employment and career advancement within art and design education programmes have had to align with those of other academic domains. The second is that it has given rise to the recognition of new modes of research and, with this, doctoral degrees and the recognition of practice and the language of practice within these. This is a phenomenon that has also grown in the areas of management and organizational studies and Action Research methodologies for these fields.

What really underpins these transformations to both the academy and the field of design research is a desire to establish relevant modes of undertaking and disseminating research that will have meaning for the ongoing practices of professionals both within and outside the academy. The academic thesis is a mode of writing in itself, and has evolved across the disciplines to have particular qualities; but as noted by Bill Green (2009: 248) the conventional thesis as a 'once only' piece of work is potentially redundant. The *once onlyness* of this statement refers to the form and the construction of the text; what is transferable is the research, critical thinking and positioning of the research into the field. Whereas for some disciplines and methodologies the construction of the thesis is the best way to articulate these aspects of the research, for practice-based design research there are many other possibilities. The intrinsic alignment of the language, or methods for undertaking the research, with the application of the research and its dissemination post-study means that there are greater possibilities for articulating research than just the writing of a thesis. The challenge that emerges on a case-by-case basis is to design the best means to articulate the research in a manner that will meet the expectations of the degree and be synergistic to the disciplinary domain.

For this is the true transferability of the research degree: designing ways to create the alignment of what a designer does as a researcher within a doctoral degree with their acts of practice outside the university. For the duration of the study the student has time to come to know their domain in new ways, outside the pressures of everyday practice, and through this to challenge and hopefully transform the practice, just as they will themselves also be transformed through the study. Congruent with all levels of education, the evidence of learning can best be found in the embodied experiences and contributions of the graduate and not in the artefacts of the study. The ability to engage with the material and intellectual aspects of a domain is the ongoing life of learning. As Max Van Manen (1990) so clearly states on the situated nature of lived experience, 'the meaning of pedagogy needs to be found in the experience of pedagogy, because the lived experience of pedagogy is all that remains' (p. 33). This is the ultimate aim of the design PhD: to enable design practitioners to develop the insight and capacities to be a designer-practitioner-researcher in all the sites of their practice once the degree is complete; this is the lived and situated experience of the pedagogy of a research degree.

Relevance to the field

A really exciting aspect of the rise of research degrees in design is not only their capacity to transform how we educate designers but also how the discoveries within design practice through research will go on to transform design in the world. However, achieving this does demand that we embrace the literacies of design and acknowledge them as being more than personal, but also disciplinary and professional.

As noted by Lawson (2004), it is difficult to pin down what designers know and what designers do across the various practices and contexts of design. Lawson proposes that it is within the ephemeral space of field expertise that the point of unity across the domains of design practice can exist. This seeming contradiction of unity in diversity through the actions of practice is in fact that which design practitioners share and make use of. 'Sometimes it is neither skill nor knowledge per se that is important but a way of seeing or perceiving that may be the crucial ability in an activity' (p. 3). The challenge for design research is to find ways to articulate these intangible but crucial aspects of design practice and design research in a manner that is both accessible to others and authentic to the practice and the research.

Translating observations of intangible or ephemeral moments of interaction whether they are social or material is a challenge for all domains of research. Developing new methods for carrying out and communicating research that will enable such communication is becoming increasingly common in anthropology, sociology, management and organizational studies, and in the sciences, through the inclusion of video and other information graphics to evidence and articulate discoveries. The drive for these innovations is both technological and episte-mological – a response to the realization that we have the capacity to do things we were unable to do before, and that we are beginning to engage with the new literacies of everyday communication.

This is true of course for design research as well, but unlike research in the social sciences and humanities and possibly more akin to colleagues' research in the sciences, arts, and the evolving domain of auto-ethnography, the acts of practice are the means both for undertaking the research and for communicating discoveries and insights. There is a potential synergy between how the research is conducted, and how it is shared. Unfortunately, within the academy there remains a reticence when it comes to embracing this perspective. Although there has been an increasing understanding and acceptance of practice as a means for doing research, there is still uncertainty about the appropriateness of presenting the outcomes of the research through practice – this is usually veiled behind a discourse of access, rigour and academic tradition. To my mind, none of these objections holds weight, and they have the potential to undermine the value of design as a professional domain of practice performing in the world outside the academy. And I should also note that, when I make such claims about the value of recognition of design literacy in the academy, I am not negating the role and value of text and academic writing as part of this. Rather, my perspective is that we need to 1.) Value both the role and literacies of design as being the most appropriate means for articulating the ideas and acts of design practice, and 2.) Embrace a designerly approach to the articulation of design research. By this I mean that we must design aesthetic, critical and articulate ways to convey actions and insights in an integrated manner, just as we would for any design project for a client or the public. We must embrace the richness and possibilities of what designers know and do, and contribute this to the growing and evolving body of knowledge within the academy and beyond. For this is surely the great possibility and contribution of design research and design researchers. As argued by Downton, '[r]esearch through designing uses the knowing of doing to achieve productive outcomes which in turn indicate the knowing and knowledge used in the production [...] [o]nce in the world of things and ideas, a design can be seen as a repositioning of knowledge and interrogated to reveal the knowledge that designers have both intentionally and unintentionally embodied there' (2003: 105).

The relationship between design artefacts and spoken dialogue is a normative practice for sharing and communicating new ideas in design. Through dialogue an idea may change, morph, expand and be identified or discarded – this is part of the iterative processes of design (Downton 2003: 109). 'The designed work is the principal purveyor of design ideas.' And, if this is the case, then we must create cultures that celebrate and acknowledge it. It is not design that needs to change but the academy and those who participate in its rules and performances. These include academic institutions, governing bodies, research supervisors and the examiners of student submissions. We must all work together if this is to be achieved, and it is at examination that this is most crucial for the research degree. For, as Allpress and Barnacle (2012) note, 'the examination process demands a relevant mode of disciplinary documentation that makes the embodied research (of the research student) legible and available to others' (p. 164). This concern about how to articulate the nuances of discovery through practice for future practice within the framework of a research degree is noted by many authors in this domain. It is only through what is presented for examination in text, artefact and embodied presentation that the examiners can make judgements regarding the success or quality of what has been done by a student, and its measure against what had been set out to do and be learnt, and what an academic institution sets as its requirements for a degree. It is a nebulous combination that requires great insights, sensitivity, and critical engagement on the part of examiners to the work that is presented to them.

Haseman and Mafe (2011) ask 'how can the findings of a practice be best represented' (p. 216), a question that I think gets to the heart of the matter. How can we devise ways to represent that which has occurred within an embodied and subjective research enquiry? How can this be articulated in a manner that is accessible to examiners and makes a bigger contribution to the discipline or profession and the academy? How do we represent the temporal and ephemeral moments of insight that occur in the studio or on site? How do we evidence design moves in a project rather than merely describing them? Having the capacity to address the nuances of these questions is possibile when we embrace design as a literacy, within the communication of design research and practice. If design is within itself a literacy that is accessible to those within its disciplinary domains, then knowing when to use design to re-present the research and when to use text to discuss or describe the research represent the means of creating an holistic and relevant mode of communication and submission.

Designing a research submission is a challenge for any research student. Identifying what to include, what to focus on and what to claim as a contribution are some of the key challenges, and although these are linked to the research process for many this is not the focus until the time comes for completion. As a poet, how do I retain a sense of poetry in my work? As a dancer, how is my body present in the text? As an ethnographer, how do I retain integrity to the words of others? As a designer, how do I use the language of my discipline in the articulation of my design enquiry? Authentic alignment between content and form is an aesthetic and linguistic challenge for all disciplinary domains, and many are still in a nascent stage of recognition within the academy. Embracing the language of design practice in the articulation of design research will be essential if we are to engage fully with the possibilities of design research in and through practice.

References

Cross, N. (2007), *Designerly Ways of Knowing*. Germany: Birkhauser.

Downton, P. (2003), *Design Research*. Melbourne: RMIT Press.

Gardner, H. (1999), *Intelligence Reframed. Multiple Intelligences for the 21st Century*. New York: Basic Books.

Green, B. 'Challenging Perspectives, Changing Practices; Doctoral Education in Transition', in Boud, David and Lee, Alison (eds) (2009), *Changing Practices of Doctoral Education*. New York: Routledge.

Haseman, B. and Mafe, D. (2011) 'Acquiring Know-How: Research Training for Practice-led Researchers', in Smith, Hazel and Dean, Roger T. (eds), *Practice-led Research, Research-led Practice in the Creative Arts*. Edinburgh University Press, 211–18.

Kellner, Douglas (1998), 'Multiple Literacies and Critical Pedagogy in a Multicultural Society', *Educational Theory* 48 (1): 103–22.

Lawson, B. (2004), *What Designers Know*. Oxford: Architectural Press.

Masny, D. (2009), 'Literacies as Becoming' in Masny, D. and Cole, D. R. (eds), *Multiple Literacies Theory. A Deleuzian Perspective*. Rotterdam: Sense Publishers, 13–30.

Van Manen, M. (1990), *Researching Lived Experience, Human Science for an Action Sensitive Pedagogy*. Canada: The University of Western Ontario.

Vaughan, L. and Morrison A. (2013), 'Form, Fit and Function, Considering the Design Doctorate', in the proceedings of *The 2nd International Conference of Design Education Researchers*, Design Research Society/Cumulus, 14–17 May, Oslo and Akershus University College of Applied Sciences.

Chapter 12

TEN GREEN BOTTLES: REFLECTING ON THE EXEGESIS IN THE THESIS BY COMPILATION MODEL

Andrew Morrison

Contexts and methods

There is a traditional British children's song that goes, 'Ten green bottles standing on the wall / If one green bottle should accidently fall / There'll be nine green bottles …'. Doctoral students in the main domains of design are typically new to conducting and writing up the processes and results of extended research inquiry. In this chapter, I include the views of ten such students in design whom I have supervised on their expectations, experience, reflections and suggestions on having taken a doctorate based on the thesis by Compilation Model. Common in the natural sciences and prevalent in doctoral research in the Nordic countries, the production of papers, articles and chapters by the student (together with a supervisor and/or project team members) over the period of their research furlough is central to such a thesis. In addition, in the final phase of this doctoral model the student formalizes an exegesis or 'kappe' (meaning mantle or cloak in the Nordic languages).

This exegesis must provide evidence of research reflection and new knowledge, weaving together the threads of the publications into an overarching expository text that is not formally published. PhD student Jørn Knutsen stated: [the 'kappe' is] a very strange genre! You can't simply read it. You have to connect to the articles and the design work. It takes time and effort. You can't read it by opening it on a page.' Examination at our university is based on this combined production of publications and exegesis which is conducted by way of a public defence, typically over several hours. This is a more academic approach than is the case in some other design schools (e.g. RMIT in Australia), where a variety of weighting practice and analysis, and the relationship between artefacts and written exegesis is permitted.

The thesis by compilation is a fruitful format for reflecting on knowledge-building situated in design practice, allowing for dissemination of design research and considered critique and interpretation. The PhD in design is now accepted as being diverse in its materializations. Models include a varied weighting of practice and critical analysis, such as that offered at RMIT University, with more formal academic demands such as those of The Oslo School of Architecture and Design (AHO) (Vaughan and Morrison 2014). The exegesis is a beguiling academic genre that is still being formed in the sense of genre building (Berkenkotter and Huckin 1995) and an approach to genre as realized by way of social action (Miller 1984). While a small and growing research literature exists, to date this does not give much attention to the thesis by compilation or to the domains of design.

This chapter is part of a larger project called EXEGESIS into the thesis by compilation that studies matters of genre and expectations, relationships between practice and reflection, and design-driven innovation in form and multimodal research rhetoric. It also draws on my own experiences as a PhD School educator and leader, a participant in diverse practice-based research projects and as a supervisor for students within and across the main domains of design. The reflections presented here are drawn from a mesh of published research, qualitative methods and experience of having written a practice-based thesis of my own, and supervising and examining others in the Nordic region. In addition, I have discussed this experience and these reflections with several colleagues embedded in research and education on PhD practice-based inquiry, locally and internationally.

I have developed this text as a transdisciplinary, ethnographically inflected essay that draws on mixed methods of inquiry to provide an account of working with the ten doctoral students. This has involved rich and dense descriptions of work underway, through discussions and dialogue between students and supervisor, presentation of work in progress in research seminars and PhD school events; and by way of an overall developmental sociocultural approach to understanding the mix of modes of inquiry and the framing of practice-based PhD research through design in the form of public defences. The completed theses by compilation amount to some sixty published articles and over a thousand pages of exegetical material.

However, as Steinar Killi, one of our PhD's, working on a thesis on additive manufacturing thesis, observed, this is not just a matter of compiling a set of articles. It is much more a looping process of drafting and rewriting what is essentially a meta view that needs to be framed and articulated analytically. I experienced numerous developmental processes of my own in negotiating students' different learning styles and research processes. I also drew on, and shared, experience across the group in order to build knowledge of the 'kappe' reflexively and to build on it over time. As Snorre Hjelseth commented (his thesis is being assessed while this chapter is under review): 'You are much tighter on getting me to connect things in my kappe than you were with earlier students! It's useful, don't worry (laughs).'

Knowledge through design

While there is much overlap in the body of work on the intricacies of making and interpretation through and about practice in the arts (Barrett and Bolt 2007), my aim here is to fashion two moves to unpack the nature and role of the exegesis in the design PhD by compilation. I orient that literature towards design and design education at graduate level in a discussion of the exegesis in design pedagogy and doctoral knowledge-building and publication. I then discuss the exegesis in the design PhD with reference to research that is typically not accessed by design research or much present in the established body of research on practice-based inquiry in the arts. The design PhD, I conclude, may be informed by practices and successes achieved elsewhere and to which design may also contribute. I close by arguing for an approach to multimodal composition that may attenuate the at times over-warranted claims of practice while tempering tendencies of academic argumentation and interpretation to overshadow the importance for design inquiry of cultural context and situated processes of construction.

At one level, the ten green bottles of the children's song reference ten new students assembled at the start of their formal taught PhD education and subsequent extensive, supervised period of research. Over the past eight years I have supervised to successful completion ten design PhDs. These have included the domains of product, interaction and service design. The group of students involved has been central to building up a cohort of doctoral research in design at the Oslo School of Architecture and Design (AHO) in Norway. Each has followed the thesis by compilation approach. These students did not embark on their research at the same time, but were all at one point 'green' to academic research in its fuller forms. They were all practising designers, however, and by no means green when it came to conceptual or developmental thinking and professional production. This deca-set of students has been part of four successive doctoral schools, and has followed individual projects of study or been part of large, funded research projects.

There was a point at which all ten students registered, or were 'standing on the wall' at the same time. That they should remain standing, as it were, was crucial to the success of the PhD school education, which was designed to be more design-centred than hitherto. It was also important for the progression of the related projects funded by the Research Council of Norway, and to each individual student or group as a whole, that none of the ten should 'fall'. Accomplishing this would also mean that at the end of their intended period and programme of research they would all still be standing, so that the cyclical nature of the song and on-going design research education in design could be maintained, improved and supported further.

The PhD by compilation offers many benefits for supporting and formalizing the developmental nature of moving into research from practice. It allows for the amalgamation of publications assessed en route. The subsequent exegesis provides a means of focusing on an analytical thematic and further situating and elaborating on the relationship between theory and practice. This is especially useful for design-based inquiry. As PhD student Anthony Rowe stated: '[practice and theory were] fundamentally intertwined, yet different. They are like vines climbing up the same tree, but in different ways, in ways that cross and umm, and are hopefully symbiotic'. Lise Hansen, working on movement as material for design, commented that she did not find an example of one single thesis, or exegesis, that dove-tailed with her own niche area of research, although devouring examples in other disciplines, and from Sweden.

As Kjetil Nordby observed – working on RFID technologies on interaction design – each kappe has to be woven and worn in its own way. Thus, each of the ten students developed an exegesis to fit the interdisciplinary configurations of their own research. This was a difficult undertaking for all involved: the format and processes of developing the thesis by compilation remain largely unstudied as a genre. One short handbook exists, which centres on the natural sciences (Gustavii 2012). The exegesis has not been widely researched as an academic genre (Paltridge 2004).

Genre-based approaches to the exegesis

The exegesis has its origins in the annotation and interpretation of texts in scriptural hermeneutics and biblical studies. The term has come to mean an extended interpretation that stands beyond given material, typically that of existing artefacts (print text or artistic work). The work of Ravelli and colleagues has been central, and draws on Genre Analysis and its con/textual methods based in Applied Linguistics, drawing together ethnography and text analysis. These researchers do not present themselves as content teachers or researchers in the domains of art, design or performance, nor as explicitly linked to them as the language and writing educators they are. Paltridge (2004) is one of few scholars to have addressed the exegesis as a form of critical interpretative discourse within English Applied Discourse Studies and ESL/EFL related academic learning. Ravelli et al. (2014: 392) present a set of core rhetorical functions that they see as applying to the practice-based thesis in the creative and performing arts. These functions map out as, 1) Research Warrant, 2) Research Capacity, 3) Research Evidence, 4) Research Effectiveness. They see these are corresponding broadly with sections of a convention thesis. However, in these disciplinary domains and in mixes of them, these elements may be interspersed and cross-hatched. This differs from models of the exegesis, as will be elaborated later, where the reflective document is more descriptive of the accompanying creative work.

Hamilton (2014: 371), referring to the Connective Model of the exegesis – one of a number outlined in more detail below – outlines a generalized overall structure of an exegesis as containing (some variation of) sections that, 1) introduce, 2) section situate concepts, 3) present precedents of practice, 4) outline the researcher creative practice, 5) conclude. She argues that such a thesis is in effect an 'amalgam' of situated perspectives (Hamilton 2014: 372ff.); the thesis by connection develops into a 'polythesis', that is, 'an exegesis that guides the reader through a coherent narrative form, enriched in resonance through the direct interplay of voices'. (Hamilton 2014: 379). Paltridge et al. (2012) examined the macrostructures of theses in the visual and performing arts across Australian universities, including close analysis of successful examples. They concluded that while theses in these domains may be moulded around formal academic conventions, and follow their macros, diversity is what is reflected in the specific nature of the works being explicated.

However, this research makes little mention of two important matters. The first is that there are disciplinary dimensions to the selection, shaping, articulation and stylistics of genre in the humanities and social sciences, and these intersect with the methodological choices and clarifications chosen as part of the wider inquiry. This could be usefully explored to position such textographic research both ontologically and epistemologically. Second, this positioning might also allow for fuller investigation of the more genre-specific elements within different disciplines and their intersections. This would still need to be a macrostructural analysis so as to be able to assist students in placing their textual strategies, writing processes and genre selections in relation to existing literature and rhetorical modes of address. Our PhD students Einar Martinussen and Jørn Knutsen frequently discussed this as a necessary braiding of practice and theory in shifting from the bounded scope of articles towards a fuller contextual framing for the exegesis. An essayistic voice or ethnographically inflected account would need to be related to the macrostructures of the thesis. In our own context we need to go a step further, in that the thesis by compilation also has to have metastructures that relate to published articles while also developing an extended expository text and tone. In addition to the Literature Review, this includes what I term a *Practice Review* and an *Artefact/Process Review*.

Thesis models, practice and the exegesis

Fletcher and Mann (2004) edited a ground-breaking special issue of the Australian e-journal TEXT which presented a diversity of views online addressing key challenges and potentials for understanding the relationship between creative works and their scholarly analysis. Referring to writing a doctoral thesis in the creative arts, Milech and Schilo (2004: online), identified three approaches to the exegesis and the practice-based dissertation: the Context, Commentary and Research Question models.

The *Context Model* refers to a thesis built around a theoretical framework and historical setting for the practice work. This is a rather traditional and formalist third-person academic thesis with claims to objectivity. The *Commentary Model* tends to have practice at its core, providing close readings of artefacts, with reflexive accounts and thick description. The *Research Question Model* offers a way of avoiding the separation between creative and written component, and conceptualizes them as an integrated whole. This allows the creative production itself to be valued as a way of gathering and composing research-related material at the same time that the creative artefact is unpacking, situated and critiqued with reference to other works, related research and intertextual interpretation. Milech and Schilo (2004: online) see this as freeing students from ambiguities of the Context Model '(how does the exegesis relate to the creative work or production piece)' and the restrictions of the Commentary Model '(my exegesis is an explanation of my creative work or production piece)'. They are able then 'to research a single question in two languages'. These two languages, however, can be more fully appreciated only through the de/construction dynamics embodied in the exegesis itself.

Hamilton and Jaaniste (2010) argued that we may usefully conceptualize an additional view, that of the *Connective Model*. This is one that applies in particular to the practitioner-researcher. They selected this name because 'by looking out both towards the established field and inwards towards the practice, it serves to connect the research outcomes to the ongoing research trajectory of the field'. (Hamilton 2014: 371). It is the dual orientation of the thesis that is significant. Hamilton (2014: 370) sees this as having one aspect toward research, with its established conventions and practices, and another as oriented towards inner voice, creative activities and related processes.

I suggest we add an additional view, namely the *Compilation Model*. This model is an exegesis that refers to a wider thesis drawing on and drawing together practice and theory, weaving together all four other models. This is the thesis model that we have adopted and developed at AHO, one in which a variety of practices, ways of knowing and modes of reflection and analysis may be included and distinguished. The Compilation Model encompasses the academic frameworks of the Context Model; it includes the descriptive and situated character of the Commentary Model; it incorporates the duality of the Research Question and Connective Models. In the Compilation Model the thesis writer must bind together a set of publications that may each involve a related if different artefact production and object of analysis. These elements need to be synthesized for analysis of the elements of content, commentary, research problematic and connection between making and critique. I would go so far as to argue that this might be the most complex and taxing model for design practitioners to follow and succeed in delivering.

A developmental process of compilation

All in all, building expertise in this format of the PhD in design has been labour intensive and personally demanding for students and supervisor. We have often been concerned about the extent of risk in the demands of moving from professional practice to processes of academic writing and formal review, and acceptance of publication in esteemed peer reviewed conferences and journals. As Lise Hansen and Steinar Killi reflected, writing articles allowed one to build expertise over time. Lise saw feedback from reviewers as invaluable (while Jon Olav Eikenes Husabø found vast variation in reviews perplexing). Over time, students have been invited to contribute to leading edited book collections. We used seminars and internal readers to deliver texts worthy of review; each exegesis and publication is sent to an external and interdisciplinary Reader. In contrast to the work of the first few students, we have increasingly moved towards developing an elaborated literature review for the overall project. This literature review is developed in conjunction with the publications, but it is now oriented toward the exegesis and provides a body of developmentally annotated, summarized and argued writing that paves the way for the extended writing of the 'kappe'.

Context, identity, voice and culture

Nelson (2004: online) observed that now that we have a body of doctoral submissions we can fruitfully look at them as compositions, so that '[r]ather than a supplier-driven approach, a reader-oriented approach is called for'. This reader-oriented approach may be expounded through closer textual analysis. It may also be revealed through dialogical approach to pedagogy and knowledge by way of a sociocultural perspective on learning (Morrison 2010) that tracks and traces the developmental in learning-as-becoming, as well as through students' reflections on processes and completion. However, as Anthony Rowe pointed out, there is still separation between artefact and exegesis, with his experiential installation 3D work not easy to mediate outside a website. He described this as a 'problem of representation'. In contrast to other students, he argued strongly for the book format to be continued but that its design should be left open to working by the designer-researcher, as is the case at RMIT. Greater clarity could also be arrived at should design inquiry look more closely at the legacies and currencies of Cultural Studies (Ravelli et al. 2014: 397). However, Timo Arnall, when looking at making visible interaction design technologies, experienced difficulty in defining an integrated analytical perspective on culture and interaction against a dominant literature from computing.

Tools, methods and multiliteracies

One further domain that might be usefully incorporated to build stronger and more stable analytical foundations (for the ten green bottles, initially and duratively), are ways that tools, technologies, expressiveness and critical reflection and interpretation have been moulded and refracted within digital media studies and electronic art. A poetics of the exegesis can be successful only if we invest more thoroughly in understanding the relationships in the methods and methodologies of an extended and relational practice-based design inquiry. We need to examine relationships between reflexive design techniques and qualitative research methods. These need to be connected to fuller theories of design as culture and communication and a more elaborated pedagogical move into the multimodally communicative, non-normative exegesis. This demands that more space and expertise be allocated to the interplay between approaches to knowledge, analytical framings, modes of writing and types of visualization, and their paralogical and summative rhetoric.

Conclusion

The time has come to leave the nursery jingle and some of the under-communicated poetics at play, and to turn up the heat in the glassworks so that, rhetorically speaking, other forms, techniques and interpretative multimodal design may flourish (Morrison 2010; Ravelli et al. 2013; Vaughan this volume). Here doctoral design thesis in the compilation model may become more experimental, draw on the very strengths of designing and its domains and offer articulations of how to move wider academic publication beyond form and formality into new modes of (electronic) scholarly publication (Andrews et al. 2012) that reveal dynamic, developmental and interpretative expertise. This, several of our students have been brave and indeed bold enough to demand, and to see through to accomplished publication. The exegesis itself needs to be composed to allow for diversity and multiple perspectives, and above all to reveal what insights and knowledge may be derived through design situated inquiry.

Acknowledgements

My thanks to all the doctoral students in design at AHO who have contributed to shared understanding of design inquiry, learning and research. For details of individual theses and related projects, please see: www.designresearch.no

References

Andrews, R., Borg, E., Boyd Davis, S., Domingo, M. and England, J. (eds) (2012), *The SAGE Handbook of Digital Dissertations and Theses*. London: Sage.
Barrett, B. and Bolt, B., (eds) (2007), *Practice as Research: Approaches to Creative Arts Enquiry*. London: I.B. Tauris.
Berkenkotter, C. and Huckin, T. (1995), *Genre Knowledge in Disciplinary Communication*. Hillsdale: Lawrence Erlbaum.
Fletcher, J. and Mann, A. (2004), 'Illuminating the exegesis: An introduction', *TEXT*, 3. Available online: http://www.textjournal.com.au/speciss/issue3/content.htm (accessed 1 September 2015).
Gustavii, B. (2012), *How to Prepare a Scientific Doctoral Dissertation based on Research Articles*. New York: Cambridge University Press.
Hamilton, J. and Jaaniste, L. (2010), 'A connective model for the practice-led research exegesis: an analysis of content and structure', *Journal of Writing in Creative Practice* 3 (1): 31–44.
Hamilton, J. (2014), 'The voices of the exegesis: Composing the speech genres of the

practitioner-researcher into a connective thesis'. In Ravelli, L., Paltridge, B. and Starfield, S. (eds), *Doctoral Writing in the Creative and Performing Arts*, 369–88. Faringdon: Libri.

Milech, B. and Schilo, A. (2004), 'Exit Jesus: relating the exegesis and the creative/ production components of a research thesis', *TEXT* 3. Available online: http://www. textjournal.com.au/speciss/issue3/content.htm (accessed 1 September 2015).

Miller, C. (1984), 'Genre as social action'. *Quarterly Journal of Speech* 70 (2): 151–67.

Morrison, A. (2010), *Inside Multimodal Composition*. Cresskill: Hampton Press.

Nelson, R. (2004), 'Doctoralness in the balance: the agonies of scholarly writing in studio research degrees', *TEXT* 3. Available online: http://www.textjournal.com.au/speciss/issue3/nelson.htm (accessed 1 September 2015).

Paltridge, B. (2004), 'The exegesis as a genre: An ethnographic examination'. In Ravelli, L. and Ellis, R. (eds), *Analyzing Academic Writing*, 84–103. London: Continuum.

Paltridge, B., Starfield, S., Ravelli, S. and Tuckwell, K. (2012), 'Change and stability: Examining the macrostructures of doctoral theses in the visual and performing arts', *Journal of English for Academic Purposes* 11 (4): 332–44.

Paltridge, B., Starfield, S., Ravelli, L., Tuckwell, K. and Nicholson, S. (2014), 'Genre in the creative-practice doctoral thesis: Diversity and unity', in Garzone, G. and Ilie, C., (eds) *Genres and Genre Theory in Transition*, 89–105. Florida: Brown Walker Press.

Ravelli, L., Paltridge, B., Starfield, S. and Tuckwell, K. (2013), 'Extending the notion of "text": the visual and performing arts doctoral thesis', *Visual Communication* 12 (4): 395–422.

Ravelli, L., Paltridge, B. and Starfield, S. (2014), 'Diversity in creative and performing arts doctoral writing: A way forward'. In L. Ravelli, B. Paltridge and S. Starfield (eds), *Doctoral Writing in the Creative and Performing Arts*, 389–406: Faringdon: Libri Publishing.

Vaughan, L. and Morrison, A. (2014), 'Unpacking models, approaches and materialisations of the design PhD', *Studies in Material Thinking* 11. Available online: https://www.materialthinking.org/sites/default/files/papers/SMT_Vol 11_Paper 02_Vaughan.pdf (accessed 1 September 2015).

Part 4

GRADUATE REFLECTIONS ON THE DESIGN PHD
IN PRACTICE

Chapter 13

WHEN WORDS WON'T DO: RESISTING THE IMPOVERISHMENT OF KNOWLEDGE

Pia Ednie-Brown

When a word is repeated over and over, it can become strange. As I wrote this essay, the word 'word' began to mutate before me into a very strange entity. Word, word, word, word, word, word, word. It starts to look awkward, which words often are. When spoken (with an Australian accent at least) 'word' voices the sound of having 'erred'; it has the act of being mistaken, quite fittingly, tied up with its vocalization. It rhymes with 'heard', 'nerd' and 'turd'. It is almost a 'sword', and nearly a 'world'. In all these ways, and many more I am sure, the word 'word' along with all other words, both finds precision and blurs into a cloud of slippage, association and variation.

Words *do* – acting in many different ways. However, they can't do everything nor can they do anything entirely alone. A PhD is tied up with words. Creative practice research occurs through the medium of practice, but a written document is always required. We can use words to get closer to, and expand upon, the ineffable, tacit and wordless actions constitutive of the depths of practice, and in that sense words are valuable, beautiful and indispensable. We often forget, however, the degree to which words are nothing without the power offered to them by the wordless dimensions of experience. What is the word 'joy' without the experience of joy? What would our awareness and expression of joy be without the word 'joy' – if, in other words, joy were not yet named. This mutual feedback between words, qualities of experience, forms and actions becomes important for the researcher because it has a deep impact on how he or she best develops, conveys and shares knowledge, raising some very interesting questions about how to 'perform' knowledge, and how and in what way knowledge performs.

An important part of the PhD examination process in the School of Architecture and Design at RMIT University is an insistence on its multiple components. There is a text (the dissertation), an exhibition and an oral presentation followed by questions and conversation between examiners and the candidate. A candidate is to be examined through offering three parts that together form a whole, each of which offers something different about the research.[1] The written document loses its status as the primary artifact of a PhD. The oral presentation and exhibition are

10.29-30 People engaging with The Shower at the Perth Institute of Contemporary Art (2006).

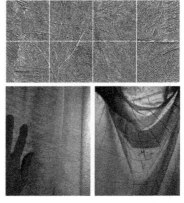

A further quite noticeable auditory attunement-misattunement arrived through the sound of the ceiling fan and *Static Tones* slipping, variably together and apart. The mechanical whirring of the fan was quite like *Static Tones* and the two were at times indistinguishable (at least to the unattentive ear). But as the skin sucked in around the body, the fan would slow down considerably, because there was, up to a point, a gradual evacuation of the air that it could suck out. This intensified a sense of creeping stillness, a slowing down and a gliding of match and mis-match between the two whirring sounds.

Certain social tensions were played out in the installation. Being inside was to be visually closed off from the outside but also exposed, with ones shape and actions inside set in a kind of naked view to others in the gallery. One was caught in a space of tension between hereness and thereness, vulnerability and protection, being naked and clothed, exposed and enclosed. It was not just the experience inside the installation that was important, but also the experience of re-entering the social field of the gallery, where we found people searching to catch the eye of another, in order to smile or laugh, to seek a shared acknowledgement of the strangeness and unfamiliarity of that experience as they departed from it, hooking back into the gallery landscape.

10.32 One of the skin texture images used to cut the particleboard. 10.33 Hand against latex inside The Shower. 10.34 Latex inset texture from first shower reveal peel.

Figure 13.1 Page spread (pp. 305–6) from Ednie-Brown (2007). Courtesy the author.

not simply to back up the written words but to work with the text, as three collaborators. When examiners arrive at the pre-examination briefing, having received the dissertation a month or so beforehand, they will often have formed a particular opinion, based on their reading of the document, of the validity and value of the research. It is extraordinarily common for this opinion to shift significantly after the presentation. This can go either way: examiners are sometimes impressed by the text but come to doubt its integrity after the presentation and questioning, and yet quite commonly come back to the conferring table after the examination with the words to the effect of: 'I get it now'. Something very important happens in that face-to-face event, which the text doesn't do. I would argue that this is because written words do different work from the acts of speaking, presenting and showing, and that it is in the collaboration between modalities that the important work of generating knowledge occurs.

The status of writing for creative practice research has long been a fascination of mine, partly because I enjoy making both with words and with other kinds of materials in the constitution of spatial entities, and because I find them to be deeply complementary practices. It struck me fairly early on in my PhD that, apparently paradoxically, the reason I feel compelled to write is to get closer to the things that I have trouble articulating and understanding in words – the things that always feel just out of reach of my comprehension. With enough effort, words can be given to concepts, experiences and ideas that were previously unknowable. In part this is about using the process of writing to discover something already lingering but previously unrealized, and in part it is about generating 'stories' that help to make sense of things. The impact of this articulation feeds into actions and practices in profound ways, and vice versa. Even though any kind of 'capture' of what I am trying to say, express, or articulate inevitably falls short, there is an enormous gain that comes from making that effort.

This double-sidedness of gain and loss has been explored with extraordinary richness in the work of Daniel Stern, which drew on detailed analyses of non-verbal interactions between adults and babies (2000), and later into how this operates across all everyday actions (2004), and is critical to creative practices (2010). Stern suggests that:

> Something is gained and something is lost when experience is put into words. The loss is of wholeness, felt truth, richness, and honesty. Is there some kind of resistance operating to counter this loss – a resistance that keeps some experiences protected in their richly complex, nonverbal, nonreflectively conscious state? Perhaps it is an æsthetic and moral true-to-self resistance, an existential resistance against the impoverishment of lived experience. (Stern 2004: 144–5)

Creative practice research is, I believe, a site of significant resistance, in the sense articulated by Stern: it is a mode of research that offers an aesthetic, 'existential resistance against the impoverishment of lived experience', also becoming a resistance against the impoverishment of knowledge. The idea that knowledge is only held in words or printed matter – a surprisingly common assumption – is one such impoverishment. Words are an important part of both developing and conveying knowledge, but the idea that they do this on their own is deeply problematic, not least because it fails to recognize that words can only do their work in ways that are deeply tied into lived particularity and experience. As you read this essay, for instance, these words do their work only amid a multitude of other factors: the environment in which the text is read, the layout and font of the text, whether it is in print or on screen, interruptions, why it is being read, the background experiences and biases of the reader, and the many slippages of meaning and association that words can move around and within. Whatever sense I am trying to make, whatever meaning I am trying to convey, there is no possibility of a fixed product or a 'pure' conveyance.

One might see this as a problem of 'fidelity': a problem of the inexactitude through which meaning is conveyed, and the infidelity of language. Scientific knowledge has worked extremely hard on the problem of fidelity, creating very sophisticated systems for conveying knowledge with finely tuned degrees of exact reproducibility. The Cartesian coordinate system, for instance, is an old and powerful invention to this end. One of the bedrocks of scientific research is, after all, reproducibility and generalizability. The complexity of the world continues to confusedly muddy the picture, however, despite the best efforts of the scientific method. This is nicely exemplified in a paper published in *Nature Methods* (Sorge 2014) showing that the presence of male researchers, as well as other nearby male animals, significantly increases the stress levels of mice.[2] This means, for instance, that a study involving mice carried out by female researchers can produce different results from an identical study undertaken by male researchers. Throwing a curveball across innumerable, controlled laboratory test results, these researchers found that '[e]xperimenter sex can thus affect baseline responses in behavioral testing' (Sorge 2014: 629). Infidelity raises its problematic head in the most surprising ways.

Creative practice research is grounded on an entirely different premise, however, in that it begins working with, and constructing itself through, idiosyncrasy, difference and the complex specificities of lived experience. It then works at producing shareable knowledge, but knowledge that is not burdened by the problem of exact reproducibility or accuracy. Many still get confused about how and why this kind of work counts as research, specifically because of its departure from reproducibility. A way to resolve this confusion lies in distinguishing between kinds of knowledge and their relevance to different situations. Creative practice research produces knowledge that is relevant to the richly complex condition of lived experience, producing shareable knowledge that is relevant to that very complexity intrinsic to all situated conditions. If you need to know how to do something in highly controlled conditions with relatively reliable pre-known outcomes, then the sciences will often serve you well. If you are seeking particular factual information, certain sciences may also serve you well, as might historical research. However, if you need to know how to do something that attends to highly variable qualities and conditions, and through which you hope to produce something that you couldn't have anticipated (something 'innovative' perhaps) then creative practice research is more likely to offer a productively guiding hand. In this context, you will be able to glean knowledge about how others have approached particular acts, problems, and practices that you may also be trying to negotiate; or perhaps ones that you never thought about negotiating before, offering something new to your own approaches.

This kind of knowledge is served reasonably well through textual means, in that we can read the accounts that others have carefully assembled for us in words. However, as suggested earlier, these words can be enriched by other means – through face-to-face, verbally and gesturally enriched exchanges, and encounters with artefacts made as part of the research. Together, these modes of encounter provide something richer and more informative than any one of them could alone. Words, as I argued above, never do their work alone, in any case, and creative practice research simply brings that fact out of the shadowy background. This is part of the resistance that creative practice research offers to the potential impoverishment of knowledge, particularly as it becomes in danger of being severed from the complexity of the lived.

When words are spoken, they become part of a multi-media performance involving sound, gesture, and situation. In everyday situations, the embeddedness of words in the complexity of lived experience becomes inescapable. A word as simple as 'yes' will mean entirely different things depending on how it is said. Work by Daniel Stern and others on the intricacies of non-verbal communication render these other intricate actions and dimensions particularly clear: once the veil of word-based meaning is removed, other kinds of meaning and action can more easily enter the foreground. These are the kinds of meaning and action that I am interested in here: those dimensions of creative practice research that collaborate with words, augmenting and enriching one another. These dimensions are, I believe, what makes the difference for examiners when they experience the presentation and exhibition.

Working across modalities is more than a process of diversifying the ways, means or modes of knowledge transfer. It is by moving across modalities, in the linking together and jostling between acts, that sense and meaning is made. When we speak, we do this at the same time as voicing the words, through tone, intonation, posture, gesture, eye contact, and so on. When we have made something, qualities of that thing can collaborate with what we write, say, and gesture about it, just as the many pieces that might constitute a body of work collaborate with one another, often in entirely non-verbal, pre-linguistic ways, in constituting a form of coherence that one can call 'a body of work'.

My own experience of doing a PhD was fraught with struggles and conflicts that touch upon these issues quite directly. Being a practitioner who largely straddled architectural theory and art practice, the status of my PhD as being undertaken by thesis or by project/practice was rarely stable. I love writing and did a lot of theorizing through writing about the work of others, but I also engaged actively in creative projects: drawings, sculptural works and interactive, architectural installations. How the theorizing and the creative practice would come together remained unclear for some time, and at some points I was sure the PhD was predominantly through creative practice, and at other times it seemed to be largely through thesis-based theoretical exploration. In the end it was examined by thesis, largely because I had written more than enough to satisfy the requirements of a thesis, and the prospect of having to design an exhibition in addition to the dissertation I had written, designed and laid out, was more than I could face at the time. My supervisors[3] became resigned to this, but had actively encouraged an examination by project. So, as things panned out, while a series of creative projects played a key role in the PhD, the examiners never experienced an exhibition, nor did I have the chance to enter into a face-to-face exchange as part of the examination process. For many years the PhD sat, uncomfortably for me, in a hybrid state – hard to publish as a book, and hard to exhibit as creative work. While it enjoyed a modicum of recognition through glowing examiner reports, and subsequently being shortlisted for a prestigious British research prize, the afterlife of this mammoth effort felt uncertain and fragile.

This was relatively early days in the history of PhDs through creative practice – for architecture at least – and the degree to which the differences have now been articulated was not as accessible to me then as it is to others now. Part of the struggle was also that the PhD process was very much one in which I, like many creative practice researchers, spent many years looping around something that evaded articulation. I felt I was choking on something inarticulable, or that my work was straining to say something that couldn't be said. Eventually I realized that the problem lay in my attention being turned somewhere other than where

Figure 13.2 Page spread (pp. 290–1) from Ednie-Brown (2007). Courtesy the author.

the critical action was happening: in the actuality of my acts of doing. While I was looking for something 'out there' to explain things, it was happening within the enactments of making: in the pattern and texture of refrains of action. And this was precisely what I kept skimming past, despite showing it to myself in everything I did.

This played itself out through not knowing how to write about my creative projects. Attempts to do so initially came out as simple descriptive accounts that seemed lacking in either worth or interest. I kept starting and quickly dropping these accounts in favour of theorization through the work of others. However, some fairly spontaneous, sometime intensely personal and poetic texts began to cross the divide because they showed me – though the *actions* of words – what was critical amid the work I was doing. As this started to become clear, my accounts of the creative project work became richer, weaving in and out of theorization and a sort of mining of the creative process for significance in moments and events that I had not previously considered significant at all.

About two thirds of the way through the PhD, I named my practice 'Onomatopœia'. This was probably what is now often referred to in our School as 'the PhD moment' – when you work out the critical discovery that has emerged through practice, and can move more directly (or less chaotically) towards completion. However, I didn't then have a clear sense of the idea of the 'PhD moment', and its significance, like many other things, was lost. This was not because I failed to attend to the significance of the naming – I actively researched 'onomatopoeia' and wrote about five thousand words on the topic and why it was an apt naming of my practice. This, however, was one of those tracts of text eventually omitted from the final document, as was the opportunity to enact the onomatopoeic through exhibition and publication. Following that trajectory more tenaciously would have involved taking the coherence of my practice across diverse media and modes more seriously. This is not without its own irony.

The thesis I submitted (Ednie-Brown 2007) revisited the idea of composition, largely seen as an obsolete aesthetic idea, offering a process and affect-oriented model of composition built alongside a study on the concept of emergence. Creative composition becomes embedded in the *experience* of emergence. Across projects it developed a related compositional technique discussed as the deployment of a 'flexible mould'. I argued that this was a way of ushering the idea of composition into contemporaneity, becoming relevant again through its affinity with emergence, which has played such a crucial role in understanding how all manner of complex organizational entities come into being. This led to the proposition that compositional expertise lies in what I discussed at length as 'ethico-aesthetic know-how', which rests on an awareness of, and sensitivity to, the 'texture' of one's own practice, in developing a broader, trans-situational sensitivity to situation and difference.

While this perhaps describes the PhD contribution in a nutshell, there are a lot of words or terms describing concepts that require unpacking and elaboration – which I won't be doing in this particular essay. What's more relevant here is that these ideas are integrally tied to experience, specificity and situated action – all things which tend to operate in the background of words. Had I done an exhibition and presentation, the particular act of naming my practice 'onomatopoeia' could have become a critical device for performing the contribution described above.

Onomatopœia is a figure of speech, usually defined as a word that sounds like that which it refers to, examples being words such as 'buzz', 'hiss', 'bump', 'whirr', 'crash', 'purr', 'squeak', 'mumble', 'crunch', and so on. They are often called 'sound-imitation' words, acting out meaning, embodying what they say.

In the naming of my practice, this 'sounding out' becomes an action of the word 'onomatopœia' itself, because it sounds like '*on a matter pia*'. The meaning of the word loops into a relation to my own name and the *matter* of my practice. The spelling of the 'pia' sound attains extra vowels in 'pœia'. Enjoyably, this spelling can be flipped into a different pronunciation wherein the 'œi' (like, 'awui') gives a distinctively Australian twang to 'pœia'/'pia' – bearing a poignant cultural resonance through its inflection. These poignancies slide a sense of a loose, playful good-fit into this choice of name, giving particular, specific relevance to a general thing (onomatopoeia). This specificity grounds the nature of onomatopoeic action, which operated across the projects in terms of their demonstration of the model of composition articulated in the PhD.

Onomatopœia is a Greek word that translates as 'name-making': it simultaneously names and makes the meaning in words. There is some scholarly debate about the limits of onomatopœia. Hugh Bredin, for instance, suggests that onomatopoeia is a linguistic universal (Bredin 1996). Walter Benjamin spent some time responding to the claim: 'Every word – and the whole of language, is onomatopoeic' (Benjamin 1986: 335) . Certainly, if we spend more time on the details, we can productively understand onomatopœia as a far broader phenomenon than a mimetic relation between the sound of a word and another sound.

When things sound like each other, what do they do? They enact similar patterns of aurally perceived movement. Likenesses share a pattern. The sound of the cat's purr and the sound we make when we say 'purr' are more or less similar in their patterning, but the differences are as significant as the similarities. When a cat purrs it enacts a ribbed or ridged topography of vibration that we can mimic through blowing out around a tongue loosely held against the front ridge inside our mouths, sending it into vibratory oscillations that bounce off the roof of the mouth (*try it*). The word 'purr' saves us the trouble of this intense tongue work, contracting its action into a simple word that distils key dimensions, where key, defining traits of the sound find an indicative shorthand. 'Purr' onomatopoeically acts in the pattern-form of the word itself where the repetition of the 'r' gives the repetitively ridged action a visual similitude.

The sound, sight and meaning of the word enter into a sympathetic vibration: they resonate. Across the sensuous dimensions there is something abstract that is not specific to any sensory modality: a temporal pattern. Daniel Stern calls this an 'amodal representation'. In the jostling of likenesses between modes or senses, their patternings gather, reinforce one another, becoming a group, a crowd, a party, a family, a collaboration. In the expressive event of the word they collaboratively insist on amodal qualities of an event-thing. Together they resonate, and this resonance is the emergence of meaning, sense and form.

Words gather meaning through their performative dimensions: all words become onomatopoeic through the situation or event in which they participate. They didn't just emerge, once, to sit on the shelf of meaning, they continue to emerge through their participation in specific conditions. The word itself, as a general thing, is a bundle of potential that is always modulated by the moment.

Without ever mentioning the word, my PhD both argued for and embodied the onomatopoeic, which can be seen as a shorthand for the complex of inter-related issues described above as a summary of the PhD contribution. In calling my practice 'Onomatopoeia', I was both 'name-making' and exemplifying a diagram of relations through which things come together, connect and produce a compositional entity, however fleetingly. The irony of the fact that I chose not to exhibit and present, but to let the written words of the dissertation do the talking, could not be more stark to me now. However, this loss is relieved somewhat by the degree to which the dissertation 'book' itself was a designed object. The document was filled with carefully placed images that played qualitative rather than just descriptive roles, and laid out with great attention to fonts, colours, and the proportion of the book itself. The words, in other words, had some measure of accompaniment and were less alone than they could have been.

Words live, like us, in events. They can be as exquisite as they can be dreary. Part of their beauty is that, like a musical score, they can be played again and again, differently each time. There are times when that music can become even richer when dance and scenography join in. When these all come together well, the symphony created across them is truly multi-modal, affectively amodal, and entirely antithetical to the impoverishment of lived experience. A PhD is not an evening at the theatre, but the act of contributing knowledge can surely have greater impact and relevance when allowed to enter the public domain in ways that attest to the fullness of their lived potential.

Notes

1 The manner in which different modalities can work together has been discussed by Professor SueAnne Ware: 'Implicit, Tacit and Ineffable: Communicating Design Practice Research', lecture and unpublished manuscript, first presented at The Fourth International Conference on Architectural Research by Design, on 8 May 2014 in Lisbon, Portugal.
2 My thanks to Professor Peter Downton for alerting me to this example.
3 Professor Leon van Schaik and Professor Peter Downton.

References

Benjamin, Walter (1986), 'On the Mimetic Faculty'. In *Reflections. Essays, Aphorisms, Autobiographical Writings*, Demetz, Peter (ed.), Jephcott, Edmund (trans). New York: Schocken Books.

Bredin, Hugh (1996), 'Onomatopoeia as a Figure and a Linguistic Principle', *New Literary History*, 27 (3): 555–69.

Ednie-Brown, Pia (2007), 'The Aesthetic of Emergence: Processual architecture and an ethico-aesthetics of composition', PhD Dissertation, School of Architecture and Design, RMIT University, Melbourne.

Sorge, Robert E., Loren J. Martin, Kelsey A. Isbester, Susana G. Sotocinal, Sarah Rosen, Alexander H. Tuttle, Jeffrey S. Wieskopf, Erinn L. Acland, Anastassia Dokova, Basil Kadoura, Philip Leger, Josiane C. S. Mapplebeck, Martina McPhail, Ada Delaney, Gustaf Wigerblad, Alan P. Schumann, Tammie Quinn, Johannes Frasnelli, Camilla I. Svensson, Wendy F. Sternberg and Jeffrey S. Mogil (2014), *Nature Meth*, http://dx.doi. org/10.1038/nmeth.2935 (last accessed 3 December, 2015).

Stern, Daniel (2000), *The Interpersonal World of the Infant*. New York and London: W. W. Norton and Co.

Stern, Daniel (2004), *The Present Moment in Psychotherapy and Everyday Life*. New York, London: W. W. Norton and Co.

Stern, Daniel (2010), *Forms of Vitality: Exploring Dynamic Experience in Psychology, the Arts, Psychotherapy, and Development*. Oxford: Oxford University Press.

Chapter 14

BEFORE, DURING AND AFTER A PHD: CURATING AS A GENERATIVE AND COLLABORATIVE PROCESS OF INFRASTRUCTURING

Katherine Moline

Before

Prompted by the paucity of design criticism in the early 2000s, I began my doctoral research in 2004 while working as a lecturer and researcher in art and design. While theatre, film and visual art were and still are frequently reviewed, very little critical commentary was published on design. What was published seemed to do little more than restate a designer's publicity material. My thesis commenced with asking whether designers were actually developing critique in their experimental work produced outside commissions. The resulting doctorate represented an intervention against the tendency in design discourse to welcome or dismiss experimental design as avant-garde without a thorough investigation of what this means. My thesis responded to a tendency in design studies to deploy the term 'avant-garde' without careful exploration of how it is understood in art history, the field with which it is most commonly associated. Accordingly, my premise was that, without a careful review and appreciation of the discourse of avant-gardism in art history and its use in design criticism, the term would continue to cover over an unjustified dismissal or uncritical acceptance of reflexive and engaged design practices. At that time in Australia practice-based research was emergent. Journals and monographs only rarely discussed examples of developments in practice-based design research, and those considered were all exhibited in the 'cultural centres' of Europe and the United States of America, not Australia. As a result only rarely did local practitioners engage with the issues of critical design practice evident internationally.

I drew on a number of previous professional experiences when developing my doctoral thesis proposal. First among these was my participation in one-day exhibitions in abandoned buildings in Sydney in the 1980s. Influenced by conceptual artists such as Art & Language, I explored how exhibitions were shaped by their contexts and developed exhibitions in alternative formats to the traditional gallery show, including features in magazines with artists' pages and in the production of artists' books. This research resulted in co-curating the work of conceptual artists into the exhibition 'In Print. Vol. 1. Artists Books' (1987), at The Power Gallery of Contemporary Art, University of Sydney. I also drew on my subsequent practice in co-design in visual communication when I led the participatory design project, 'Brushed with Care', at a hospital in the outer suburbs of Sydney between 1997 and 1999. These early experiences informed my proposal for doctoral research that would explore experimental design practices and their critical interpretations of the accepted conventions and standards of design.

PhD: Experimental design and the artistic avant-gardes between 1998 and 2007

Doctoral research is an institutive practice that articulates and questions tacit assumptions that underpin everyday practices. My doctoral research broadly addressed the interplay between critically engaged experimental design and artistic avant-gardes, and drew on empirical evidence from exhibitions staged between 1998 and 2007. My specific focus was on three key points: experimental design that proposed alternatives to dominant paradigms of functionalism; the historical design discourses evident in selected experimental designs; international exemplars of this experimental practice that proposed new social pacts in design. I defined experimental design as the reflexive critique of historical and emerging design protocols initiated by designers. Avant-garde was in turn defined as a range of artistic strategies that aimed to destabilize prevalent or institutionalized definitions of art, and proposed to sublate art into life. I contended that the connections between design and artistic traditions were worthy of investigation, rather than contradictions and ambiguities that needed to be resolved 'once and for all'.

My doctoral research explored the proposition that experimental designers, like avant-garde artists, rework at particular historical moments the technical and social conventions – the rules of making and judging – of design. I contended that experimental designers sought to remake the social pacts of design in changing circumstances. Exploring these social pacts also helped to explain aspects of experimental practices that engaged with prevailing concepts in design discourse, which recommended, for example, that design imitate nature, and redefined design as a form of management. I also argued in this context that experimental designers were intentionally renegotiating conceptions of design that could be traced through design history. The thesis concluded that experimental practitioners were not avant-garde in the sense of being preoccupied with self-expression – a poor imitation of romantic conceptions of artistic creation – but rather that experimental design was a practice of contestation and dissent. In questioning assumptions about the behaviours that everyday design practices and products created, experimental design made the norms and protocols of design visible.

As I will show, while my doctorate took the form of a traditional written thesis, the process of research was practice-based, as it motivated me to explore my own curatorial approaches as generative, in the sense of producing new insights for public debate. The resulting exhibitions, therefore, became a site for exploring curating as a form of collaboration, with exhibitors, audiences and co-curators, and sought to sustain an opportunity for debate about design's approaches to addressing significant challenges over time and in different locations.

During: 'Connections: Experimental Design' 2007

In 2007, early in my candidature, I curated 'Connections: Experimental Design' for Ivan Dougherty Gallery, in Sydney, a space managed by the faculty of Art and Design at the University of New South Wales Australia. This exhibition brought to Australia a number of designs by international practitioners who were critical of established norms and conventions. My catalogue essay explained that the exhibition aimed to 'challenge enduring myths that design is ahistorical and simply pursues innovation for its own sake' and that experimental design renegotiated social pacts with design users to do this (Moline 2007: 3). It featured experimental designs that engaged with complex social, environmental and technological issues. For example, *Technological Dream Series Number 1 (Robots)* (2007), by English designers Anthony Dunne and Fiona Raby, animated props to emulate emotional robots as an exploration of fears about Artificial Intelligence (Figure 14.1). Social issues were addressed in designs such as *HotBox* (2003) by Spanish firm Emiliana, which proposed a hypothetical outdoor heater design for street sex workers and attended to a social class often omitted from commercial design. Environmental issues featured in the installation *Autoband* (1999), by Spain-based Marti Guixe, a design that showed how a children's toy – a tape printed with road markings for playing with toy cars – could be used to discuss road design and environmental politics.

The exhibition included designs from a range of fields, including interaction design, engineering and textiles, and sought to show that experimental designs that challenged conventions could be found in many, if not all, fields of practice. My argument was, however, that undue emphasis on field or specialization distracted design discourse from larger issues connected to the futures that design practice has the potential to create. By offering visitors exposure to critiques of design norms, the exhibition sought to challenge impediments to design criticism created by the 'logic of specialization' (Draxler 2006: 151).

A 'low-key' exhibition design was aimed at focusing gallery visitors' attention on the objects on display, as this was the first time examples of international experimental design had been shown in Australia. To encourage gallery visitors to see that these were not artworks but designs intended for use, the objects were placed directly on the floor rather than on plinths. Rather than display printed matter in a vitrine as is common for design in gallery settings, visitors were invited to read experimental design magazines at the entrance of the exhibition in comfortable seating. Further, a number of videos were dispersed throughout the exhibition showing the experimental designs in use, and their sound tracks created a low, vibrating hum throughout the gallery. The absence of plinths and vitrines, and the invitation to engage with the practical application of the objects as designs rather than as artworks was supplemented in the accompanying exhibition catalogue with descriptions of the established norms and protocols that were being challenged by the experimental designs on display.

The exhibition provided a valuable opportunity to show Australian audiences international experimental design. Positive audience responses and reviews of the exhibition were encouraging (Dokulil 2007), and the exhibition established conversations within a community of practitioners who were exploring design critique locally.

There were, however, issues that demanded further exploration. I was frustrated that my intention to display a selection of experimental designs had inadvertently framed the works as exceptions rather than as examples of an activity in which many international designers were engaged. I feared this corresponded too closely to the conventional understanding of design as an elitist practice that produced expensive luxuries. A second concern was that my curatorial approach mirrored conventional understandings of curating as caretaking, connoisseurship and conservation, and that as a result it had overlooked how consumers also critiqued design conventions. I felt these oversights had limited audience appreciation of the far-reaching implications of what experimental design made possible in opening design conventions up to more rigorous scrutiny.

During: Teaching and Myths of the Near Future

Doctoral research influenced my practices as an artist/designer, curator and as a university lecturer. While completing the doctorate, I developed new coursework on experimental practices as a form of research that reflected my concern that exhibiting experimental design concealed and immobilized critiques of convention and obscured the role of design users. I initially tested the course content by visualizing my experiences as a design user of mobile media and smart phones in a series of sculptures titled *Equipment for the Actual Complexities and Intricacies of String* (2010–11) shown in Figure 14.1 in their more recent iteration as *Myths of the Near Future 2* (2015). The sculptures were made with readily available everyday materials, such as rubber, plumbing parts and mobile phone cords. In studio tutorials I demonstrated the equipment as a model for engaging design users in conversations about stories and urban myths about mobile media, media consumption and information privacy. The aim was for students to reflect on how users interpreted design experiences by doing this themselves with a device that they treated as private, but which they knew also stored traceable data that could be made public.

The workshops, titled 'Myths of the Near Future: Social Experiences Mediated by Phone', which I have also run at other universities, invite participants to

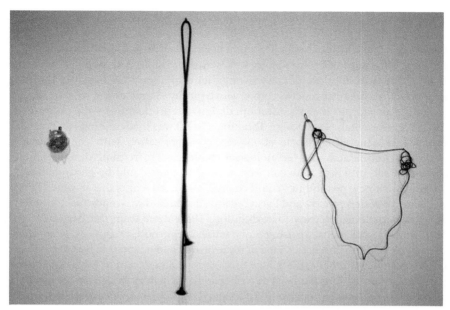

Figure 14.1 Katherine Moline, *Myths of the Near Future 2* (2015). Photography: Carl Warner. Image courtesy of Griffith Artworks, Brisbane. Courtesy the author.

choose from a number of activities from my teaching practice. For example, in *Spoken Portraits*, participants explore another's phone and then describe the phone's user based on what they found in the digital records. In another instance, participants were invited to take the *Equipment* sculptures apart and encouraged to reflect collaboratively on their experiences of smartphone technology while making photographs and videos. These workshops entailed extensive discussion about how the ethical implications of everyday practices that defined private and public were changed with mobile media (Funnell 2015; Moline 2015b, 2015c). In short, the workshops encapsulated my ambition to explore design as an experimental space that questioned emerging conventions, protocols and the emerging consumer behaviours that were facilitated by design.

The shifts in my practice over this time would not have been possible without the doctoral research and the resulting articulation of my thinking about experimental design in the 2007 'Connections' exhibition. The transformation of my practices as an artist/designer, lecturer and curator during the doctorate grew to take greater account of the collaboration between designers and design-users, as well as producers and consumers, in making and critically engaging with experimental design.

After: Generative exhibitions and Feral Experimental: New Design Thinking

On completing the doctorate I commenced research for another exhibition focusing on trajectories in design practice that challenged popular conceptions of the field. In place of conceiving of an exhibition that displayed the end product of an iterative process – that was typically characterized as a sequence of consecutive steps (analysis, ideation, design and production) – the premise of 'Feral Experimental: New Design Thinking' (2014) was that curating is a practice engaged in generating debate about design's imbrication with contemporary social, environmental, and technological challenges. To reframe design exhibitions as a site in which new connections and insights could be generated, and within which new possibilities could emerge, I selected works that deviated from the iterative design process and I also organized a three-day symposium and series of workshops to accompany the exhibition. These drew from the 'Myths of the Near Future' workshops, focusing on how users repurpose design and adapt it to their context. At the time, this idea of repurposing and adaptation was debated in co-design practices that explore how users understand design in ways not anticipated by designers. This has been described in participatory design debate as users 'appreciate[ing] and appropriate[ing] designed devices in totally unforeseen ways' (Binder et al. 2011: 170).

In another faction of design discourse, known as speculative design, greater user-engagement is described as resulting in 'overspilling', that is the 'enablement of unforeseen participant actions' or 'misbehaviors' (Michael 2012: 537). I aimed to bring the practices of participatory and speculative design together in 'Feral Experimental', as I saw these approaches to drawing user engagement into design as a significant and shared reconceptualization of the field, although they were separated by methodological differences. The exhibition therefore included participatory designs, including: *Community Centred Innovation: Co-designing for Disaster Preparedness* (2009–14) by Melbourne based Yoko Akama; the speculative designs of *Avena+ Test Bed — Agricultural Printing and Altered Landscapes* (2013), by Stuttgart-based designer Benedikt Groß; participatory artworks such as *Veloscape* (2014) by Sydney-based Volker Kuchelmeister, Laura Fisher and Jill Bennett at the UNSW National Institute of Experimental Arts, Sydney (Figure 14.2). The curatorial emphasis was on large-scale projects that were developed with substantial design-user engagements.

The combination of works included in 'Feral Experimental' explored design approaches that investigated significant contemporary challenges connected to global warming, data visualization, social inclusion and bodily engagement in the digital era, and also included both International and local Australian practitioners. The aim of this exhibition was to show design as a process that engaged design users. Rather than exhibit completed static works, as in 'Connections: Experimental Design', this exhibition included workbooks with which the designs had been developed in workshops, design games, photographic and video documentation, as well as prototypes, so as to solicit user feedback, instead of the completed final products. Exhibiting design development also interrupted

Figure 14.2 'Feral Experimental: New Design Thinking' (2014). Installation detail – Heather Daam with Maartje van Gestel, *An Empathic Adventure, Grey But Mobile* (2013–2014); Volker Kuchelmeister, Laura Fisher, Jill Bennett, *Veloscape* (2014). Photography: Britta Campion. Image courtesy of UNSW Galleries, Sydney. Courtesy the author.

expectations that a design could be understood just by looking at it, as if it were a work of art. This mode of display sought to show designs that developed over time and engaged many other people at significant turning points. The rationale was that this would facilitate audiences' seeing experimental design as an approach in a number of communities of practice grouped by methodologies: speculative, participatory and co-design, as well as exploratory experimentation by artists and designers.

Provisional definitions of these design frameworks were provided in the exhibition catalogue, and with this information visitors were invited to find connections between works that were otherwise often seen through sharply defined categorical lenses (Moline 2014: 11). Speculative design was described as aiming to provoke debate about design and engage people in thinking critically about their interactions with design, that is seeing it as 'fictional worlds', 'what-if scenarios' and 'cautionary tales'. (Dunne and Raby 2013: 3). Co-design was referred to as a collaborative process that engaged many stakeholders including the users of designed products and services, with the purpose to design *with* rather than *for* stakeholders. Elizabeth Sanders, an early advocate of co-design, describes it as 'social or collective creativity' (Sanders and Stappers 2012: 58). Participatory design shares with co-design the principle of creating legitimate participation for all stakeholders, but it is explicitly engaged with ethical and political issues in design. Exploratory experimentation was articulated as a research approach shared between artists and designers. The catalogue stated that the exhibition brought these diverse approaches together to show areas where they converged and to demonstrate that 'the influence and impact of design is now so extensive it has infiltrated every facet of everyday life' (Moline 2014: 10). Public reception of the exhibition drew attention to these insights that the exhibition provided into leading edge design (Scully 2014; Leimbach 2014; Periz 2015).

In recognition of the multiple agencies involved in discourse around design's purpose, the symposium accompanying the exhibition was organized to create conversations with practitioners and audiences, and invite critics to test prevailing and newly established orthodoxies about the differences between speculative design, participatory co-design and experimental practice in art and design. Papers explored theoretical propositions concerning experimental practice and the implications of case studies for emerging methods in sessions on experimental design thinking, experimental design combines, experimental design and environmental sustainability, and experimental interaction design. The symposium was complemented by workshops in which participants were invited to test issues discussed in the symposium panels.

My symposium paper explored participatory and speculative approaches to design research and proposed that what constitutes productive research was a contested issue. I looked at how participatory research's commitment to understanding user experiences and the involvement of diverse stakeholders had much in common with speculative design's reflections on how design-users repurpose products for their own desires and create narratives that enrich understandings of social conundrums. I pointed out that participatory and speculative design were rarely considered together in exhibitions or anthologies of contemporary design research, despite recent design examples that intermixed aspects of each approach. I also presented case-studies that demonstrated that the differences between participatory and speculative design were not always clear cut. These included: *Design Anthropology Innovation Model (DAIM)* (2008–10), by design researchers Joachim Halse, Eva Brandt, Brendon Clark and Thomas Binder at the Royal Danish Academy of Fine Arts, School of Design (KADK), Copenhagen, and *Energy Co-Design Communities (ECDC)* (2010–14) by Bill Gaver, Mike Michael, Tobie Kerridge, Liliana Ovale, Matthew Plummer-Fernandez, Alex Wilkie and Jennifer Gabrys at the Interaction Research Studio at Goldsmiths College, London. The paper extended the reflection in my doctoral thesis that design specialization distracted discourse from larger and more pressing concerns, and proposed that factionalism was occurring in emerging practices that defined themselves with specialist jargon about design methodology.

The 'Feral Experimental' exhibition effectively generated a network of designers, academics and curators, and community concern around the similarities and differences between experimental, speculative, and participatory or co-design. The network generated discussions that led to further co-curated exhibitions in Melbourne and Brisbane, and this in turn provided opportunities for me to extend what I learnt – from the doctoral research, the exhibition I curated in 2007, and the subsequent workshops – towards developing a new curatorial model for design exhibitions that involved greater user engagement in symposium debate and workshop experiences. The co-curators in each city were intrinsically involved in customizing the construction or framing of the issues and concerns that were relevant to each community in which the exhibitions were situated.

'Experimental Practice: Provocations In and Out of Design', 2015

'Experimental Practice: Provocations In and Out of Design' (2015) is one of the exhibitions that was a direct result of discussions that began after the 'Feral Experimental' symposium, and an invitation to collaboratively curate an exhibition in Melbourne with Royal Melbourne Institute of Technology (RMIT) academics, Brad Haylock and Laurene Vaughan. The resulting exhibition focused on encouraging debate about a number of design projects that aimed to make a difference within the specific communities of practice in Melbourne, specifically works that explored data interactions. The show included works such as *They Rule* (2001/11) by Josh On and Little Sis, who used a data interface to show connections between members of corporation boards, *The Institutional Harvest* (2013), in which Mitchell Whitelaw developed a data visualization interface that showed changes to Australian Women's services and agencies between 1970 and 2013, and *Text, Vodka & Le Rock'n'Roll* (2015) by Chicks on Speed (Alex Murray-Leslie and Melissa Logan in collaboration with Kathrin Krottenthaler). The exhibition attended to the specific concerns of Melbourne and aimed to 'challenge expectations of what we expect and believe design can do, or should do, as either a strategy or a provocation for future action' (Vaughan 2015: 1). It focused on more recent iterations of projects and included new works that were contextualized as 'works in progress' rather than fixed or finished in a gallery context (Moline 2015a: 2).

Collaborating with other curators on this project provided a significant opportunity to shift my curatorial approach away from audience interpretations of exhibitions as a theatre stage or a medium of the curator's self-expression (O'Neill 2012: 97). My hope that curated exhibitions could generate debate shared affinities with curator Ute Meta Bauer's description of exhibitions as 'about an exchange of experiences', and the idea of exhibitions as a dialogue that does not necessarily result in consensus (Bauer in Brand and Molnár 2013: 75; Bauer in Bauer and Babias 2011; p. 74). Collaborative curation has been described by writer Paul O'Neill as an act of 'denouncing of the individual author position' (O'Neill 2010: 6). Extending this idea, I found that co-curating enriched the experience as it brought different opinions and new questions not only to the exhibition, but also more broadly into the debate about what it means to curate as a practice. The differences between our approaches further transformed my thinking on curating exhibitions from one of compelling collaborators or gallery visitors to agree with a curatorial vision to one designed to provoke debate. 'Experimental Practice: Provocations In and Out of Design' elaborated my understanding of exhibitions as generative – which I had gained when curating 'Feral Experimental' – into seeing exhibitions as collaborations not only with the exhibitors and gallery visitors but also with other curators. Refiguring exhibitions as sites for generative production had begun to create a community of practice that connected disparate design communities and increased the visibility and tangibility of experimental practices for Australian audiences.

After: 'Experimental Thinking/Design Practices' 2015

The network that developed following 'Feral Experimental' and 'Experimental Practice' prompted the Griffith University's Queensland College of Art (QCA) to invite me to co-curate an exhibition in Brisbane. Meetings with QCA design academics Peter Hall and Beck Davis, discussed the exhibitions in Sydney and Melbourne, and with input from Brad Haylock and Laurene Vaughan we explored the visceral thematic that occupied artists and designers concerned with wearable technology in Queensland. Works that emphasized visceral engagement, included the video *Footwerk: Improvisations in Gender, Sound and Space* (2015) by Alex Murray-Leslie, which deployed computer-enhanced footwear to generate soundscapes by different minority groups including transgender pole dancers in Singapore, and *Robotic Spider Dress 2.0 (Intel version)* (2014) by Anouk Wipprecht, a mechatronic dress that defended the wearer's personal space when triggered by biosignals (breath for example) to detect when the wearer felt threatened. Embodied experiences of design and knowing were also explored by Tristan Schultz in *Drawing 'Together' Indigenous Futures* (2015), where he presented a map of cultural competency developed with a group of Aboriginal and Torres Strait Islander academics at the College of Indigenous Australian Peoples at Southern Cross University, Lismore (Figure 14.3).

This QCA invitation meant that my doctoral research – into experimental designs that critiqued the norms and conventions of design – could explore and critique design conventions not only collaboratively, as the curatorial team had in Melbourne, but also meant the exhibition model was sufficiently robust to become a flexible infrastructure that invited critical debate. Creating such an infrastructure means creating a platform that is connected to other platforms or networks, rather than being limited to a one-off event. In other words, what is referred to as *infrastructuring* in design helps to describe how a platform, such as the Internet or a series of exhibitions, 'reaches beyond the single event (temporal) and any one particular site (spatial); it is not reinvented every time, and is embedded in other sociomaterial structures' (Binder et al. 2011: 172). *Infrastructuring* is one way to support the development of polemical debate about design that transforms opposition and antipathy to constructive conflict that produces positive change (Bjögvinsson et al. 2012: 109). The term *infrastructuring* described many aspects of the series of exhibitions I was involved in curating after the doctorate, namely the flexible systems that supported collaborative curation at a distance and with fellow curators with whom negotiation relied on acknowledging differences as well as shared interests.

Figure 14.3 'Experimental Thinking/Design Practices' (2015). Installation detail – Tristan Schultz, *Drawing 'Together' Indigenous Futures* (2015); Laurens Boer and Jared Donovan, *The Sensitive Aunt* (2012), Griffith University Art Gallery, Brisbane, Australia, 2015. Carl Warner. Image courtesy of Griffith Artworks, Brisbane. Courtesy the author.

The exhibition in Brisbane completed a series of exhibitions I curated in Australia following my doctoral research. The significance of this exhibition was in the realization that curating could become a practice that produced and *infra-structured* an approach that could generate debate by drawing on the experiences of design in specific communities and emphasizing local issues. In sum, generating debate through co-curation developed an alternative to the conventions of curating. *Infrastructuring* the processes of curation became a viable alternative for collaborative co-creation of exhibitions, and generated a dialogue that multiplied connections between practitioners dispersed in a number of remote locations and specializations.

Conclusion

This chapter has outlined the development of my curatorial approach in design exhibitions, and my work as a lecturer in relation to my doctoral research on connections between experimental design and artistic avant-gardes. The exhibition titled 'Connections: Experimental Design', early in my candidature

(2007) laid out the problematic of my doctoral thesis: What is the agency of designers who explore alternatives to the dominant design paradigms based in consumerism, and what kinds of social pacts does experimental design make possible? The exhibition traced connections between experimental practices in design and an understanding of artistic avant-garde to indicate the concerns of designers whose practices critique dominant design paradigms and the organization of the field according to specialization. The doctoral research transformed my practices as a lecturer and researcher when I developed new teaching approaches in the workshops 'Myths of the Near Future'. The combination of these activities led to further analysis of the dialogue between art and design and, on completion of my thesis, the 2014 exhibition 'Feral Experimental: New Design Thinking'. This exhibition generated an expanded network of practitioners interested in experimental approaches to design, in particular speculative design and participatory/co-design.

Following my doctorate, my approach to curating was transformed again when I collaborated with curators in Melbourne for the exhibition 'Experimental Practice', and related symposium. The dialogue was then further extended to include other curators and audiences, and the *infrastructuring* of co-curating became evident in the subsequent exhibition and panel debates for 'Experimental Thinking/Design Practices' in Brisbane in 2015.

These experiments in curating since completing the doctorate developed my understanding of curating, shifting it from generative, to collaborative to *infrastructuring*. The experience changed my practices to help find connections between disciplinary silos that my thesis had argued were inhibiting the critical potential of exhibitions of experimental designs that challenged the norms and standards of the field. Reconfiguring exhibitions so that audiences had opportunities to see and actively engage in practice-led research was an exciting process.

As the exhibitions unfolded, they renewed my commitment to making space for design exhibitions. Curating three exhibitions in eighteen months brought with it logistic complexities, but it taught me in practical terms how to formulate exhibitions as sites for experimentation not only with exhibitors and audiences but also with co-curators. The institutive process of doctoral research is evident in the differences between my curatorial approach in 2007 and the exhibitions, symposia and workshops I have curated since completing the thesis. These examples demonstrate how a traditional thesis transformed my practices in a range of contexts. While 'Connections: Experimental Design' introduced strategies that addressed the challenges of exhibiting design research in a gallery context ordinarily associated with art, the workshops that culminated in 'Myths of the Near Future' helped me to see how active engagement with ideas raised important questions about design. This informed my curatorial approach for 'Feral Experimental' and developed a process that generated dialogue about design research. Co-curating the subsequent exhibition, 'Experimental Practice', taught me about the value of collaboration in the curatorial context, and 'Experimental Thinking' infrastructured processes and practices that made co-curation in multiple locations viable. The *infrastructuring* practices developed so far will be tested in an exhibition that is being developed by a curatorial team for Carnegie Mellon University in Pittsburgh in 2016, which is intended to explore further the social pacts created in design.

References

Bauer, U. and Babias, M. (2011), 'Easy Looking – Curatorial Practice in a Neo-Liberal World. Uta Meta Bauer in an interview with Marius Babias', *OnCurating: Curating Critique* 9: 72–6.

Binder, T., Ehn, P., Jacacci, G., De Michelis, G., Linde, P. and Wagner, I. (2011), *Design Things*. Cambridge MA: MIT Press.

Björgvinsson, Erling, Ehn, Pelle, Hillgren, Per-Anders (2012), 'Design Things and Design Thinking: Contemporary Participatory Design Challenges', *Design Issues* 28 (3): 101–16.

Brand, A. and Molnár, M. (2013), 'Authorship (ext)ended: Artist, artwork, public and the curator: Ute Meta Bauer and Yvonne P. Doderer interviewed by Annemarie Brand and Monika Molnár', *OnCurating: On Artistic and Curatorial Authorship* 19: 75–80.

Dokulil, H. (2007), 'Connections: Experimental Design. An Interview with Katherine Moline, Curator', *Inside: Australian Design Review* 48: 36–9.

Draxler, H. (2006), 'Letting Loos(e): Institutional Critique and Design', *Art after Conceptual Art*, Alberro, Alberto and Buchman, Sabeth (eds), 151–60. Cambridge MA: MIT Press.

Dunne, A. and Raby, F. (2013), *Speculative Everything: Design, Fiction, and Social Dreaming*. Cambridge: MA: MIT Press.

Funnell, A. (2015), 'Myths of the Near Future', *Future Tense*, 1 Nov., available online: http://www.abc.net.au/radionational/programs/futuretense/myths-of-the-near-future/6888830 (accessed 10 May 2016).

Griffith University (2015), *Griffith Artworks: Experimental Thinking/Design Practices*, available online https://www.youtube.com/watch?v=9fSXUp_c2cc (accessed 12 May 2016).

Leimbach, T. (2014), 'Design goes wild: boundary crossing in Feral Experimental', *The Conversation*, 19 August, available online http://theconversation.com/design-goes-wild-boundary-crossing-in-feral-experimental-29974 (accessed 12 May 2016).

Michael, M. (2012), 'What Are We Busy Doing?', *Engaging the Idiot, in Science, Technology, & Human Values*, 37 (5): 528–34.

Moline, K., (2007), 'Connections: Experimental Design', *Connections: Experimental Design*, ed. Moline, Katherine, 3–15, Sydney: Ivan Dougherty Gallery UNSW.

Moline, K., (2014), 'Dingo Logic: Feral Experimental', *Feral Experimental*, ed. Moline, Katherine, 6–11, Sydney: UNSW Galleries and the National Institute of Experimental Arts.

Moline, K., (2015a) 'Experimental Practice: Provocations', *The Design Hub*, ed. K. Moline, B. Haylock, L. Vaughan, 2–3, Melbourne: RMIT University .

Moline, K., (2015b), 'Bringing Experimental Practice and Thinking Together', *Experimental Thinking/Design Practices*, ed. K. Moline and P. Hall, 8–9, Brisbane: Griffith University Art Gallery.

Moline, K. (2015c), 'On Researching Mobile Media', *Researching Digital Cultures: Methods & Ethics Symposium*, UNSW School of Arts and Media, 5 November (Unpublished).

O'Neill, P. (2010), 'The Politics of the Small Act', *OnCurating: The Political Potential of Curatorial Practice* (4): 6–10.

O'Neill, P. (2012), *The Culture of Curating and the Curating of Culture(s)*. Cambridge, MA: MIT Press.

Periz, I. (2015), 'The Skullbone Experiment: A paradigm of art and nature, Feral Experimental: New Design Thinking', *Eyeline. Contemporary Visual Arts* 82: 74–5.

Sanders, E. and Stappers, P. J., (2012), *Convivial Toolbox: Generative Research for the Front End of Design*. Amsterdam: BIS.

Scully, J. (2014), 'Interview with Dr. Katherine Moline – Feral Experimental at UNSW Art & Design', *So Hot Right Now*, 26 July, available online http://www.2ser.com/component/k2/item/10178-feral-experiment (accessed 10 May 2016).

Vaughan, L. (2015), 'Exhibition as Experimental Practice', *Experimental Thinking/Design Practices*, ed. K. Moline and P. Hall, 7, Brisbane: Griffith University Art Gallery, 7.

Chapter 15

THE RESEARCHERLY DESIGNER/THE DESIGNERLY RESEARCHER

Joyce Yee

Introduction

A 'researcherly designer' is a practising designer trained in research and a 'designerly researcher' is a practising researcher trained in design. These terms are used in this chapter to highlight and discuss how design skills contribute to a research practice and similarly how research skills contribute to a design practice. I do this by reflecting primarily on my personal experience through my PhD, my more recent supervision experience of design PhDs, and I ground my situated knowledge with existing literature. I will start by providing a brief background to my practice and discussing how I transitioned from a design practice into a hybrid practice consisting of research, teaching and design. It is worth noting that I have only focused on what I consider to be key skills and attributes, since there are many other skills that benefit both practices.

My introduction to design research

I followed a fairly standard route into design. I completed a Bachelors of Arts in Graphic Design, before enrolling on a Masters of Arts in Visual Communication. Both degrees were studio-based programmes designed to provide practical and technical skills to prepare me for a professional environment. I had relatively modest research training at postgraduate level but insufficient for what I needed at doctoral level. Although trained in graphic design, I moved into digital, interactive and web design in my professional practice and slowly transitioned into what is now described as a service and interaction designer. In total I was practising as a professional designer for twelve years, where five of those overlapped with my PhD study. My PhD was practice-led, using a mixed-method research design consisting of action research, reflective practice and semi-structured interviews. The focus of the PhD was to develop a framework to promote the practice and understanding of typography across different design domains. I continued to practise as an Interaction Designer for three years after I obtained my PhD before moving away from day-to-day design work. Although I am now in a full-time lecturing post, I am still strongly connected to the practice through industry-based student projects and my research work in the area of design practice.

When I began my PhD, I was only marginally aware of the seismic changes happening in the educational and professional sector. I wanted to pursue a PhD because I was simply curious. At that time, I was employed as an Interaction Designer at the university's design research centre. Through the work that I did and the people I met, I was introduced to the idea of design research, which was mostly (to use Frayling's term), research *for the purpose of* design. It was research undertaken solely for the purpose of addressing a design brief. Most of the design briefs we worked on did not have an inherent research question but were practical issues and problems that needed to be resolved. At the same time, I was also introduced to research *into* design – studies about how designers worked, thought and practised. Findings from Melican et al. (1998) suggest that the majority of design researchers' decisions to pursue a PhD were motivated by two main considerations: personal intellectual development, and professional advancement. My own main motivating factor was personal intellectual development. Intellectually and professionally, I was interested in using a research lens to help me understand what I do and to help me do it better.

How a research lens informs design practice

This section will introduce and discuss how my research training has informed my professional practice.

Articulating the why, how and what

Design and the creative arts are often talked about as a 'black box', where the process and activities are difficult to define and are often not very well articulated. This perception has been based to some extent on a lack of understanding of and study in the subject, due to its practice-based nature. One of the most important skills I developed through my PhD research training is the ability to shine a light into my own 'black box'. A fundamental principle of research practice is to make the research process explicit so that others can interrogate and learn from the process. This approach is almost the antithesis of the design culture I trained in, where process is something you did rather than described and shared.

At that time I was (in Hubert and Stuart Dreyfus' skill-based model, 2003) operating at the level of a 'competent' designer. The Dreyfus brothers distinguish seven distinct levels of expertise, corresponding with seven ways of perceiving, interpreting, structuring and solving problems. Becoming more aware and reflective of what I was doing helped me transition from a competent designer to a proficient designer. Someone who is operating at the proficient level is able to draw on personal experiences and observe the experience of others to identify the most important issues and create an appropriate plan. Action Research and Reflective Practice models offered me the scaffolding required to help me reflect, plan and act in a systematic and deliberated way. It enabled me to track my actions and to evaluate objectively whether my plan had led to the desired outcome. Through Reflective Practice, I was able to recognize how important it was to be evidencing and reflecting on the 'why', 'how' and 'what' of my practice. As a designer, I am better able to articulate the thought process at different stages of my design process. This helps me to communicate my design decisions to stake-holders and generate a shared understanding of the project.

Developing critical thinking skills through writing

In order to develop a coherent argument, one requires the ability to think critically. It seems widely accepted that being able to write well reflects clarity of thought. According to Applebee (1984: 577), the role of writing in thinking is usually attributed to four factors: 1) the permanence of the word allowing reflection and revision; 2) the explicitness required for writing in order for it to retain meaning beyond its original context; 3) the resources provided by conventional forms of discourse for organizing and thinking through new ideas and explicating the relationships between them; 4) a medium for exploring implications contained in unexamined assumptions.

Despite my research training, I find writing hard and tedious, not something that comes naturally to me. I am not alone in this sentiment. Art and design students commonly express frustration when it comes to academic writing. This is due to the fact that the creative disciplines tend to privilege intuitive rather than analytical thinking (Apps and Mamchur 2009). However, despite my struggle, writing has been the single most important factor in helping me to develop critical thinking skills. One could argue that anyone would benefit from developing better critical thinking skills. Why should it be particularly important to design practice?

Designers, like it or not, have to produce a surprising amount of written documentation throughout a project – for example a project proposal, a research report, a concept proposal and a final project case study. Although these consist for the most part of descriptive writing, I would argue that the simple act of noting down what happened helps designers articulate their design process and exposes intuitive considerations and decision-making. It helps them develop a coherent narrative to support their work and explain the work to others.

In a similar way, the process of writing has enabled me to record my thoughts and actions, interrogate my line of argument, and subsequently reflect and revise my understanding of the subject. Writing allowed me to 'connect the dots' in my knowledge and allowed others to evaluate my ideas. As a designer, I am used to thinking through making, and in my research practice I had to relearn how to think through writing. Academic writing is about presenting a point of view and supporting it with the relevant literature. In a way, designers do this through their design work – they present ideas and use supporting research to support their solution. Writing offers me a different mode of thinking (through a more linear and systematic approach) and helps situate design knowledge with other types of knowledge in the field.

Understanding the importance of epistemology

Epistemology according to the Merriam Webster Online Dictionary is 'the study or a theory of the nature and grounds of knowledge especially with reference to its limits and validity'. Epistemology is the branch of philosophy that deals with the nature of knowledge, with questions of what we know and how we know it. It is an important element of a research study as it places the research in a particular tradition of knowledge, and influences subsequent research methods used in the study. It helps form the research's standpoint. On an individual level, one's epistemological position is instrumental in shaping a person's worldview.

Prior to my PhD, I confess that such key philosophical questions hardly featured explicitly in my day-to-day life. I had my own values, which developed over time, but was not overly concerned with where my knowledge came from and how I knew it to be 'true'. I did not explicitly question my worldview and it often did not feature in my practice. However reflecting back I realized that many of the questions that I have been grappling with are in one way or another epistemological questions.

Anastas (2002: 9) emphasizes why epistemology is important to a researcher in the context of social work: it affects the kind of research undertaken, how the scholarships of others will be valued, how the work is understood politically and how the work is situated in relation to others. As a researcher, it was extremely important that I should locate my research in relation to the work of others, and that it helped place my overarching worldview in relation to others. As a designer, this philosophical lens has made me more aware of underlying assumptions and helped me understand people better by critically questioning their politics, behaviour, habits and motivations. This is particularly important as many of the projects that I worked on were focused on using digital tools to encourage behaviour change.

How a design lens informs research practice

In the previous section I discussed how a research lens can inform a design practice. In this section, I would like to offer a complementary view on how a design lens can inform a research practice.

Being a creative researcher

The Frascati Manual's[1] definition of research is:

> Research and experimental development (R&D) comprise *creative* work undertaken on a systematic basis in order to increase the stock of knowledge, including knowledge of man, culture and society, and the use of this stock of knowledge to devise new applications. (2002: 30, my emphasis)

The word 'creative' features prominently in the definition and suggests how important the creative mind is to the research process. The role of 'creativity' and 'imagination' however are not always associated with academic research. Instead, terms such as 'systematic', 'rigorous' and 'repeatability' are more commonly used to describe research. Yet 'without an imaginative insight into what data "might" mean and the variety of ways in which it "could" be interpreted, science would have made little progress in extending the body of knowledge' (Swann 2002, p. 54). Hart (1998) emphasizes how important it is to develop an imaginative approach to research. For him, a research imagination is about: 'having a broad view of a topic; being open to ideas regardless of how or where they originated; questioning and scrutinizing ideas, methods and arguments regardless of who proposes them; playing with different ideas in order to see if links can be made; following ideas to see where they might lead ...' (1998: 30).

According to Vitae's[2] Research Development Framework the definition of a creative researcher (2010: 2) is someone who:

- develops new ways of working;
- has novel ideas and realizes their potential;
- identifies new trends; creates new opportunities;
- develops convincing and persuasive arguments to defend research;
- takes intellectual risks; challenges the status quo.

At the beginning of my PhD, I was too preoccupied with trying to be systematic, rigorous and repeatable, worried that my creative and intuitive way of working was in opposition to a research practice. However, reflecting back it was hard to ignore my 'creative' side, and it was clear I was developing new ways of working that felt more natural to me. This was evident early on when I started to coalesce my literature review process. At that time, there was very little literature on typographic education for screen-based media due to the fact it was an evolving technology. Hence, my initial literature review was very wide ranging, and I was following ideas that sometimes led to a dead end. I had to be 'creative' in my search terms and had to make intuitive leaps in connecting ideas from different disciplines. For example, I referred to an evolutionary biology theory, 'punctuated equilibrium' by Eldredge and Gould (1972), to suggest that disciplinary knowledge goes through long periods of stability alternating with periods of radical change. I also took intellectual risks, challenging the relevance of traditional typographic knowledge for a digital medium and making radical suggestions as to what should be taught to students.

Embracing uncertainty and ambiguity

A designer's ability to embrace uncertainty and face ambiguity is one of five attitudes central to the culture of professional designers, according to a study of top executives in design-intensive organizations by Michlewski (2015). This ability to accept the messiness of people and circumstances allows designers to adjust to different developments and unexpected circumstances. A research project is inherently messy, despite how it is often reported. In design research, and especially practice-based research (where variables are difficult to 'control'), this attitude has certainly helped to build researchers' resilience in overcoming difficulties encountered in their study.

They have been many occasions during the course of my PhD when plans had to change due to unexpected outcomes (for example unexpected insights from data collection) or delays (due to accessibility issues during fieldwork). For example, I had to reduce the scope of my study to focus mainly on the use of the framework in an educational setting due to delays in setting up action research projects with students. Instead of being able to test the framework with professional designers, I had to settle for a peer review process to provide a limited level of validation to the framework.

Visualization as a research tool

It is generally acknowledged in design theory and thinking literature that visual representation of complex information in different forms is a central feature of design activity (see, for example, Cross 2001; Kolko 2011; Lawson 1980). It is not surprising, then, that my own PhD and many others that I have read or examined are either very visual in their representation or use visual strategies in their processes. This strategy not only uses skills suited to the designers' cognitive styles (Durling et al., 1996), it also enables design researchers to leverage their more developed visual communication skills in support of their written argument.

Based on my own experience and subsequent research into how others have used visual techniques in their PhD studies (Yee 2010; 2012), there are three key benefits of visualizing information during a research process. First, as a reflection and exploration tool (see Yee 2003); second, as an analysis and knowledge generation tool; third, as a communication, facilitation and discussion tool.

Insights gained from my own experience and my observation of others suggest that the use of visual mapping is a highly appropriate method of contextualizing knowledge for visual thinkers like designers. Its main value seems to be sense-making, enabling design researchers to clarify and transform their thoughts by externalizing various ideas through the process of visualization. Visuals are used both as an internal process (for example facilitating a researcher's understanding) or an external process (for example to communicate or support discussions).

Adopting a bricolage approach

In my earlier work (Yee 2010, 2012), I reviewed a number of Design PhDs and found that a majority of them followed what I would consider a bricolage approach in their research design. The notion of 'bricolage' coined by Lévi-Strauss (1966) can be crudely translated as the English phrase of 'making-do'. In a general sense, a bricoleur (someone who employs the bricolage method) is described as a resourceful and creative 'fiddler or tinkerer', and one who uses available materials to create new objects out of existing ones. A bricolage approach in a research methodological context was first articulated by Denzin and Lincoln (2000). It goes beyond what some might describe as a mixed method. Kincheloe (2001) describes it as multi-perspectival research methods using tools from different disciplines that enable the researcher to compare and contrast multiple points of view. A key difference in using this multi-perspectival and interdisciplinary approach in research is that the researcher must be knowledgeable in differing epistemologies and social theoretical assumptions in order to confidently select, adapt and apply the methods in an appropriate and defendable manner.

The propensity to borrow and adapt strategies, tools and materials at hand has served designers well (see, for example, Louridas 1999). Personally I have used a mixed method approach in my PhD, which combined a number of approaches such as survey, interview and reflective practice. In many of my subsequent research projects, I have usually adapted existing research methods to suit my way of working (for example using a visual template tool or creating design probes to collect user insights). Based on my experience and observations of others, the skill to borrow from others, adapt and use what is at hand, has led to methodological innovations in the form of new research tools, creative combinations of research methods and thesis-structural innovations.

Using empathic skills to uncover hidden insights

The ability of a designer to engage in deep empathy has often been discussed in user-centred design (Coleman et al. 2003; Wright and McCarthy 2008), design thinking (Brown. 2009 Michlewski 2015) and service design discourse (Segelström 2009; Polaine et al. 2013). In current qualitative research discourses, empathy is generally regarded as a positive attribute to have as a researcher. There is an acknowledgement that empathy between the researcher and participant will result in better (more reliable and authentic) research data (Sciarra 1999). Rather than undermining my objectivity as a researcher, the ability to put myself in someone else's shoes has helped me to draw out key insights that would otherwise be hidden. Being able to build a rapport with participants is also really important since people will be more open if they have trust in the researcher. Additionally, as a researcher aiming to deliver relevant and useful outcomes to different types of audiences, my empathic skills have helped me frame outcomes in a language and format suited to the different audiences.

Conclusion

In this chapter, I have shown that skills learned as a researcher and as a designer are mutually beneficial and enhance both practices. Having a creative- and making-based training that embraces uncertainty, uses visual thinking and a 'make-do' attitude brings a very positive contribution to research practice. Equally, research training brings insightful reflection, critical thinking and deeper understanding of practice to a designer. Prior to my PhD, I believed that design and research activities were two separate practices. I have come to embrace the richness provided through both practices, and this has enabled me to develop a multi-faceted hybrid practice.

By oscillating between a researcherly designer and a designerly researcher, I am better able to reflect, evaluate and articulate what I do and why I do it. I am able to select the right research tools for different purposes and understand how important it is to be able to rationalize and explain my choices. I now draw from a wider contextual and theoretical pool of knowledge. Most importantly, I have developed a consciously critical approach to my actions and their consequences.

Notes

1   The Frascati Manual published by the Organisation for Economic Cooperation and Development (OECD) is a document that sets out the methodology for collecting statistics about research and development. The Higher Education Statistical Agency (HESA) in the UK uses this definition of research to help track and report research activities.
2   Vitae is a not-for-profit registered UK charity dedicated to active career learning and development for the researcher.

References

Anastas, J. W. (2002), 'Why Epistemology Matters', Keynote address at the Fourteenth National Symposium on Doctoral Research in Social Work College of Social Work. April 20.

Applebee, A. (1984), 'Writing and Reasoning', *Review of Educational Research* 54 (4): 577–96.

Apps, L. and Mamchur, C. (2009), 'Artful Language: Academic Writing for the Art Student', *The International Journal of Art and Design Education* 28 (3): 269–78.

Brown, T. (2009), *Change by Design*. New York: HarperCollins Publishers.

Coleman, R., Lebbon, C. and Myerson, J. (2003), 'Design and Empathy'. In Clarkson, J., Keates S., Coleman, R. and Lebbon, C. (eds), *Inclusive Design*, 478–99, London: Springer.

Cross, N. (2001), *Design Thinking: Understanding How Designers Think and Work*: Oxford and New York: Berg Publishers.

Denzin, N., and Lincoln, Y. (2000), *Handbook of Qualitative Research* (2nd edn). Thousand Oaks, CA: Sage.

Dreyfus, H. and Dreyfus, S. (1986), *Mind over Machine: The Power of Human Intuition and Expertise in the Era of the Computer*: New York: The Free Press.

Durling, D., Cross, N. and Johnson, J. (1996), 'Personality and Learning Preferences of Students in Design and Design-related Disciplines', IDATER 96 International Conference on Design and Technology, Loughborough University.

Eldredge, N. and Gould, S. J. (1972), 'Punctuated Equilibria: An Alternative to Phyletic Gradualism'. In T. J. M. Schopf (ed.), *Models of Paleobiology* 82–115. San Francisco: Freeman, Cooper.

Hart, C. (1998), *Doing a Literature Review: Releasing the Social Science Research*: London: SAGE.

Kincheloe, J. (2001), 'Describing the Bricolage: Conceptualizing a New Rigor in Qualitative Research', *Qualitative Inquiry*: 11 (3): 679–92.

Kolko, J. (2011), *Exposing the Magic of Design: A Practitioner's Guide to the Methods and Theory of Synthesis*. Oxford: Oxford University Press.

Lawson, B. (1980), *How Designers Think: The Design Process Demystified*: Oxford: Architectural Press.

Lévi-Strauss, C. (1966), *The Savage Mind*. Chicago: University of Chicago Press.

Louridas, P. (1999), 'Design as Bricolage: Anthropology Meets Design Thinking', *Design Studies* 20 (6): 517–35.

Melican, J., Barros, I. F., Holguin, R. and Joh, M. J. (1998), 'So, You're Going to Be … A Doctor of Design?' Paper presented at the *Doctoral Education in Design*, Ohio, Carnegie Mellon University, 8–11 October.

Michlewski, K. (2015), *Design Attitude*. London: Gower.

OECD (2002), Frascati 'Manual 2002: Proposed Standard Practice for Surveys on Research and Experimental Development', *The Measurement of Scientific and Technological Activities*. Paris: OECD Publishing.

Polaine, A., Reasons, B. and Løvlie, L. (2013), *Service Design: From Insight to Implementation*. New York: Rosenfield Media.

Sciarra, D. (1999), 'The Role of the Qualitative Researcher' in M. Kopala, L. A. Suzuki, (eds), *Using Qualitative Methods in Psychology*. California: Sage.

Segelström, F. (2009), 'Communicating through Visualizations: Service Designers on Visualizing User Research', *The First Nordic Conference on Service Design and Service Innovation*. Oslo.

Swann, Cal (2002), 'Action Research and the Practice of Design', *Design Issues* 18 (2): 49–61.

Vitae (2010), *Introducing the Researcher Development Framework*, Vitae Website. Available online: https://www.vitae.ac.uk/vitae-publications/rdf-related/introducing-the-vitae-researcher-development-framework-rdf-to-employers-2011.pdf (accessed 15 July 2015).

Wright, P. and McCarthy, J. (2008), 'Empathy and experience in HCI', in *Proceedings of the SIGCHI Conference on Human Factors in Computing Systems* (CHI '08). New York: ACM: 637–46.

Yee, J. (2003), 'Dynamic Literature Mapping: Typography in Screen-based Media', *European Academy of Design Conference*, 28–30 April, Barcelona, Spain.

Yee, J. (2006), 'Developing a Practice-led Framework to Promote the Practise and Understanding of Typography across Different Media', Doctoral thesis, Northumbria University, Newcastle upon Tyne.

Yee, J. (2010), 'Methodological Innovation in Practice-Based Design Doctorates', *Journal of Research Practice* 6 (2): M15.

Yee, J. (2012), 'Implications for research training and examination for design PhDs', in R. Andrews, E. Borg, S. Davis, M. Domingo and J. England (eds), *The SAGE Handbook of Digital Dissertations and Theses*, 461–92. London: Sage.

Chapter 16

MAKE HAPPEN: SENSE-MAKING THE AFFORDANCES OF A PRACTICE-BASED PHD IN DESIGN

Lisa Grocott

Making Known / The Design PhD

Let me start by saying, when I look at my PhD dissertation I engage in a conversation familiar to many PhD survivors that goes something like this: 'Really – that's it? Years of research, of your life, and this is what you've got to show for it?' I like that this invitation to reflect upon doing my project-based design PhD challenges me to not conflate my dismissal of the thesis with a discounting of the PhD journey.

Figuring is a practice of sense-making I refined through my PhD (2012). It is a practice of sketching that is equal parts speculation and reflection. In this chapter, I oscillate between writing and figuring to troubling, disclosing and making visible my journey of becoming as a researcher. This recursive act allows for an emergent, non-linear process – less hypothesis-testing, more solution-seeking. Here I trace backwards from the work I do today to my PhD. The conceit being to compare alternative scenarios as a tactic for questioning the possibility of a different kind of doctorate – or not doing one at all.

I began my PhD with the conviction that making was my research methodology and by making I meant the crafting of visual artefacts. If I could have got away with submitting a 100 per cent visual thesis project I would have. I understood Scientific research as my nemesis. I rejected the research paradigm of evidence-based, data-driven research in search of 'the truth' as the antithesis of what design research sought to be.

Jump ahead ten years and I spend more time making conversation than I do making diagrams. I am more likely to sketch on a post-it than in Illustrator. Today the idea of designing experimental studies with my learning scientist collaborators is what quickens my heart. I even want to see the data on whether our hunches are holding up. Does this mean my PhD led me to foreclose on the very expertise I sought to strengthen? I think the opposite. The PhD invited me to step outside my comfort zone and question many assumptions I held to be true. Negotiating the challenges along the way was not pretty, but here I am doing the work I wanted to be doing, so ultimately the PhD directed me to the end goal I was invested in.

You see, a core objective of my PhD was to enhance a practitioner's understanding of his or her own expertise by investigating the affordances of design research. The goal being to 'articulate the value of design to a partner in an interdisciplinary collaboration' (Grocott 2010). Motivated like many designers to forge new practice spaces beyond the world of commerce, I sought to 'communicate what design thinking brings to complex socio-cultural situations'. Through an introspective, reflective read of my own practice I set out to explain the contribution design offers to large-scale systemic problems. Paradoxically, even though my objective was to work on interdisciplinary, collaborative, large-scale social problems I did not work with other disciplines, in teams or on systemic issues. In hindsight this seems a fatal flaw. Funny even, if it were intentionally ironic. And yet.

I now do the work I dreamed of doing. Daily I am reminded how my PhD set me on this trajectory. By the end of my PhD I had tactical moves for amplifying the back-talk of my practice to make known the tacit understandings of an experiential practice. Turns out meta-understandings of design can be gained from an inward-facing, design-led investigation after all. Transcending the crafting of the material artefact my newfound understandings disclosed the affordances of tolerating ambiguity; negotiating the fixed and contingent nature of knowing; deploying speculation to mine the future-oriented realm of possibilities and potential. In my current practice I regularly co-create with non-designers, and my ability to manipulate these capacities is one way I persuade my collaborators of the value of design.

The stories I will share illustrate the ways I have re-framed the act of making. I still use the material intelligence that comes with making and putting artefacts out into the world. I find comfort in this known expertise, yet I value more the challenge to push my definition of making to include ideas of becoming, forging, bringing into existence and carrying out an action. These stories touch on how I maximize a designer's capacity to make tangible, make sense, make possible, through tracing the connections between the here and now and the PhD projects. The comparisons highlight three integrated components of my research practice: the mindset of designing, the nature of design knowing and the potential of design research.

Making tangible/design mindset

A design PhD is about making ideas tangible. What is interesting is how different research artefacts engage audiences in different ways. The material artefacts afford multiple ways for people to engage briefly, in contrast to written texts that call for deeper engagement by fewer people. A common lament is that PhDs are read by few people. In my case I can confirm only that my final PhD was read by my examiners, a copy editor and my mother. I am not presuming that document views on academia.edu translate to anyone reading it. In contrast, upwards of two

Figure 16.1 Deep Peer Review or Sustained Critique and Engagement.
LEFT Represents the number of people who reviewed chapters or the entire PhD.
RIGHT Illustrates the number of community members who engaged with the projects
and presentations of the PhD. Courtesy the author.

hundred people had some touchpoint with the research projects. The community stakeholders, a broader audience of designers and researchers all experienced, discussed, critiqued, or reflected on the work through presentations, exhibitions, publications and town hall meetings. The making of tangible artefacts, scenarios and futures offers an alternative feedback mechanism to conventional peer review – reframing a focus on impact, audience and engagement. A normal orientation for a designer but a shift in mindset for a researcher.

Researchers at the HPI Stanford Design Thinking Research Program identify tenets that they observe as central to the practice of design thinking (Menial and Leifer 2011). The four design thinking principles are that: all design activity is social in nature; design thinkers must preserve ambiguity; all design is re-design; making ideas tangible always facilitates communication. It is interesting to consider how these tenets play out in the mindset a researcher brings to practice.

There are many ways to embody these principles in practice. My design mindset has shifted over a decade from an orientation to craft clear communication artefacts to co-designing with project stakeholders open-ended artefacts. As an alternative to the scientific diagram that 'figures' to lock in knowledge, the verb 'figuring' highlights the discursive agency of ambiguity. Post my PhD I had to concede that my refined diagrams failed to live up to the democratic goal of inviting others into the conversation since they yet relied on a designer's expertise to continue the conversation.

Now, I design workshops where I bring along a box of playmobils to facilitate the *figuring* of the situation. This move from abstract poetic diagrams to situations grounded in people's stories shifts the social interactions – successfully inviting the scientists, teachers and students into a shared conversation. If you use miniature people to refer to learning spaces, the dialogue is implicitly human-centred. More surprising is the playful, generative way participants layer meaning onto, for example, the headless playmobil, the latino father, or the random soccer ball. There is simultaneously a subjective ambiguity built into the plastic personas and a situational tangibility that promotes debate as to the authenticity of the script enacted. Ten years ago I dismissed the practice of co-designing for negating the material intelligence of the designer. Today I better understand that co-designing does not negate my expertise so much as turn it inside out. *How* I make is now more important than what I make.

Make sense/design knowing

The most explicit thread between my PhD and current practice is the commitment to making sense of design practice. The final PhD project was a poster series that made visible the meta attributes I understood to be inherent to design research. The battle I chose (sadly, I saw it as a fight) was to align the attributes of a design research methodology with the criteria for rigorous research (2011). I sought to make sense of how design might honour a practice that is performative, negotiative, adaptive, grounded and discursive, while claiming that it could meet Cross's assertions that research should be methodological, purposive, inquisitive, informed and communicative (2007). I wanted to honour the unique nature of

Figure 16.2 Career transformation through Professional Practice or Practice-based Research.
LEFT Represents the vortex of professional practice. Client-commissioned projects present a breadth of learning opportunities with little time for reflection beyond the specific project. RIGHT Illustrates practice-based research. Speculative research grounded in situated projects space explores new terrain and scaffolds new practice futures. Courtesy the author.

knowing mined in research through designing. Today, my workshops use different exercises to ask similar questions. I continue to make sense of the gaps between experimental scientific research and practice-led design research – yet I no longer see science as the enemy. Today I am convinced that design needs to develop authentic metrics for making evident (or not) the impact of an intervention. My ten-year-old self would be horrified by that last sentence. This is a good thing.

The PhD offered a space for amplified sense-making of my practice and in so doing an incessant habit was formed. I now practise with a heightened state of speculative reflection into how I have worked and how I might work. As a professor in a graduate programme in Transdisciplinary Design I meet a lot of designers interested in practice spaces beyond the corporate sphere. I relate to the ambition to seek out new partners and to have social projects to dive into. Today I work with researchers invested in not what we teach but how we learn. My PhD offered an onramp into this new practice space and a way of naming how I might work with my interdisciplinary partners.

Bryan Lawson and Kees Dorst propose a pyramid with *project* at the base, followed by *process,* then *practice* next, with *profession* at the top (2009, p. 61). The authors describe a pathway to mastery as moving upwards through these phases. In positioning *profession* at the apex they are referring to a time when the field of design is the focus of inquiry. The opportunity to reflect and analyse at this meta level is a luxury few get to exercise in professional practice. In contrast, the potential transformative agency of research to change our collective practice calls on the insights gained from practice to advance design knowing.

In my PhD I developed design-led adaptations of auto-ethnography and grounded theory methodologies. Today, I deploy this expertise to bridge practices as I negotiate my experiences collaborating with learning scientists. I use this knowing to facilitate co-design workshops that explore the sweet spot between design and science methodologies. How might a *human-centred orientation* back up quantitative data? How might a *speculation-driven approach* refine the right hypothesis? How might *solution-seeking tactics* amplify the impact of the knowledge? The inward-facing orientation of my PhD seemed paradoxical when the end goal was to chart new terrains for practice. And yet. My capacity to read the affordances of design accelerated my transition from the dominant practice spaces of design towards a social design context.

Make possible / research practice

Peter Jarvis characterizes practitioner research as a process where learning experiences surface through situations in the workplace, personal theories emerge, then the practitioner investigates these theories in a subsequent situation (1998: 39). These micro-moves make way for new meta theories to emerge and for practice to evolve over time. In recent design discourse there has been a focus on the seismic shifts emerging in design practice due to technological advances, and necessitated by the scale and social context of problems we seek to tackle. The convergence

Figure 16.3 Fixing the Known or Disclosing the Potential
LEFT Illustrates the disciplinary orientation to lock in the truth: to fix how things are in the world. RIGHT Represents design knowing as being possibilities-driven: to speculate how things might be. Courtesy the author.

of imposed changes and calls for action drive an impulse to not simply evolve current practice situations but to radically explore new practice spaces, methods and partnerships. I understand the agency of a project-based PhD, to train to be a practitioner-researcher, is to forge new pathways. Through this lens my investigations into design research are a study into future potential.

The first time I read Clive Dilnot's writings on design operating in the realm of possibilities, I recall my heart quickening at the characterization that design asks not what is but what could be (Dilnot 1999). Today subfields like design fiction and design futures represent a more widely held understanding of design as a future-oriented practice, but last century I confess I was guilty of using problem-solving as a shorthand for what designers do. These philosophical understandings promised a way to see anew a practice I tacitly believed to be more poetic than strategic, more about becoming than resolving. Reflective practice was the go-to solution for many early practice-based PhDs, where I studied (Schön 1983; Von Schaik 2010). Uninterested as I was in being a philosopher or historian it seems inevitable that I would do an auto-ethnographic study of my practice. And yet. I loved when my design bias was challenged by adapting other disciplines' methods.

Of course the close readings of design practice directly informed my attempts to develop hybrid methods. One PhD exercise experimented with grounded theory as a methodology for coding 500+ pieces of material ephemera from my practice. Grounded theory aligns with the emergent nature of design knowing, so the challenge was to tweak the coding protocols for artefacts instead of an interview transcript. The systematic approach was foreign, and yet, as patterns brought to the surface insights that challenged basic assumptions I held dear, I found familiarity in the disclosive experience of illumination. I became evangelical in my enthusiasm that we could *make possible* new ways of researching by splicing social science methods with design expertise.

I foresaw the potential of interdisciplinary teams being able to forge new methods that respect the disciplinary orientations of the collaborators. Who could argue with that? And yet. The first year I worked with learning scientists was a study in learning from failure. I was challenged by what I saw as a reductive, prescriptive path of inquiry and felt diminished by the facile compliments my work received around 'looking good'. To learn from these failed collaborations I continued a practice evolved during my PhD. I triangulated the acts of designing, writing and presenting to reflect on the meta challenges of these interdisciplinary collaborations (2015). The potential to amplify the lesson to be learned from each new situation comes from this act of questioning my own assumptions and empathically respecting the disciplinary values my collaborators hold true. Nigel Cross's generalizations about the different disciplinary values presented to me an insight into how we might enlist the scientist's quest *for truth* while honouring the designer's commitment to the *appropriateness* of the solution (Cross 2007).

My latest attempt at adapting hybrid methods has focused on the affordances of prototyping as a sense-making strategy at the pre-intervention phase in learning sciences research. I have been exploring the quick-and-dirty process of rapid prototyping for surveying and synthesizing the potential of future learning interventions. The 4P framework that I evolved presents an approach to rapidly surveying the potential landscape of a future intervention through the four frames of: place, people, product and participation (2015). In contrast to the convergent nature of hypothesis-testing, setting out with a divergent move offers researchers a space for gathering a broad range of data points before investing in the experimental study.

Conclusion

The upside to questioning the relevance of my PhD is to see how far we have come. With a more confident understanding of the agency of practice-based research it is possible to be more inclusive and humble in defining design's contribution to interdisciplinary collaborations. The real heart of my reluctance lies in the title of my PhD: *Design Research and Reflective Practice: the facility of design-oriented research to translate practitioner insights into new understandings of design.* I was unconvinced by my emphasis on reflective practice before I got to the conclusion.

My experiments into grounded theory made tangible what design could learn from methods that explicitly sought to question assumptions and expose bias. I was unsure what to do with this information. Assured that the only good PhD was a finished one I persevered – even though the PhD felt diminished by what I now knew.

I now see that the story of my PhD need not conclude with 'I did it, I'm not proud, but it's done!' Knowing we get to craft our life stories, I can now rewrite the story of my PhD (Gottschal 2012). A second motivational speech by my supervisor (I needed several) gifted the reminder that the PhD was not the end game. The PhD is simply a researcher's driver's licence. Through this lens it becomes possible to honour the learning and the knowing that evolved into my current practice. Liberated from my PhD I now get to explore and adapt methods from narrative psychology, auto-ethnography, storytelling and motivated reasoning. Still, I also concede that Schön's reflective practitioner theories grounded in design case studies were pretty good training wheels.

In contextualizing my PhD in the narrative of my career trajectory I also see how my work is the same but different. This is as it should be. Shifting from a design-led approach to a transdisciplinary orientation has transformed my day-to-day work. I have transitioned from figuring crafted diagrams to performing with playmobils. Yet consistently I leverage ambiguity to propose temporarily fixed solutions as a strategy to *make tangible* tentative ideas open for discussion. Even as I move away from graphic design towards design research I continue my meta focus on *making sense* of design practice and research. Even my interest in *making possible* authentic metrics for evaluating research interventions traces back to my curiosity about hybrid methods.

The design researcher's commitment to make tangible, make sense and make possible ground a practice propelled to design preferred futures. To make happen. Each incremental move a designer makes is ultimately about using generative, creative, material, performative, critical action to better assess potential. Design is less about fixing solutions and more about crafting futures. A design-based PhD is also an investment in future potential.

In the service of examining the integrated components of design research my PhD required me to disassemble my practice. A curriculum of iteratively designing, writing and presenting scaffolded the learning experience that had me toggling between paying attention to the what of the design artefacts, the why of design research and the how of designing. This holistic agitation of troubling all that I knew is what accelerated the evolution of my practice. The extent to which I held on dearly to my visualizing expertise is an example of how hard it can be to budge long-held beliefs. My PhD led me to understand design as a discursive, social practice – yet my work embodied this knowing only after I had finished. Interrogating my figuring practice post my PhD marked the transition to facilitating workshops where my visualizing skills are reduced to no more than the sharpie pen + post-it note sketches of this chapter.

Five years past graduating I can now share the story of how the practice that was pulled apart has been pieced back together. Since completing my PhD I have learned new bodies of literature and asserted the relevance of a designer's joining a research team. Significantly, this post-PhD era represents a greater shift in the transformation of my practice than the candidature of my PhD.

This is the real story. The PhD is the start line. If we understand a practice-based PhD as an exercise in perseverance and transformation then when we have the courage and curiosity to break down our practice again our embodied PhD experiences will define our capacity to build it up again. My current research

Figure 16.4 A Practice Deconstructed and Reconstructed Again (and Again)
Both diagrams represent the three components: design projects, research practice, designer's mindset.
LEFT Represents how a practice is examined then disassembled by the process of a PhD.
RIGHT Illustrates the interlacing of these components to (re)form a more expansive definition of practice. Courtesy the author.

is into how we make visible the mindsets, essential skills and habits that build resilience and promote thriving. The capacity to learn from failure, to keep persevering when no end is in sight, to work round in-your-face obstacles and to embrace new challenges – these are some of the attributes that shape a positive mindset for learning (Dweck 2006). So I would resist reducing the contribution of a PhD through the single dimension of academic knowledge. I'm going with the story that it's an experiential training into how you might find your purpose and keep reinventing your practice over a lifetime. Knowing that with each evolution of practice the potential impact of the work is concentrated and amplified. All you have to do is make it happen.

References

Cross, Nigel (2007), *Designerly Ways of Knowing*. Basel: Birkhauser.
Dilnot, Clive (1999), 'The Science of Uncertainty: The Potential Contribution of Design to Knowledge'. In *Proceedings of the Ohio Conference*, Carnegie Mellon University.
Dweck, Carol (2006), *Mindset: The New Psychology of Success*. 1st edn Ballantine Books.
Gottschall, Jonathan (2012), *Storytelling Animal: How Stories Make Us Human*. New York: Houghton Mifflin Harcourt.
Grocott, Lisa (2010), 'Design Research & Reflective Practice: The Facility of Design-oriented Research to Translate Practitioner Insights into New Understandings of Design'. researchbank.rmit.edu.au/eserv/rmit:10830/Grocott.pdf. (accessed 30 April 2016).
Grocott, Lisa (2011), 'Designerly Ways of Researching: Design Knowing and the Practice

of Researching'. *Studies in Material Thinking* 6 (Special Issue: Research Outputs in Art and Design). www.materialthinking.org. (accessed 25 April 2016).

Grocott, Lisa (2012), 'The Discursive Practice of Figuring Diagrams'. *Tracey*, Drawing Knowledge: Special Issue (May). http://www.lboro.ac.uk/microsites/sota/tracey/journal/edu/2012/PDF/Lisa_Grocott-TRACEY-Journal-DK-2012.pdf. (accessed 25 April 2016).

Grocott, Lisa (2015), 'The Affordances of Designing for the Learning Sciences'. In *Proceedings of the 3rd International Conference for Design Education Researchers* 3: 1180–95. Chicago, USA: Aalto University, Finland. doi:10.13140/RG.2.1.2904.6880.

Jarvis, Peter (1998), *The Practitioner-Research: Developing Theory from Practice*. San Francisco: Jossey-Bass.

Lawson, Bryan, and Dorst, Kees (2009). *Design Expertise*. New York: Routledge.

Menial, C. and Leifer L. (2011), *Design Thinking Understand – Improve – Apply*. Heidelberg, Dordrecht, London and New York: Springer.

Schön, Donald (1983), *The Reflective Practitioner: How Professionals Think in Action*. New York: Basic Books.

Von Schaik, Leon. (ed.) (2010), *The Practice of Practice 2: Research in the Medium of Design*. Melbourne: Onepointsixone.

Chapter 17

FROM PARATEXTS TO PRIMARY TEXTS: SHIFTING
FROM A COMMERCIAL TO A RESEARCH-FOCUSED
DESIGN PRACTICE

Zoë Sadokierski

Introduction

This chapter reports how doctoral research shifted my design practice from one
that was primarily commercial to one that is primarily research focused.

My commercial practice is book design. Since 2003 I have designed hundreds
of books for Australian publishers and won multiple book design awards.
Although I enjoy commercial book design, I turned to academia in order to
engage with design practice in a more reflective and critical way.

One reason I returned to study was the appeal of practice-led research. In
Designerly Ways of Knowing (2006) Nigel Cross proposes that, in addition to
sciences and humanities, design is a third way of knowing the world – a 'third
culture'. Cross concedes that even a three-culture view of human knowledge is
limited, but suggests that contrasting design with the more established disciplines
of the sciences and humanities is a useful way to articulate what is unique about
design. What is it that design knows or does that is different from other ways of
knowing?

Practitioner-researchers are well positioned to answer this question. By
conducting scholarly research, practising designers can expand design discourse
by offering insights into practice-led ways of researching. Alongside borrowing
methods and language from other disciplines, design can adapt methods and
language from its own practice: how can tacit knowledge and methods (strategies
to reveal insights) from design practice inform scholarly research?

In the first section of this chapter I explain how my doctoral thesis 'Visual
Writing: a critique of graphic devices in hybrid novels' (2010) is practice-led
despite not having an original design artefact created at the centre of the study. I
report that several key insights from my doctoral research have shaped my post-
doctoral research practice: a distinction between primary texts and paratexts as
a way of understanding how book designers conventionally practise and how I

aspire to practise; a distinction between the 'good eye' of the practitioner and the 'curious or critical eye' of the practitioner researcher; identifying non-fiction as an area which allows designers to collaborate with writers beyond paratext.

The second section of this chapter discusses current research into experimental publishing models, particularly for scholarly research. Publishing is in a state of flux. Digital publishing platforms are changing the speed and efficiency of publishing, and also the way publications are composed, using word, image, audio-visual and interactive elements. The two projects discussed are the MediaObject book series, for which I am a series editor and designer, and a collaborative research project, Words from the First Walk, which includes book design in the research and dissemination phases of the project. Both projects demonstrate how my practice has shifted from working at the final, production stage of a publishing project (paratext), to an initial research and development role (primary text) that leads to a design outcome.

From commercial design practice to doctoral research

Following my bachelor degree in Visual Communication at the University of Technology Sydney, I joined publisher Allen & Unwin in 2003. Although I enjoy designing books, I soon missed the critical engagement I'd enjoyed at university so I sought tutoring work to re-engage with a critical practice. Lecturers encouraged me to consider postgraduate study, but I didn't seriously consider this until a problem emerged through my practice that seemed worth investigating.

One of the publishers at Allen & Unwin approached me with a pile of uncon-ventional novels; these books had images embedded within the written text, such as line drawings, photographs and strange typesetting. These books are unusual because novels are conventionally a purely written literary form. The puzzled publisher came to me because, within the publishing house, a designer – who works closely with images – seemed most capable of explaining these novels with pictures. Instinctively I knew this was an interesting phenomenon, but couldn't immediately explain what was going on.

At the time, I hoped this was a sub-genre of literary fiction in which the designer had a more active role in the creation of a book's primary content as well as its packaging (cover and typesetting). Gerard Genette's paratextual theory helps to clarify what I mean by this. Genette (1997) distinguishes between the 'primary text', which is the author's manuscript – the work of literature in unmediated form – and 'paratexts', the collection of supplementary elements that frame and present the primary text as an object that can be held and read, everything from the paper stock to the title of the book. In my experience, the commercial book designer is responsible for the material paratext (cover design and typesetting, through negotiation with editorial and marketing departments), rather than the primary text (the content of the book, through collaboration with the author).[1] I was interested in ways designers and writers could work together earlier in the publishing process, developing a collaborative creative relationship, as opposed to the designer providing a service to the publisher.

I hoped that by identifying and researching an emerging area within commercial publishing I would uncover new opportunities for my future practice. Although my doctoral research did not reveal opportunities to collaborate in creating a primary text, my post-doctoral practice has. To explain how this happened, I will begin with a brief overview of my doctoral research.

Visual Writing: A critique of graphic devices in hybrid novels

My research examined a publishing phenomenon that I labelled 'hybrid novels': novels in which graphic devices such as photographs, drawings and experimental typography are integrated into the written text. I hoped this phenomenon would reveal designers collaborating with writers to produce the primary text. However I quickly realized hybrid novels are not the product of such collaboration, but of writers working in a designerly way. Access to digital images (through digital cameras, scanners and online image libraries) coupled with desktop publishing programs such as Adobe InDesign mean authors are able to embed graphic devices into their manuscripts quickly and without specialized training. Rather than collaborating with designers, in some instances writers are replacing them. This uncomfortable insight shifted the focus of my research to critiquing the phenomenon through a kind of content analysis, rather than through practitioner-research.

Hybrid novels are identified as an insufficiently explained phenomenon by literary critics and academics, particularly in the field of Visual Studies (see Sadokierski 2010: 55–8). Critics ask: What are these images? What are they doing in novels? How does one 'read' them? These questions point to the need for new approaches to the analysis and critique of hybrid texts, approaches that account for the interplay between words and images. My thesis proposes that visual communication designers – those versed in both the verbal and the visual – offer useful analytical tools and critique for the study of hybrid texts. The research asks: How could a designer's particular knowledge of word-image interplay explain the function of graphic devices in hybrid novels?

Despite not having an original design artefact created at the centre of the study, my doctoral thesis was practice-led in three ways. First, an under-explained literary phenomenon identified through my design practice led to the research. Second, I adapted analytic and critical tools from my design practice as research methods; I developed practice-led methods to demonstrate how designers can contribute to scholarship. I have since expanded and written about developing practice-based research tools in more detail (see Sadokierski 2013; Sadokierski and Sweetapple 2015). Third, the thesis is itself a hybrid text; the argument is formed through a combination of writing and graphic devices.

On reflection, I realize there is a design artefact at the centre of my doctoral research – the thesis itself. In presenting an argument about hybrid texts as a hybrid text, I use the 'language' of my discipline to express scholarly research

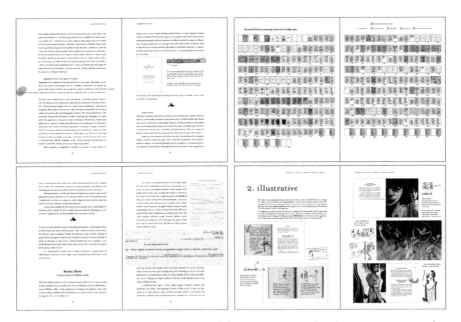

Figure 17.1 Spreads from 'Visual Writing' showing ways graphic devices are integrated into the written text. Courtesy the author.

about design through design. Significantly, designing the thesis as a hybrid text I reflected that non-fiction provides more opportunities for collaboration between writers and designers. Since completing my thesis, I have worked with non-fiction texts, particularly finding ways to enhance or elaborate scholarly publications using graphic devices.

The second significant insight developed through the research is that my particular knowledge as a design practitioner – what I labelled my 'curious eye' – is an asset when it comes to scholarly research. Commercial practice and academia are not mutually exclusive: one can practise across both arenas.

The Curious Eye of the practitioner-researcher

Coming to scholarly research from practice, I spent time reading around and thinking through the muddy line between design practice and research. My thesis proposes a distinction between the 'good eye' of the practitioner and the 'curious eye' of the practitioner-researcher (Sadokierski 2010: 79–84, developed from Rose 1998 and Rogoff 1998). Both 'eyes' are critical, but to different ends. I claim that the practitioner's good eye is informed by tacit knowledge developed across three domains: scholarship (pedagogical and self-initiated study), reflections on personal process, and professional experience. The good eye focuses on knowing how; it critically informs decisions in practice.

The curious, or critical, eye of the practitioner-researcher foregrounds and explicitly articulates the tacit knowledge of the good eye, in order to extend a discipline. The curious eye asks questions, researches and theorizes. Through doctoral research, I turn my practitioner's good eye into a researcher's curious eye. My understanding of practice deeply informs my approach to scholarship, both in the questions I ask and the analytical approaches I take.

Post-doctoral practitioner-research: thinking through making

Confident that I could use practice as a mode of inquiry, and understanding that non-fiction offers more opportunities for designers to collaborate with writers to create hybrid texts, in the five years since completing my doctoral research I have developed collaborative relationships with writers that allow me to work across both practice and research.

Below, I report two research projects that blur the line between design practice and scholarship: the book series MediaObject, and the exhibition Words from the First Walk.

Open Access publishing for art and design: MediaObject

MediaObject is a peer reviewed Open Access book series published through the University of Technology Sydney ePress, which I co-edited with Dr Chris Caines. These publications include audio-visual material to critique practitioner-research in which showing or hearing a creative work is imperative to understanding it.

Open Access (OA) is a form of academic publishing made possible by the internet. Peer reviewed journal articles and books are available online free of charge, with unrestricted access and free of most copyright and licensing restrictions, which allows research to be quickly and broadly disseminated.[2]

For practitioner-researchers in art and design, OA publishing has two key benefits. First, publications are available to readers in industry who rarely have access to expensive scholarly journals. This allows researchers to bridge the gap between academia and professional practice without having to publish twice. Second, web-based and digital publishing (on tablets and other handheld devices) allows researchers to include visual and audio content that cannot be published in print. Due to production costs and restricted space in printed journals and books, inclusion of images is limited in quantity and often quality. Images are usually reproduced small, printed in black ink only. This means research is reported primarily through the written word, which can be an insufficient way to report practitioner-research.

Investigating the visual communication opportunities afforded by digital and OA publishing is fertile ground for design research.

Experiments in digital publishing

The first two books in the MediaObject series – *Live A/V in Australia* by Grayson Cooke and *Voice/Presence/Absence* edited by Malcolm Angelucci and Chris Caines – both critique the practices of audio-visual artists and scholars in Australia. The publications are enhanced ebooks; as well as substantial written texts (10,000 and 80,000 words respectively) they include video interviews, documentation of events, audio tracks and slideshows of images. Richly describing audio-visual practice requires audio-visual material; this is not possible in a print publication.

For these first two MediaObject books my role was designing the publishing model as well as the layout; the challenge was figuring out how best to present the various types of content for readers to navigate in a logical and meaningful way. Being involved from the start allowed me to test various soft- and hardware options and distribution platforms, and to prototype different formats and design approaches. Through this slow, iterative research practice I came to deeply understand the possibilities and limitations embedded within different digital publishing models. This kind of scoping research is difficult to fund in commercial practice; publishers are struggling financially, few have resources to fund experimental technological research and development. Reporting these first MediaObject books in both scholarly and publishing industry forums, it is clear that this is a timely project, of value to both academia and industry.[3]

Designing a format that suits the content

For the third MediaObject publication, I extended my previous research by creating a unique publishing model designed around a specific practice: the work of contemporary lace-maker Cecilia Heffer. In this instance, I also shift from designing the paratext (design and format) to collaborating on parts of the primary text (writing and imagery).

I approached Heffer to write *Lace Narratives,* a monograph of her innovative textile practice between 2005 and 2015. Acting as both editor and designer, I formulated a unique model that best communicated Heffer's particular practice. To understand Heffer's innovative lace-making practice we need to observe her creative process, to hear and read her reflections on process and outcomes, and to touch the material artefact itself. In order to achieve this, the publication comes in two parts: a process video and a printed book with fabric samples.

With videographer Chris Caines, I recorded Heffer in her studio creating a lace-length and talking through her creative process. This footage was later cut together with photographs, additional audio and motion graphics, with the help of video editor Esther Chung, to form a cohesive narrative. The final video is freely available to view online from October 2015.

The printed book includes a ten-thousand-word critical reflection on practice written by Heffer, extended with images of her creative process and final laceworks. Produced in a limited edition of ten, each book includes six fabric swatches of different laceworks. These editions are to be held in libraries, accessible to the

Figure 17.2 *Lace Narratives* limited edition book, with fabric swatches. Courtesy the author.

public. Watching the process video, reading Heffer's reflections on her research and design process, and handling the lace swatches gives a holistic sense of her practice and output that cannot be achieved through a single publication.

A PDF of the book is freely available to download, and a print-on-demand version is available to purchase at cost price for interested readers who cannot access one of the limited-edition books in a library collection.

My input into the primary text is evident through the visual narrative in the video, which I directed, and through visual juxtapositions in the layout that demonstrate how Heffer's research influences her final work. Developing this visual content involved multiple sessions in Heffer's studio, talking and searching her archives to find ways to communicate visually her tacit process. Heffer reflected that this collaborative process led her to see her own work from a new perspective.

My background in commercial book design, doctoral research into hybrid texts and post-doctoral research into alternative publishing models synthesize in this project, resulting in a unique publication, the aim of which is to communicate the innovation embedded within Heffer's practice. It is an example of my own practice shifting from designing paratexts to primary texts, through active collaboration.

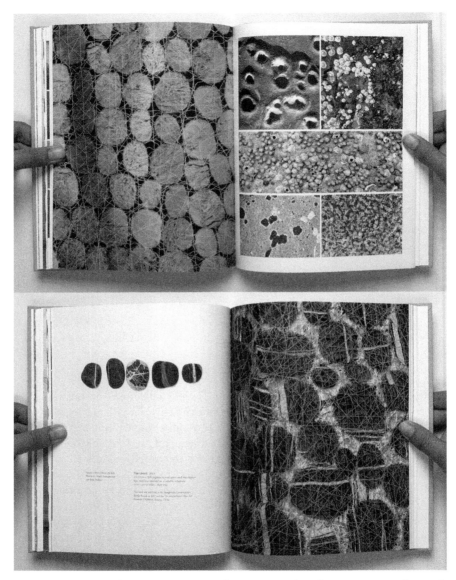

Figure 17.3 Spreads from *Lace Narratives* showing examples of juxtapositions I designed to demonstrate links between Heffer's visual research and final design artefacts. Courtesy the author.

Book making as research and articulation: Words from the First Walk

My research practice involves generating practice-led projects of my own, and in collaboration with other practitioners/scholars. The output of these projects is primarily shared through exhibitions, accompanied by talks and workshops whose purpose is to disseminate the research outcomes. In addition, I produce two types of publication: exhibition catalogues and experimental books created as part of my research process. Below, I explain the scholarly aims driving these two types of books through a single project, Words from the First Walk.

Words from the First Walk is a research collaboration between myself, photographer Jacqueline Lorber-Kasunic and writer Tom Lee, which culminated in an exhibition of works on paper in 2013. Lecturing together, we discovered a shared interest in communicating narratives about the Australian landscape through writing and design practices. The exhibition presents our different perspectives of a three-day walk around 'Coorah', a property in central west New South Wales managed by Lee's family.

For the exhibition, Lorber-Kasunic created a photographic essay documenting the impact of farming technology on the landscape. My work includes a suite of collages, etchings and artist's books that respond to a passage from Murray Bail's novel *Eucalyptus*, set on a farm similar to Lee's property. I also created a ninety-page exhibition catalogue, including two of Lee's essays about Coorah. The catalogue synthesizes the three projects as one body of collaborative practice.

Exhibition catalogues

To extend exhibitions, I produce catalogues which include documentation of my design process and prototypes, as well as writing about the context, aims and findings behind the designed artefacts. I do this to situate the practice clearly as scholarly research.

By clearly articulating research questions and aims underpinning the practice, reflecting on the creative process and outcomes, and situating a body of work in a scholarly context I can demonstrate how practice constitutes research. In producing a document that exists beyond the duration and location of a physical exhibition, I allow the research to find broad audiences, and my background as a book designer is an asset when it comes to controlling the dissemination of my research beyond traditional scholarly publications.

Experimental books as a way to think through making

Exhibition catalogues are produced at the end of a creative process to document and contextualize the work. I also create experimental books during my research process, as a way to think through or test ideas. One example from the Words from the First Walk project is a small book titled 'Paragraph/Paddocks' (Sadokierski 2013b). It is a collection of formal graphic experiments (collages, drawings, photographs) that I created to analyse an excerpt from Bail's *Eucalyptus*.

Figure 17.4 Words from the First Walk catalogue. Top row: Cover and spread from Lee's essays with Sadokierski's design. Below: spreads from Sadokierski's documentation on site and process leading to final works on paper. Courtesy the author.

Figure 17.5 Spreads from Paragraph/Paddocks book. Read more about the aims and findings of the individual experiments at: bookworkpress.com/Paragraph-Paddocks. Courtesy the author.

Occasionally, a passage of text resonates with me after I have shelved a book; I sense something significant is contained within the pages, waiting to be known. The passage of text transcends the context of the book and demands further, isolated attention. The text in question, here, is a passage in which Bail juxtaposes paragraphs and paddocks: city and country, written accounts of the land and our physical experience of the land. This passage draws together ideas about book publishing and the environment, two areas of ongoing interest to me.

The experiments respond to the question: How could I analyse/interpret a written text through visualization, borrowing methods from my professional design practice?

This is an example of an interpretative process described by Galey and Ruecker as one in which:

> the goals of the designer [are] deliberately to carry out an interpretive act in the course of producing an artifact. As Lev Manovich has publicly phrased it, 'a prototype is a theory'. One of the functions of the artefact then becomes to communicate that interpretation, and to make it productively contestable. (Galey and Ruecker 2010: 406)

Presented as a book, the experiments are organized in a sequence that directs the reader to follow my analytical thinking. My understanding of visual narrative, developed through years of design practice, allows me to present analytic experiments in a way that communicates my findings. As artefacts these graphic experiments act as both the analytical tool and the visual explanation of thinking-through-making (for more on this, see Sadokierski and Sweetapple 2013).

Conclusion

Since completing my doctorate, I have shifted to a primarily research-focused design practice. Undertaking doctoral research equipped me with research and writing skills that allow me to bridge the gap between commercial practice and academia, engaging with research projects in which design practice is used both as a mode of investigation and a way to disseminate research outcomes.

The MediaObject book series allows me to test ways to practise within publishing, beyond the conventional practice of a commercial book designer. Editing and designing Heffer's monograph, I was integrated within the project from the beginning, and this shifted how and what I designed, and allowed me to shape the primary text as well as the material paratext.

Reflecting on five years of practice-based research projects I realize that the catalogues and experimental books I create are of more scholarly value than the exhibitions and public talks they accompany, because these publications are a means to disseminate broadly research process and findings. Yet they are easily lost among the 'main' work in my exhibitions: in a gallery space visitors rarely take the time to read longer texts, or slowly engage with the pages of a book in sequence (as the designer intends them to). In response to this reflection, I began to produce catalogues by way of print-on-demand (POD) services, making them accessible beyond the duration of the exhibition and to audiences outside Sydney.[4]

In 2015 I launched Bookwork Press – bookworkpress.com – to present my research catalogues and books in one place on line. This is not a business venture (the books are sold at cost price) but another iteration of my ongoing experiments with OA publishing as a means to disseminate practitioner-research. These self-published books do not 'count' as scholarly publications. The aim of the site is to make my research openly accessible to both design practitioners and scholars working in similar territory, bridging the brackish water between professional practice and academia.

Notes

1 See Sadokierski (2010: 16–25) for a detailed critique of how paratextual theory can explain the role and value of book design.
2 For a detailed explanation of Open Access, see Director of Harvard Open Access Project Peter Suber's overview (Suber 2015).
3 Chris Caines and I presented the MediaObject books at the Fibreculture Digital Publishing and Open Access Publishing seminar hosted by the School of Arts and Social Sciences at University of New South Wales in December 2013, and I described the design process at the Small Press Network Independent Publishers Conference in November 2014.
4 See Sadokierski 2014 for detailed explanation on how POD works, and the catalogue Books On Demand for analysis of pros and cons of different POD platforms.

References

Angelucci, M. and Caines, C. (2014), Voice/Presence/Absence, MediaObject and UTS ePress, Sydney.

Bail, M. (1998), *Eucalyptus*, Text Publishing, Melbourne.

Cooke, G. (2013), Live A/V in Australia, MediaObject and UTS ePress, Sydney.

Cross, N. (2006), *Designerly Ways of Knowing*. Springer-Verlag, London.

Drawn Threads: A process video (2015), [short film] Dir. Z. Sadokierski, Sydney: MediaObject. October 20.

Galey, A. and Ruecker, S. (2010), 'How a prototype argues', *Literary and Linguistic Computing*, 25 (4): 405–24.

MediaObject. (2013), [website] Online: http://www.mediaobject.net/ (accessed 14 August 2015).

Rogoff, I. (1998), 'Studying Visual Culture', in Mirzoe, N. (ed.), *The Visual Culture Reader*, 14–26, London: Routledge.

Rose, G. (2007), *Visual Methodologies: An introduction to the interpretation of visual materials*, 2nd edn. London: SAGE Publications.

Sadokierski, Z. (2010), Visual Writing: A critique of graphic devices in hybrid novels. Doctoral thesis.

Sadokierski, Z. A. (2013), 'Photo-graphic Devices in Jonathan Safran Foer's Extremely Loud and Incredibly Close' in Pedri, N. and Petit, L. (eds), *Picturing the Language of Images*, 177–99. Newcastle upon Tyne: Cambridge Scholars Publishing.

Sadokierski, Z. (2013b), 'Paragraphs/Paddocks', artist book. Sydney: Page Screen Publications.

Sadokierski, Z., Lorber-Kasunic, K. and Lee, T. (2013), 'Words from the First Walk', exhibition catalogue, Sydney: Page Screen Publications.

Sadokierski, Z. (2014), 'Shelf Promotion: How everyone can be a publisher with print-on-demand books', *The Conversation*, October 13. Online: https://theconversation.

com/shelf-promotion-how-everyone-can-be-a-publisher-with-print-on-demand-books-30923 (accessed 14 August 2015).

Sadokierski, Z. A. and Sweetapple, K. (2015), 'Drawing Out: How Designers Analyse Written Texts in Visual Ways' in P. Rodgers and J. Yee (eds), *Routledge Companion to Design Research*, 248–61. London: Routledge.

Suber, P. (2015), 'Open Access Overview', SPARC Open Access Newsletter, Earlham College, 15 December 2015. Online: http://legacy.earlham.edu/~peters/fos/overview.htm (accessed 21 December 2015).

Chapter 18

FROM PRACTICE TO PRACTICE-LED RESEARCH: CHALLENGES AND REWARDS

Neal Haslem

I began my doctoral research in March 2008. It is perhaps more accurate to say that this was when I officially began my doctorate, since the process of embarking upon a doctoral study seldom aligns with a university year schedule. It would be somewhat more accurate to say that my doctorate began with the writing of my research proposal the previous year. If I look a little deeper, however, many of the concepts articulated in that proposal arose during the final work of my master's research, which was completed in 2007. My master's research of course also began with a written proposal, and this was motivated by my twelve years in industry practice. This industry practice commenced following my undergraduate degree – a degree that was a product of my motivations, concerns and understanding of the world, my place in it, and how I felt I might be able to contribute to it. The point being that it is somewhat difficult to extricate the discrete starting points and origins for the endeavour of postgraduate research. Doctoral research often originates in one's practice as a whole; it is this holistic depth of motivation and interconnectedness that leads to many of the challenges, as well as the rewards.

The key motivation behind my entry to postgraduate research was to re-engage my curiosity about the practice of communication design. Re-entering higher education and completing a master's research degree marked the first stage in this, through which I was later able to embark on my doctoral research. Through my master's research I gained an understanding of practice-led research as a mode of research. I came to understand what it was to undertake research into the area of communication design, and I became familiar with current discourse and the world of academic design research. Although challenging and unfamiliar in many ways, my master's experience also felt like a 'homecoming'. Through it I re-initiated an aspect of my practice that had lacked stimulation and community during my years in industry. Specifically, this was a lack of a *sense of inquiry* – the desire to better understand the *why* and the *how* behind the work of communication design.

I first started articulating this curiosity around the *why* and *how* of communication design during my final Honours year at the University of Tasmania in

1991. I very quickly found my sense of inquiry discouraged, as I started working as a designer. In the commercial environment there appeared to be neither the time nor the interest to ask *why*, and *how* was limited to the concrete commercial imperative of how to produce an effective response to the requirements of a client brief within the constraints of timeframe and budget. During the next ten years of my industry-based practice, *why* and *how* remained in the background. While I might occasionally take time to reflect upon these issues personally or with friends and family they were not validated within the commercial communities of my work. While the pragmatic constraints of commercial endeavour might provide one explanation, I was also aware that these kinds of questions appeared somewhat impolitic; it did not appear seemly to ask *why* or *how*, nor was it seen as part of my role as a designer. This being so, my lived experience of design included research *for* design but not *about* or *through* design.

In his book *Design Research* (2003), Peter Downton, the Australian design researcher and academic, follows Professor Christopher Frayling (1993), in defining three categories for design research. The first, research *for* design (Downton 2003: 17) he defines as research conducted during a design project to support the designing process. This research directly helps designers to produce design outcomes. The second, research *about* (or *into*) design is research which aims to understand the practice of design more clearly: 'research into what design should be' (design methods), 'research into what designers (actually) do', 'teaching and learning design' and 'history of design and designed things' (p. 35). The third, research *through* design is arguably the most important category for practice-based design researchers. In defining research *through* design, Downton, following Frayling, makes an argument for design as knowledge; the knowing of the designer, embedded within design outcomes, makes material transferable knowledge *through* design as research. As Frayling states, 'the practice-based doctorate advances knowledge partly by means of practice' (1997: 18).

When I entered the world of higher degrees research – and practice-led research at RMIT University – I entered a community within which research *about* design and *through* design was valued. The research community I joined provided validation of my sense that the practice of design itself deserved in-depth investigation. It provided support that my questions about the *how* and *why* were important questions for the future of practice – not just for my own continuing practice but also for the practice of communication design as a whole.

Occasionally, during this industry-dominated time, I might attend a lecture, see an exhibition or read something that brought considerations of the *how* and *why* back to consciousness. Another reminder, and in retrospect clearly a step on the way to postgraduate research, was provided through my developing practice as a teacher of design. In 1998, when I started teaching part-time at undergraduate level, the need to ask questions returned. A discussion with novice designers about *how* one might design inevitably raises for consideration the underlying questions of *why* one might design and *how* design operates.

As my desire to re-engage my inquiry into practice became more active, I discussed this with my professional contacts. On the suggestion of a client, who was completing his own candidature at RMIT, I attended a candidature presentation at RMIT's Architecture and Design Graduate Research Conference (GRC). These graduate conferences are largely in-house events staged twice-yearly for current research candidates, although open to the public. The presentation I saw was given by a candidate working on an investigation of the potential use of nanotechnology within architecture. In listening to this candidate present, and from the feedback he received from his panel, I realized that here was a discourse that gave serious attention to the *why* and *how*. Excited by my glimpse into the world of practice-led research I made further inquiries and began to imagine that I might be allowed to take part in, and perhaps even contribute to, this discourse.

My tentative search for an entry point to the world of postgraduate studies then moved on to a series of challenging encounters with potential supervisors. To one of these potential supervisors I showed an early page of writing. Although in retrospect I can see this writing was a proposal of sorts, it was not conceived in that way when I wrote it; rather I felt that I had written down 'an idea'. The person I showed was a client – and friend – whom I was working with on an arts-based project. Her reading of my text, and the insightful and considered response she gave me, took me aback. I was surprised by the seriousness with which she approached my writing and by the clarity and depth of her critical appraisal; she gave it her full attention and read it as though it might be important. She gave it serious consideration, took it apart, looked through it, beneath it, and then questioned me on its underlying motivations. She did all this in the space of ten minutes or so. I felt a little awestruck following this encounter and somewhat deflated by her incisive questions and critique.

This experience of a postgraduate supervisor's depth of criticality was, while momentarily damaging to my ego, highly stimulating. As Richard Ingleby states in his discussion on forming the research question, 'the development of a critical approach marks the crux of the transition to graduate research study' (2007: 45). Perhaps our brief discussion about my one-page 'idea' marked an early stage in the commencement of my own 'transition'. The event described occurred in 2002, almost two years before I applied for postgraduate candidature. There is an indication here of the length of time – and the transition – that needed to be negotiated by a mature practitioner (myself) returning to higher education and a research degree.

Some months after this event, another potential supervisor told me, somewhat flippantly, that I should be aware that there was only a 30 per cent completion rate with new candidates. It took me a little while to realize what she meant – that it was likely that I would be one of those 70 per cent who start and do not complete. She was also blunt in communicating that her institution currently had no suitable supervisors for me and that she herself already had too many candidates. This fairly frosty response did not dissuade me from continuing my search for research.

Finally I met the person who was to be my first supervisor. She worked for RMIT University – coincidentally so, it seemed at the time. I visited her off-campus at her design studio and was introduced to other designers who worked with her. All the members of the studio seemed to be undertaking research degrees at RMIT

University. I later came to understand that she had brought together a group of promising undergraduate students to form a research-based commercial studio. The work they produced in the studio provided the projects through which they pursued their research objectives (Grocott and Marshall 2003). At the time of this first meeting I wasn't aware of this quite deliberate positioning; all I perceived was that I had entered another world, and it didn't look anything like a university or the academy – nor the design studios I was accustomed to.

The studio, and the members of that studio, seemed incredibly edgy and stylish. Not stylish in the mannerist, swanky client-impressing interiors I had encountered previously in industry, but avant-garde and convention-breaking, driven by a sense of inquiry. I was intimidated by this first interview. I continue to think that the probable reason I was granted an interview – or any consideration at all – was a lucky mistake. In my initial email enquiry I included a scan of a small cross-stitch (Figure 18.1) I was halfway through completing. I had started

Figure 18.1 The scan of the cross-stitch experiment that I sent with my early research proposal (image and work: Neal Haslem). Courtesy the author.

the cross-stitch based on a hunch, and I was using it to investigate and represent a 'real' digital visual language. I was struck by its handmade yet pixelated materiality. I can see now that this minor material investigation – un-knowing yet intuitive – was an example of practice-led design research. Making and externalizing the cross-stitch experiment allowed me to start to investigate a hunch that I could not otherwise articulate.

My first supervisor would have been able to see I was already working in a practice-led research mode. During that initial meeting – as we discussed my research proposal – I started to understand that she was, like me, motivated by a desire to better understand the *how* and the *why* of communication design. This was enough for me to decide that I wanted to be part of this practice-led design research culture and the community she represented. I can only surmise that from her point of view I must have exhibited some traces of postgraduate potential. As Mark Tennant and Susan Roberts remark in their overview of the conditions regarding the agreement between supervisor and candidate, 'A common feature [...] is that much of the process is informal, and potential supervisors have the opportunity to screen candidates prior to agreeing to supervise' (2007: 20).

I have outlined some of the steps I took on my way into design research and discussed that those steps took time and were developed over years, through conversations and experiences. It is also worth noting that these were not easy steps for me to take. It was very challenging to re-enter the academic world, with self-doubt arising often: did I have the aptitude and ability to become a design researcher and take part in this discourse – or not? It gradually became clear that I did, and that I enjoyed it greatly.

This challenge of 'finding my feet' in the new world of academic research is not solely my own experience. As Natalie Moltschaniwskyj and George Moltschaniwskyj discuss in their essay 'Setting the scene: Initiating the supervision relationship', 'the starting graduate has to undergo a social, academic and intellectual transition from their former life [...] into a new life as a graduate candidate' (2007: 28). However, it is not to overstate my experience to say that returning to higher education and becoming involved in design research made me feel that I had found a place where I belonged. Here was an environment in which other people, design practitioners like me, were also – like me – interested in questioning the *how* and the *why* of communication design. Here was an environment in which the open and frank search for understanding and knowledge – a search that quite frequently wished to articulate the seemingly ineffable in practice – was taken seriously and supported institutionally. In many ways I felt as though I had found a community that could become home.

As a research candidate I discovered that all my areas of practice: commercial design work, design education and design research acted to support one another. Events and experiences in one sphere of activity could be reflected upon, and investigated further, in the others. I came to see that my practice as a communication designer was composed of all three of these roles, practitioner, educator and researcher, and that they supported and amplified one another. During this time I became aware of the existence of a name for a life of considered agency in the world: *praxis*. I understand now that the experiences I went through during those first years of research were those of the discovery of personal *praxis*.

Location and community are also important for providing the capacity to engage in research. During 2007, while lecturing within a small visual communications programme at my undergraduate university, I attempted to initiate a communication design research discourse. It proved difficult to establish significant interest. Within the university, graphic design was viewed simply as an instrumentalist application of visual communication, and therefore not a practice necessitating postgraduate research. Within local industry, the existing discourse was one of 'show and tell'. While there was potential to develop a research discourse, it was nascent. Perhaps eventually I would have been successful in initiating this discourse but it would not have happened easily, and was unlikely to be supported, at least initially, by the local academic institution. At the time I had only recently finished my own master's; I did not feel particularly well-equipped to single-handedly initiate a research culture.

This experience helped me to realize the advantage of having a supportive community of research practice within which to be situated. My practice was no longer one of professional design alone. My practice had become a three-part practice of design, education and research. It was with these considerations in mind that I applied for a doctorate and scholarship at RMIT University. Again, I felt the trepidation, the sense of the audacious overreach I might be making to imagine that I would be accepted as a PhD candidate or that I might have the capacity to complete such a venture successfully.

I was successful in my application for doctoral research and also received a scholarship. A little over three years later I submitted my exegesis, a 40,000 word document. Three months after that, in June 2011, I exhibited my project work and gave a final presentation in front of my three examiners, my supervisors, family members, and some twenty other friends and colleagues. My doctorate was passed, with minor amendments. I submitted the amended doctorate in September 2011.

I was lucky to find myself at RMIT University, an institution that has a developing tradition in practice-led research. There is a temptation for designers, when they come to undertake research, to turn towards the more established traditional research modes. However, practice-led research relies on one's expertise as a practitioner to drive the doctoral investigation. As Brent Allpress and Robyn Barnacle point out 'project-based research is [...] centred on and through disciplinary ways of knowing and, as such, is crucial to the understanding and advancement of disciplinary knowledge' (2009: 159).

Doubt is always going to be the companion of the researcher, and perhaps it is part of the supervisor's job to occasionally allay those fears. Sometimes the fears might be well-grounded, and a highly developed sense of self-criticism becomes the researcher's friend. In the pursuit of new understandings and new knowledge one is inevitably engaged in a process of opening up new ground – and that ground will necessarily be uncertain. This can lead to doubt and uncertainty in the candidate and affect their communication of their research to others: 'At a review meeting, it is not unusual for a candidate to feel a range of emotions – including feeling exposed and vulnerable – and to have some anxiety and uncertainty about the process and likely outcomes' (Denholm 2007: 64).

One's supervisor will not necessarily know where a candidate is going; they might have managed to glean a sense of it, but it is the candidate who drives the research and communicates the findings. A large part of the work of the candidate is in the clear articulation of knowledge that does not yet exist as articulated 'knowledge'. While a supervisor can provide support, it is the candidate who must rely on their own sense of the new understandings they are trying to articulate. As Elain Martin and Ron Adams express it, 'typically as candidates develop insight and knowledge of their research area, a struggle arises concerning how to express that knowledge' (2007: 215).

An important part of the work of the postgraduate supervisor is to ensure that their candidate does their work thoroughly – regardless of their research question. As Carey Denholm and Terry Evans point out in the introduction to their book *Supervising Doctorates Downunder* 'nowadays the doctoral graduate is expected to be a flexible and adaptable researcher as well as an effective communicator [...] [supervisors] are seen as primarily responsible for ensuring that many of these graduate attributes accrue during candidature' (Denholm and Evans 2007: 3).

Yet for a candidate the successful investigation of their research question is the most important work at hand. Thus supervisors' roles are complex and can become somewhat ambiguous: 'as a researcher, the candidate should exhibit autonomy, independence of thought and originality; as learners, they are dependent on guidance and feedback and need to be prepared to take direction. Playing out this dual role is complex and demanding' (Tennant and Roberts 2007: 20).

Added to this are a number of other roles the supervisor often takes: mentoring, coaching, sponsoring and ensuring the progress of the candidature (Grant and Pearson 2007). From my own perspective as a candidate, the supervisory relationship was all these things and more. In many ways I feel wholeheartedly indebted to my supervisors for the critical roles they played in enabling my doctoral research to be completed successfully. As Tennant and Roberts (2007, p. 21) point out, it is possible to itemize the essential consistent factors of successful candidature:

- the critical importance of the sense of belonging to a group or a research culture;
- frequency of meetings and structure of activities between meetings;
- the centrality of a good interpersonal working relationship.

There is a tension at work on candidates; while they are embedded deeply in understanding and communicating their research enquiry they are simultaneously required to successfully acquire key – but somewhat prosaic – fundamental research skills. One way RMIT University manages this tension is through the twice-yearly Graduate Research Conference. This is a largely in-house conference, with a select scattering of guest panel members brought in to provide a healthy injection of outside dialogues and points-of-view. These regular conferences synchronize with candidate's exams, so that candidates-in-progress get an experience of the examination while examiners have the opportunity to sit on research-in-progress panels. As Ingleby comments, 'the requirement to present directs the candidate to the need to communicate to an audience; and the requirement to respond reveals the difficulty of trying to understand as a "first time" audience' (2007: 49).

With the help of regular events like the RMIT University Graduate Research Conference a vibrant community of fellow postgraduate researchers can be cultivated. This can, in effect, remove some of the onus of support from the supervisor and develop the strength of the candidates' discipline and rigour. In addition to this, supervisors can include other structured group activities, from design camps to shared reading: 'candidates gain a greater connectedness and a sense of attachment within a research community when provided with opportunities to work through ideas that are core to the discipline, challenge each other's perspectives, exchange narratives of their experience and justify decisions [...] Group supervision as part of the supervisory process serves as a complement to individual candidate-supervisory team meetings' (Conrad 2007: 37).

For me, the opportunity to work with a community of established practitioners, under the guidance of higher degree research supervisors, and to think, talk, research and write about matters of importance in the field I have chosen to make my life's work, has been an affirming one. There are not many opportunities for professional development in communication design; once the initial training or undergraduate degree is complete one is often left to find some form of professional development through other colleagues and clients, or bigger and better projects and budgets.

Entry into the world of higher degree design research gave me the opportunity to re-engage with my inquiry into practice and to contribute to the practice and the field. My research has allowed me to establish what I hope is a lifelong multi-faceted practice as a designer, educator and researcher. I know that there are many other practitioners in the world, in industry, with the same sort of need for inquiry that I have. Higher degree research, and in particular practice-led research, has the capacity to offer this opportunity for inquiry – and provide a supportive yet critical community for those who might still be wondering *how* and *why*.

References

Allpress, B. and Barnacle, R. (2009), 'Projecting the PhD: Architectural design research by and through projects', in D. Boud and A. Lee (eds), *Changing Practices of Doctoral Education*, 157–70. Abingdon: Routledge.

Conrad, L. (2007), 'Developing the intellectual and emotional climate for candidates', in C. Denholm and T. Evans (eds), (2007) *Supervising Doctorates Downunder: Keys to Effective Supervision in Australia and New Zealand*, 36–44. Melbourne: ACER Press.

Denholm, C. (2007), 'Conducting reviews of candidature', in C. Denholm and T. Evans (eds), *Supervising Doctorates Downunder: Keys to Effective Supervision in Australia and New Zealand,* pp. 54–61. Melbourne: ACER Press.

Denholm, C. and Evans, T. (eds) (2007), *Supervising Doctorates Downunder: Keys to Effective Supervision in Australia and New Zealand.* Melbourne: ACER Press.

Downton, P. (2003), *Design research.* Melbourne: RMIT Publishing.

Frayling, C. (1993), *Research in Art and Design.* (Royal College of Art Research Papers vol. 1 no. 1) London: Royal College of Art.

Frayling, C. (1997), *Practice-Based Doctorates in The Creative and Performing Arts and Design.* Coventry, UK Council for Graduate Education.

Grant, B. and Pearson, M. (2007), 'Approaches to doctoral supervision in Australia and Aotearoa New Zealand', in C. Denholm and T. Evans (eds) *Supervising Doctorates Downunder: Keys to Effective Supervision in Australia and New Zealand,* pp. 11–18. Melbourne: ACER Press.

Grocott, L. and Marshall, T. (2003, April), 'Poetic process and professional practice: A case study for practitioner-led design research'. Paper presented at the 5th European Academy of Design Conference TECHNE Design Wisdom, Barcelona.

Ingleby, R. (2007), 'Helping candidates form their research question', in C. Denholm and T. Evans (eds) *Supervising Doctorates Downunder: Keys to Effective Supervision in Australia and New Zealand,* pp. 45–52. Melbourne: ACER Press.

Martin, E. and Adams, R. (2007), 'Degrees of uncertainty: Writing and demystifying the thesis', in C. Denholm and T. Evans (eds) *Supervising Doctorates Downunder: Keys to Effective Supervision in Australia and New Zealand,* pp. 215–23. Melbourne: ACER Press.

Moltschaniwskyj, N. and Moltschaniwskyj, G. (2007), 'Setting the scene: Initiating the supervisory relationship', in C. Denholm and T. Evans (eds) *Supervising Doctorates Downunder: Keys to Effective Supervision in Australia and New Zealand,* pp. 28–35. Melbourne: ACER Press.

Tennant, M. and Roberts, S. (2007), 'Agreeing to supervise', in C. Denholm and T. Evans (eds) *Supervising Doctorates Downunder: Keys to Effective Supervision in Australia and New Zealand,* pp. 20–7. Melbourne: ACER Press.

Chapter 19

GROKKING THE SWAMP: ADVENTURES INTO THE PRACTICAL ABYSS, AND BACK AGAIN

Jeremy Yuille

In the varied topography of professional practice, there is a high ground overlooking a swamp. (Schön 1990)

Let me tell you a story ... the tale of how I grokked my PhD.

Grok is coined as an untranslatable Martian concept and word in Heinlein's 1961 science fiction novel, *Stranger in a Strange Land*, and has since worked its way into geek and counterculture. To 'grok' some knowledge or technique is to claim that this knowledge has become part of you, that your understanding of this knowledge is more than a detached instrumental learning.

Somewhere in the third year of my PhD, one of my supervisors offhandedly mentioned to me that it 'might be time I started finishing'. Talking with my other supervisor a few weeks later, a word dropped out and sat on the table. I can't remember who said it first, but it wasn't me who picked it up and used it strangely in the next sentence, bringing it forward in my awareness ...

That word fitted the gap I'd been discovering for the last few years. A word rendered my thinking in a direction, and helped me to see what might be a way out of 'The Swamp'. I seized the word, and started on the road back.

Reflecting on this moment, I see it as a critical point in my PhD. In an effort to resist the temptation to see this as THE critical incident in my PhD, I examined the wider timeline of my research.

My Master of Design (2003–5) and PhD (2007–12) were both undertaken in a practice-led culture at RMIT University, where I have been an academic faculty member since 2000. In our practice-led research culture, 'The Swamp' is a trope used to describe the necessary state of sophisticated complexity that a practice-led PhD needs to pass through. Being 'in The Swamp' is a state often accompanied by confusion and self-doubt on the student's part – and relief or anxiety on the critical reviewer's part – depending on their experience with this form of research. The trope draws on Schön's swamp, featured in the epigram that begins this story, and – like every useful trope – the etymology is never explicit. Our Swamp has taken mythical form, invoked at many formal review presentations, its use often signifying 'insider' or 'initiated' status. As I reflected on my experience during both of my practice-led research degrees, it became clear that the next logical step would be to locate our Swamp within a larger, more familiar, and more useful, narrative structure.

In the following chapter I reflect on the state of being in The Swamp, locating it within the narrative cycle of Joseph Campbell's monomyth from his 1949 book, *The Hero with a Thousand Faces*. I draw from Christopher Vogler's interpretation of Campbell's monomyth, and map key elements of The Hero's Journey to stages I have observed in my own and others' practice-led PhD studies.

To begin, I'll give a brief overview of Schön's swamp and Campbell's monomyth.

The Swamp

Donald Schön's *Educating the Reflective Practitioner: Toward a New Design for Teaching and Learning in the Professions* (1990) begins with a compelling picture of 'relatively unimportant, manageable problems overlooking a swamp of messy, confusing problems […] of greatest human concern' (Ch. 1). Schön's model is useful as a way to set up what you might be doing when you embark on a practice-led PhD: you're venturing into The Swamp. It's going to get messy and confusing,

Figure 19.1 The practitioner's choice. Courtesy the author.

but this is an expected – even necessary – experience for a PhD student to go through. The Swamp reminds people that practice-led research has a rationality that differs from traditional academic research.

Schön sets up two very different worlds: the high ground of technical rationalism, and the low ground of important – albeit non-rigorous – inquiry. His separation of these two worlds builds a sense of their incompatibility, best exemplified in his framing of 'the Practitioner's Choice' (ibid.). The uninitiated practitioner sometimes believes that these two worlds are irreconcilable, that they have to choose *between* them.

This perceived duality seems at odds with Schön's constructionist stance and staunch rejection of technical rationality. What if we approach this situation from a different angle? Instead of focusing on the *knowledge* or *situations* a student engages with, let's think about what *happens* to the practitioner, the PhD student. What's their narrative? How do they experience change? How might they conceptualize their PhD as a *journey* – understanding which stage they might be in – and how do they approach the challenges ahead of them? To do this, let's look at Campbell's monomyth as a guide.

The Hero's Journey

Joseph Campbell's monomyth draws from extensive analysis of human mythology, and identifies a series of archetypal stages common across culture and time. The term monomyth is drawn from James Joyce's *Ulysses*, of which Campbell was a noted scholar.

Christopher Vogler's 1998 book *The Writer's Journey: Mythic Structure for Writers* recasts and simplifies Campbell's monomyth, with an emphasis on the narrative structure of movies. Specifically relevant to the practice-led PhD experience, Vogler focuses on both the external narrative and internal character motivations experienced by the journey's hero (pp. 211–13). Vogler's terminology is less mythical than Campbell's, and for that reason I will use Vogler's terms for most of this chapter, referring to Campbell's terms only when they help to better reconcile The Hero's Journey with The Swamp. The important thing to remember is that Campbell and Vogler are both writing about the same 'few common structural elements found universally in myths, fairy tales, dreams, and movies' (p. 1), described by Vogler as follows:

> Heroes are introduced in the ORDINARY WORLD, where they receive a CALL TO ADVENTURE. They are RELUCTANT at first and REFUSE THE CALL, but are encouraged by a MENTOR to CROSS THE THRESHOLD and enter the Special World where they encounter TESTS, ALLIES AND ENEMIES. They APPROACH THE INMOST CAVE, crossing a second threshold where they endure the ORDEAL. They take possession of their REWARDS and are pursued on THE ROAD BACK to the Ordinary World. They cross the third threshold, experience a RESURRECTION, and are transformed by their

experience. THEY RETURN WITH THE ELIXIR, a boon or treasure to benefit the Ordinary World (Christopher Vogler 1998: 26).

In the sections following, I'll take us through some phases of this journey, mapping them to experiences and stages I have observed in my own and others' practice-led PhD studies. In doing so, I hope to speak to two audiences: students undertaking practice-led PhD study, and colleagues mentoring these students through their journey. I hope to help both audiences step back from their immediate experience and see their progress as different points on a similar journey.

The Call to Adventure: Charting a map

Once upon a time […] our hero stands in her normal world and heeds a call to adventure. What is that thing over there?

I was wary of what the spotlight of a PhD might do to my design practice. I wasn't entirely sure about what my practice *was*. I had studied architecture, then throughout the 1990s applied the conceptual skills gained from that study to music, performance and interactive media. In the early 2000s I found myself an academic and Interaction Designer with a unique take on the field, and a network to help me understand some of the hidden motivations and forces this new professional field was experiencing. I didn't want to lose the practical aspects of my design practice to the academy, yet I knew that it is essential to move through stages of instinctual ability to explicit capability during the course of a PhD.

Often you move backwards, to outflank a blockage or aspect of your practice that resists examination. In fact, backwards isn't exactly correct – many of the moves, particularly in the early stages of a PhD, are orthogonal to your practice. You're making progress, but not in a direction that's practically apparent.

You're gaining altitude, looking for that helicopter view of things, charting a map of your field. You're also learning there are such things as fields, and that fields are contested, created by relationships of power and status as much as by history and technology. One way to think of this stage is that you're building a map, because you'll need to find its limits and leave them if you're to ever find the change you're seeking.

This is important at the outset. *You need to want to change the world*. Even just a little part of it. Even if it's just your *understanding* of a little part of the world. Change runs through the middle of design, and it's no coincidence that you'll find change a constant partner in a practice-led design PhD. You need to be passionately invested in your quest, because there are challenges ahead, and not the kind you're prepared for. *That would be too easy.*

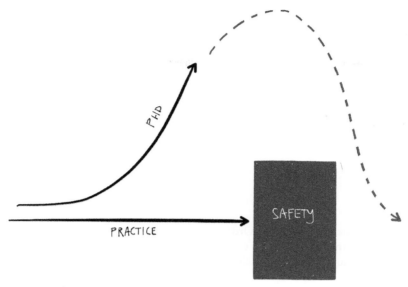

Figure 19.2 PhD moves are often orthogonal to your practice, to help you skirt blockages. Courtesy the author.

Meeting with the Mentor

The function of the mentor is to prepare the hero to face the unknown. (Vogler 1998: 18)

Supervisor, Committee, Professor, Industry Partner… the practice-led PhD has many forms of mentor, and you need to find one if you're ever going to make it across the threshold and back again. I remember my supervisor talking about 'taking the high road' – as though it was something I wasn't on. On reflection, I suspect this was said in an effort to plant the model of a 'high road' in my mind so that I might take it on my return. At this stage I already understood my PhD as a journey, I just had no idea it was a round trip. We'll discuss this later, after The Swamp.

Crossing the Threshold

Our hero looks across the threshold, into the unknown. Off the map. Eager to get there, but she needs to get past the Guardians.

At RMIT University we have formalized some aspects of this stage and have called it the 'Confirmation of Candidature'. Jokes about its religious nature abound. This is the first Threshold in your journey: being released to seek your fortune and fate. The challenge here is to align yourself with the rationality of the academy, when everyone knows you're about to leave its protective walls and start making it all up as you go. Your Mentors will all have been here before. They all know what it's like to be in the state you're in, even if they're not entirely sure about what you're going to do.

By this stage you should have a map of the territory you want to explore. Your Mentors want to know the direction you'll set out on, and they've got a pretty good sense of what you think you'll encounter before you hit the edge of the map. They're largely interested in knowing if you'll make it off the map and – once there – whether you'll return alive.

Threshold Guardians – friend and foe

This first Threshold between the Ordinary and the Special World can also be seen as a shift from the known to the unknown. At this Threshold, our hero is tested by Guardians, another useful archetypal character to bring to the practice-led PhD discourse.

What is the role of a Guardian? What do they stand guard against? Vogler characterizes different narrative roles played by Guardians, ranging from a threat to be vanquished, a special power to be integrated by our Hero, to a Mentor-in-waiting.

Models of Guardian inside the academy – particularly with respect to the PhD – include the formal *Opponent* of some PhD models, *panellists* of RMIT's Practice Research Symposia, *examiners* – and often one or more established contributors to the field, with differing approaches to yours.

Tests, allies, enemies

Across the first Threshold, our hero is beset by tests, joined by allies and unmasks enemies.

In a practice-led PhD, you need to locate yourself with respect to the map – that you just left – and the new fields you're now discovering. Who are you like, who are you not like, who's going to help you? Who will be your allies on this stage of the quest? Who do you want to vanquish, or just steer clear of? Where are the boundary objects, and how do they help you pass – or skirt – the tests?

The Ordeal, The Swamp and The Abyss

Schön talks about The Swamp. Campbell's monomyth describes The Abyss. Vogler's hero endures The Ordeal. They're all the same thing, and it's useful to have a range of frames for the state you find yourself in when confusion, fear and despair set in.

Everything is everything. Nothing makes sense. The map you've created looks like a serial killer's collage. You're in deep, head underwater, struggling to see how you'll keep your practice together, let alone deliver something back to the academy.

… also, you're nearly there …

It's during this point that you'll start to see how useful the word 'useful' is.

For instance, The Swamp is really useful here. You've found your way into a messy, ill-defined and scary morass of ideas, theories, practices, fields, forces, pressures, emotions and opinions. The only way is forward, and you're off the map. At least you think you are. Oh yeah, and your compass doesn't seem to work anymore. Schön's Swamp frames The Abyss as a place you need to pass through, a set of increasingly complex interconnections and relationships between the forces that sent you here and the forces you've encountered since setting off. The Swamp can only be found off the map.

… you're almost there …

The good thing about The Abyss is that it's quiet. If you let it be. You can think differently here, away from the noise of the Ordinary World. I like to frame RMIT's twice-yearly graduate critique and reviews as semi-formalized ways of making room for the kind of slow thinking that Daniel Kahneman describes in his 2011 book *Thinking, Fast and Slow*. This kind of explicit reflective thinking is difficult to do as a regular part of practice, whereas a practice-led PhD is the perfect way to develop this capability.

To be fair – all research is a jump across an Abyss. The thing to remember is that a 'deductive' or 'inductive' abyss is quite different from an 'abductive' one. Abductive sensemaking – well described by Jon Kolko in his 2010 article 'Sensemaking and framing: A theoretical reflection on perspective in design synthesis' – is a jump into the unknown. When we embark on a quest to create new knowledge in a field using this mode of rationality, we're already starting with The Swamp in mind. This brings a key difference, one of the secrets to practice-led research: in the middle of The Swamp, where you find yourself neck deep in the mire, it comes to you as a whisper: 'You need to design your way out of this situation'.

You need to design your way out of a problem space the PhD puts you in. Yes, the practice-led PhD is (just) an elaborate game to position you in a situation that requires you to think and act differently. To break your normal.

Embrace it. It's terrifying, but it's also the only way you're ever getting back.

Resurrection: Transformation and the road back

You've looked into The Abyss, traversed The Swamp, faced your demons and achieved transformation. Or not. Either way, the aim is that you've learned, you've changed, and you emerge from The Swamp with new powers that you must now bring back across the 'Threshold of Knowing'. From the unknown, back to the known, the world that you left behind.

It's useful to begin with this return in mind, before you set out. Reminding yourself about why you need to describe things *while* you're thinking about them, not just after you've worked them out. Why you need to describe *how* you're going about an experiment, not just its result. Why you need to get more and more comfortable with reflection *in* action, not just reflection *on* actions. All of this builds your new practice, and will help you in your next task, which is where the grokking comes in.

Design practice rarely sends us clients who are itching to reframe their assumptions, take things up a level (or three), or constantly question their approach. This is shifting as design becomes more aligned with fields like management, capabilities like leadership, and situations like organizational change – but still only slightly. Traditional design practices can quickly become a prisoner of their own success, taking insights gained through smaller experimental projects and rendering them into fixed processes and approaches that can scale to the types of project that monographs are built around.

This is fine – if the aim is to produce monographs, or win awards – and there's more than enough room for this kind of design practice to go around. This kind of practice is relatively safe. This kind of practice is not what you build a practice-led PhD on, because this kind of practice doesn't include *you* in the design problem.

Your practice-led PhD isn't about carving off a safe piece of knowledge and becoming an expert in it. A practice-led PhD is about becoming aware of your becoming. It's about pushing through the hyper-analysis that a technical rationalist stance can bring to your work. It's about transcending the navel-gazing state of reflection that undisciplined thinking about your practice may impose. It's about forgetting that you're on a path – so that you can get lost enough. It's about waking up one evening and realizing 'I'm in The Swamp!'

The key here is to let this change you. The challenge here is to concentrate on what the swamp is telling you, not on getting out. This sounds easy, but there's actually a good reason why we don't get a lot of clients who are brave enough to go here. Transformation is a difficult change to self-initiate. One way of framing the practice-led PhD is that *it contrives the circumstances within which you have a greater chance of achieving meaningful and positive transformation of your practice.* To do this, you need to change yourself. To do this you need to listen for what the abyss tells you, when it looks back.

Return with the Elixir

You'll return from beyond the edge of the map with gifts that few can immediately recognize, particularly those who'll benefit most from them. You now need to learn how to tell the story of your new gifts, without resorting to your story of how

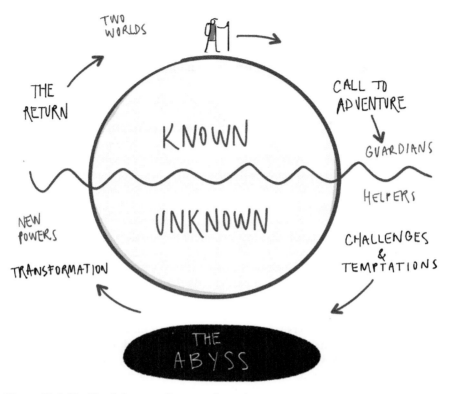

Figure 19.3 The Hero's Journey. Courtesy the author.

you came by them. Time to don that Ordinary World rationality again, because you're going to need to make sense to people who couldn't go on your journey, even if they wanted to.'

This is the point at which Vogler's model ends, and Campbell's monomyth has this final stage, particularly relevant for the practice-led PhD.

You didn't think it was over yet, did you?

Once our hero has returned transformed, with their gifts for the Ordinary World, Campbell describes their ability to inhabit two worlds at once. Be they the inner and outer world, the known and unknown – or any other duality – our hero finds herself able to integrate previously irreconcilable rationalities. She finds herself back at the beginning of the cycle, with new powers of action and perception.

The Cycle

You've been able to spend precious time in the wilderness. You've made your own map of rationality, your own language and models of why things work the way they do. It was quiet there, and you were able to think differently about your practice for perhaps the first time in ages.

You positioned yourself in a corner and then designed your way out, learning how to see your new powers in practice from afar. You've returned to noisy normality and convinced everyone that those things you saw really exist, and that they're useful in the Ordinary World. Now you need to find a way to integrate your new powers and perspective with the existing normal of the Ordinary World. As the monomyth describes, you need to master the two worlds.

This is what I grokked. Not the critical incident and the word *forensic* that eventually became part of how I described my contribution to knowledge. Not the methods that I used to design my way out of the problem my PhD had led me to. Not the new capability that the PhD helped me develop. No. What I grokked just now – as I sit here writing this for you – is the cyclical nature of explicit and disciplined reflective practice, and particularly that the cycle extends far further into the future than it does into the past.

Campbell's monomyth and Vogler's journey highlight extrinsic and intrinsic motivations that researchers face during the course of undertaking a practice-led PhD. This lens also helps us to see the PhD as a network of human capability development, where we may play the role of hero, mentor, guardian and helper interchangeably – often at the same time – in different interlinked narratives. I learn from my journey through The Swamp, and subsequently mentor my PhD students to face their Abyss and – hopefully – return transformed to begin the next cycle. As a lens, Campbell's monomyth has helped me to integrate the worlds of the hero and the mentor, to sustain a practice that grows in interest and inquiry. As a lens, the Hero's Journey can help us to guide others and ourselves through repeated journeys to The Swamp, and back again.

> 'no matter what lens you use, everything you see through that lens is actually there.' Donella Meadows (*Thinking in Systems: A Primer* 2008)

Acknowledgements

Thank you to my mentors – Soumitri Varadarajan for the high road, Linda Brennan for the turning, Dave Gray for the Hero's Journey, and Laurene Vaughan for (repeatedly) showing me how to put it all together.

References

Campbell, J. (1949), *The Hero with a Thousand Faces* 2nd edn (1968). Princeton, NJ: Princeton University Press.

Heinlein, R. A. (1961), *Stranger in a Strange Land.* New York: Penguin Publishing Group.

Kahneman, D. (2011), *Thinking, Fast and Slow* 1st edn. New York: Farrar, Straus and Giroux.

Kolko, J. (2010, July), 'Sensemaking and Framing: A Theoretical Reflection on Perspective in Design Synthesis'. Paper presented at the conference of Design Research Society, Montreal. Retrieved from http://www.jonkolko.com/writingSensemaking.php.

Meadows, D. H. (2008) *Thinking in Systems: A Primer.* White River Junction, VT: Chelsea Green Publishing.

Schön, D. A. (1990), *Educating the Reflective Practitioner: Toward a New Design for Teaching and Learning in the Professions.* San Francisco, CA: Jossey-Bass.

Vogler, C. (1998), *The Writer's Journey: Mythic Structure for Writers*, 2nd edn. Studio City, CA: Michael Wiese Productions.

INDEX